Praise for the Books of Linda Reilly

"A very fun cat-centric novel, along with strong writing, fun characters, and a crowd-pleasing finale." —*Kings River Life Magazine*

"I thoroughly enjoyed this puzzler of a mystery. Reilly cooks up a perfect recipe of murder and mayhem in this charming cozy." —Jenn McKinlay, *New York Times* bestselling author

"Smart, sassy, and a little bit scary. Everything a good cozy should be!" —Laura Childs, *New York Times* bestselling author

"Foodies and mystery lovers will come for the red herrings and stay for the cheese." —*Kirkus Reviews*

"Masterful misdirection coupled with a pace that can't be beat, Linda Reilly has grilled up a winner for sure!" —J. C. Eaton, author of the Sophie Kimball Mysteries, The Wine Trail Mysteries, and The Marcie Rayner Mysteries

"A well-crafted and fun start to a new series! Carly and her crew serve mouth-watering grilled cheese sandwiches while solving crime in a quaint Vermont town. Plenty of twists and turns to keep you turning the pages and guessing the killer to the very end." —Tina Kashian, author of the Kebab Kitchen Mysteries

"A delightful and determined heroine, idyllic small town, and buffet of worthy suspects make this hearty whodunnit an enticing start to a decidedly delectable new series! This sandwich-centric cozy will leave readers drooling for more!" —Bree Baker, author of the Seaside Café Mysteries

Books by Linda Reilly

Grilled Cheese Mysteries

Up to No Gouda
No Parm No Foul
Cheddar Late Than Never
Brie Careful What You Wish For

Cat Lady Mysteries

Escape Claws
Claws of Death
Claws for Celebration
Claws of Action
The Girl with the Kitten Tattoo

Deep Fried Mysteries

Fillet of Murder
Out of the Dying Pan
A Frying Shame

Apple Mariani Mysteries

Some Enchanted Murder

Brie Careful What You Wish For

A Grilled Cheese Mystery

Linda Reilly

BEYOND THE PAGE
PUBLISHING

Brie Careful What You Wish For
Linda Reilly
Copyright © 2024 by Linda Reilly
Cover design and illustration by Dar Albert, Wicked Smart Designs

Beyond the Page Books
are published by
Beyond the Page Publishing
www.beyondthepagepub.com

ISBN: 978-1-960511-62-1

This book is dedicated to the memory of my uncle, Ret. Massachusetts State Police Captain John J. White, not only for sharing my love of books but for patiently answering all my law enforcement questions over the years. John, you are dearly missed.

ACKNOWLEDGMENTS

I have so many wonderful people to thank for bringing this book to fruition. My editor, Bill Harris, for eagerly embracing the Grilled Cheese Mysteries and for his spot-on editing. Bill, it is such a pleasure to work with you.

Roberta Baker, attorney extraordinaire, for her expert advice on Vermont probate procedures. Wendi Murphy, for suggesting the taco salad as a summer favorite of Carly's—and for making the recipe for me! Judy Jones, for her always insightful comments and advice, and for being my ever-present cheering squad. Abby White, for suggesting the name Paisley for a sweet little pug. Melody Walker, for naming a character—real estate agent Penelope Primrose. Melody, I hope you'll also like your walk-on role! And Meezan Hassan Ford, for suggesting the delectably cheesy title *Brie Careful What You Wish For*. Meezan— you totally nailed it.

More than anything, I owe a world of thanks to all the readers who gave me such encouragement throughout the writing of the Grilled Cheese Mysteries. A special shoutout to Kelly Vaiman, Jennifer Kovaleski, and all the hardworking admins and moderators of the Fans of Linda Reilly Facebook page. You all did a phenomenal job spreading the word about the series.

CHAPTER 1

CARLY HALE LOOKED UP FROM BEHIND THE COUNTER OF HER GRILLED Cheese Eatery. She smiled when she saw Ross Baxter lope through the front door. Over six feet tall with a mop of curly black hair and sunglasses perched on his head, the eighteen-year-old flashed a grin that made his chocolate brown eyes twinkle.

Carly gave him a thumbs-up. "Perfect timing, Ross. Grant's just finishing up your order."

"Excellent! Hey, Grant." Tilting his chin in greeting, Ross set his insulated carrier on a free stool and unzipped the top. "Man, it's hotter than a sauna out there. I sure hope the AC in my grandpa's old Dodge makes it through the summer."

Ross was the founder of Fab Food on Wheels, a business he started just over a month ago for pickup and delivery of restaurant takeout. His clientele consisted mainly of senior citizens, most of whom were either unable or unwilling to order food online, let alone pay with a debit card. They preferred buying lunch the old-fashioned way—cash in hand.

It was Ross's maternal grandmother, Helen Quigley, who planted the seed in her grandson's mind for his fledgling business. Since he was saving money to attend college in the fall, it was the ideal summer job.

His business model was simple. Customers called him with their orders in the morning. Ross then placed his orders online to the restaurants he delivered for. He charged his customers a flat fee, and cash payments were a must. Delivery fees were based on the size of the order, but he often scored tips that were larger than the fee. Carly attributed that to the young man's bubbly personality and efficient service.

Grant Robinson, the eatery's grill cook extraordinaire and an aspiring chef, set five takeout boxes on the counter. "You're all set, Ross. There's an extra bag with Mrs. Gray's five pickles, just like you asked."

"Thanks." Ross's expression darkened, and his mouth curved into a frown. He began stacking the takeout boxes into his carrier. "I really wish she wouldn't call me anymore. She's like, so impossible to please, you know? That's not polite to say, but she's really a nightmare customer."

From the cooler, Carly fetched the drinks that went with Ross's order and placed them in his carrier next to the takeout boxes. Since Mrs. Gray was also Carly's customer, she refrained from commenting. She was curious, though, as to the reason Ross found her so difficult.

"If there's anything we can do to help, just let us know," Carly told him. "We're always glad to accommodate special requests."

"I know. You guys all rock." With a parting smile, Ross lifted his carrier and headed for the door. "Gotta bounce!"

"Such a great kid," Suzanne Rivers commented, leaning across the counter to give three order slips to Grant. "If my Josh grows up to be half that polite, I'll drop down and kiss the ground."

Suzanne was Carly's part-time server, a thirtysomething who took orders and served customers at whirlwind speed. Their regular customers adored her—she knew every one of their kids' and grandkids' names, as well as those of their pets. Suzanne's own son, Josh, was in middle school. According to Suzanne, he'd been having some growing pains and was going through a grumpy stage.

"Aw, your Josh is terrific," Carly reminded her. "Any time he's been in here, he's been an angel." That was a slight exaggeration, but basically Josh was a good kid.

"Angel?" Suzanne barked. "You haven't seen his flip side—you know, the side where horns are sprouting from his head? Every night when I tell him it's time to shut off his phone and go to bed, I get lip like you wouldn't believe."

"Maybe he needs you to cut him a little slack," Carly suggested.

"Says the woman who hasn't had a kid yet," Suzanne quipped. "You wait, your turn is coming."

I hope so, Carly thought.

She stared through the eatery's front window at the perfect June day. Across the main drag was the town green—a patch of land where visitors and locals alike stopped to relax, read, and recharge. Winding walkways and curved wooden benches graced the small area. Massive concrete flowerpots—maintained by town volunteers—overflowed with red geraniums, multicolored impatiens, and bright pink petunias.

More than two years had passed since Carly lost her husband, Daniel. He was on a mission of mercy when his pickup, laden with wood, skidded on an icy road and tumbled down an embankment. They were living in northern Vermont at the time, but soon afterward Carly relocated to her beloved town of Balsam Dell in the southern part of the state. The grilled cheese restaurant she'd daydreamed of opening suddenly became a reality. She took over the lease of a failing ice cream parlor and made the space her own.

It was during the renovation of her eatery when she met Ari Mitchell. A local electrician, Ari had installed the overhead lighting that reminded Carly of lamps hanging in an old barn. Her initial feelings for him terrified her. She'd been racked with guilt over her attraction to someone so soon after Daniel's death. It didn't take long for her to see Ari for the man he was. Caring and kind, he was also quite adorable with his dark curly hair and deep brown eyes, and a smile with enough wattage to outshine the sun.

Her insides fluttered when she thought of how close they'd grown over the past year. More recently, Ari had made it known that he was ready for the ultimate commitment—the "M" word. Carly thought she was, too—except for that annoying *Caution* sign in a corner of her brain that occasionally popped up without warning.

Carly's near deadly encounters with killers didn't help to soothe her apprehensions. That she'd aided the police in nabbing a few "bad guys" was only a slight consolation. She vowed to let the police handle all future murder investigations with no interference from her. Besides, how many more murders could happen in a quiet town like Balsam Dell?

"You're in la-la land." Valerie Wells, Carly's assistant manager, came up behind her and poked her in the side.

"Oh! I didn't hear you. Everything okay?" Moving past Valerie, Carly made a point of clearing dishes off a vacated table.

"Everything's great, but you looked far away there, girl. Daydreaming about Mr. Right?" she teased.

Carly felt her cheeks flush. "No," she fibbed. "Just thinking about how lucky we are to have Ross doing his delivery gig for the summer. It's brought us a lot of extra business, especially at the lunch hour."

"Yeah, but who's going to take over once he's in college?" Valerie chewed one glossy lip.

"A question that remains unanswered. For now, let's enjoy the windfall."

Carly went behind the counter and deposited the dirty dishes in a large plastic tub. Valerie trailed behind her. "Hey, Carly, is it okay if I take my break around one fifteen? I'm bringing lunch over to Fred. We're going to eat in his office."

"Lunch with the chief again, huh?" Carly cupped one ear theatrically and leaned closer to Valerie. "Wait. Are those . . . wedding bells I hear in the distance?"

"Oh, you." Valerie fussed with her brunette topknot—a nervous gesture Carly knew all too well. "You read too much into things."

Fred Holloway, Balsam Dell's chief of police, had been widowed years earlier. When Valerie began working at the eatery about seven months before, she and the chief had been drawn to one another. It was a joy to watch their friendship bloom into an easy romance. Holloway was also a longtime friend of Carly's family. His daughter, Anne, was the veterinarian for Carly's sweet little dog—Havarti.

The chief was also the person who threatened to toss Carly in a jail cell if she didn't stop trying to solve murders. Carly never took him seriously, of course. It was only his way of spouting off steam because she'd placed herself in peril a few too many times.

Thankfully, those days were behind her.

After Valerie left for her lunch break, the eatery quieted down. At the small table in the kitchen, Carly enjoyed a salad, while Suzanne opted for a bowl of tomato soup and half of a Sweddar Weather—grilled cheddar and Swiss on artisan white bread.

"You're really on a salad kick these days, aren't you?" Suzanne shoved a corner of her melty sandwich into her mouth.

"I'm only trying to eat a bit healthier. Plus"—Carly patted her abdomen—"I've definitely put on a few pounds since I opened this place. And besides, Grant's salad is delicious."

Suzanne nodded and swallowed. "That I agree with."

The eatery's salad, a favorite side dish Grant had created, was a combo of field greens, dried cranberries, crumbled goat cheese, and sunflower seeds. He dressed it with a light blend of almond oil, balsamic vinegar, and delicate herbs that had customers begging for his recipe.

Suzanne's expression turned serious, and she softened her voice. "What are you going to do, Carly? Grant'll be leaving for culinary school by the end of the summer."

Carly stabbed her fork into a clump of greens. Every time she thought of losing Grant, her stomach hardened into a knot. The young man had been with her from the beginning. His short dreads had grown longer, and his boyish features had transformed into a devastatingly handsome face. Most important, he'd supported her through the tough times, especially when local murders had threatened to consume her.

"Carly?"

"I know," Carly finally responded. "By the end of July, I need to start interviewing. I'm honestly not sure where to start."

"You don't think you should start sooner?" Suzanne said. "Where are you going to advertise?"

"I don't know." Carly set down her fork and took a swig of her iced tea. "To tell you the truth, I'm so afraid of running this place without him that I wake up nights in a cold sweat."

The swinging door into the kitchen opened. Grant stood there for a few seconds. In one hand he held a plate with half a grilled cheddar sandwich. From his pained expression, Carly knew he'd heard at least part of their convo.

"Grant, we—" she began to explain.

He went over and set the sandwich on the table beside Carly, then quirked a smile. "Hey, listen, no worries, okay? You've been eating a lot of salad this week, so today I think some real comfort food is in order."

Carly grinned at him, the aroma of grilled butter and melted cheddar revving up her taste buds. She picked up the sandwich. "You're a mind reader, you know that?" She bit off a corner and chewed slowly, savoring the sharp cheddar.

"Listen, Carly," Grant said, "it's not going to be as hard as you think to replace me. I'll help you interview if you'd like, but it's going to end up being your choice. There's a ton of competent cooks out there to choose from. Once you land on someone, I'll be glad to do some training. You'll find the right match, I promise."

Carly swallowed. "Thank you, Grant. I appreciate that more than I can say."

"Any time. Hey, as soon as you guys finish, I'll take a quick break. And stop worrying, okay?"

"Okay," the women said in unison.

But Carly knew deep down they were only paying him lip service.

• • •

Valerie left an hour early to catch a movie with the chief. After six, customers tended to trickle in, allowing Carly and Grant time to start closing up.

The surprise of the day arrived in the form of a glum-looking Ross Baxter. He came into the eatery about ten minutes before its seven o'clock closing time, his usual bright smile absent.

Grant was finishing up a few things in the kitchen while Carly tidied the grill area and put away the perishables in the fridge beneath the counter.

"You look bummed," Carly said, immediately sensing his mood.

Ross shrugged and held out his arms. "I'm like, in a tough spot, Ms. Hale. Can I talk to you for a minute?"

"Of course. Come on, let's sit. Want a cold drink?"

"I wouldn't mind a cherry soda."

Carly fetched his drink, and they slid into opposite sides of a booth. Ross twisted off the cap and took a long gulp.

"Mrs. Gray called my grandmother today," he explained. "She told Gram I was rude and refused to follow her instructions, and that she wasn't going to pay for my services anymore. She . . . also told Gram I spied on her."

Carly was shocked. "That doesn't sound like you. Do you know why she said that?"

"I think I know why, but she's wrong! Ms. Hale, I'm polite to all my customers, and I go out of my way to please them. But Mrs. Gray—*no one* can please her. She's like, just the most awful person. I hate saying that, but it's true."

Carly wasn't sure if something else was going on, but she trusted that Ross was being honest. "It's fine with me if you tell her you can't deliver our food to her anymore. If she still wants to order from us, I'll arrange to have it delivered another way. I'm not sure that will solve your problem, though."

"That's just it. I can't refuse her. Gram's a stickler about respecting your elders. She says dealing with people like Mrs. Gray is part of being an adult."

"I see her point, but why would Mrs. Gray say you spied on her?"

He pulled in a long breath, and his muscular shoulders sagged. "Okay, this was like, about three weeks ago, right after I started my business. I had an order for her from the sub shop. I knocked on her screen door, like I always do. The inside door was open, but when I peeked through the screen, I didn't see her. The kitchen's at the back of the house, so I knocked again, louder. When she still didn't answer I waited another minute. You know, in case she was in the bathroom or something. Then I heard voices coming from the back of the house. Mrs. Gray was having an argument with a man, and it was getting louder. I heard the guy say he was sick of doing her bidding, that he'd had enough."

"Yikes. Could you see who it was?"

Ross shook his head. "No, but she called him a very nasty name. After that, the guy told her she could stuff her threats in a sack because he was done taking her crap. And then he said if she didn't give it back, she was going to regret it."

"Give what back?" Carly prodded.

"He didn't say, but I heard that part clearly." He gulped back a mouthful of his cherry soda, and for several beats he remained silent.

"There's something else, isn't there?" Carly pressed.

Ross nodded, his young face a picture of misery. "I heard a door slam, and then a loud crash, like . . . something metal hitting the floor or the wall. At that point I got scared that the guy might've hurt Mrs. Gray. I dropped my carrier and rushed inside."

"Wait," Carly said. "The screen door wasn't locked?"

"No." He folded his hands on the table. "Anyway, when I got to the kitchen, the man was nowhere in sight. On the floor there was a big metal spoon, like the one Gram uses to stir sauce. I asked Mrs. Gray if she was okay. She gave me this awful look, and then she ripped into me like a wolverine."

"What did she say?"

Ross blew out a shaky breath. "She accused me of eavesdropping on her private conversation. She said I was a creepy little spy and a thief."

"That's terrible. Did you tell her what really happened?"

"I tried, but she kept screaming over me so I couldn't get a word in."

"Why did she call you a thief?"

"One day last week she complained that she got stiffed on potato chips. She accused me of stealing some of hers and eating them in the car!"

Carly sat back in the booth and thought for a moment. If everything happened exactly as Ross had described, maybe she needed to refuse delivery orders from Octavia Gray. Even though Ross wasn't Carly's employee, he performed a service that brought in extra business for the eatery. He shouldn't have to tolerate abusive behavior from a customer.

Still, it was her job to sell grilled cheese, and boycotting a customer would be bad business.

Ross sagged. "I'm like, almost sure she's going to order from me tomorrow. She's totally addicted to your Smoky Steals the Bacon. Plus, I honestly think she enjoys torturing me."

Oh boy.

"You never know. Maybe she'll change her mind by then," Carly said. "Ross, that man—do you have any idea who he was?"

"No, not a clue. I only heard his voice. But the only car in Mrs. Gray's driveway was her own."

"And she definitely lives alone?"

He shrugged. "Yeah, far as I know. Gram told me her husband died a long time ago."

"Would you recognize the man's voice if you heard it again?" Carly asked.

"I'm not sure. Maybe. It was kind of nasally."

"And you heard a door slam, so whoever he was," Carly surmised, "he must've left through the back door. Unless it was another door that slammed, like maybe a closet or a bathroom door?"

Ross's eyes widened. "I didn't think of that. That would mean the guy could've still been there when I raced into the house." He drained the soda in his bottle and replaced the cap.

Carly felt at a loss. She didn't know how to advise Ross, but maybe she could offer a temporary solution. "If Mrs. Gray does order tomorrow, would it help if I delivered her lunch? She's obviously a fan of grilled cheese, but I don't want you to take any more abuse from her. Either Valerie or I could run over with her order and maybe talk to her. She doesn't live that far from here."

He gave Carly a lopsided smile. "Oh man, I'd love to take you up on that. But it's my job and I'm going to do it. I have to take the bad with the good, right?"

Carly admired his work ethic, and his determination. "Okay, but I'm glad you confided in me. Let me know if I can do anything to ease the tension with Mrs. Gray, okay?"

"Will do. And thanks for listening, Ms. Hale."

After Ross left, Carly sat for a moment and mulled their conversation. Not that it was her personal business, but she couldn't stand by and watch Ross be mistreated by a customer—even if that customer was an elderly widow.

If need be, she'd have a chat with Octavia Gray herself.

CHAPTER 2

AFTER CLOSING THE RESTAURANT CARLY HEADED HOME, STOPPING FIRST for a bouquet of fresh-cut flowers at one of the local farm stands.

Located only a mile or so from the restaurant, her apartment occupied the second floor of a beautifully maintained two-family home. Painted yellow with gray trim, the house had a small yard flanked by a wooden fence. Carly's landlady, Joyce Katso, was a sweetheart of a woman. Because of her challenges with MS, Joyce shared her first-floor apartment with her caretaker, Becca Avery, who was studying to be a licensed nurse assistant. The arrangement worked perfectly for the pair. Becca also checked on Havarti during the day, a huge blessing for Carly.

The moment Carly stepped inside her apartment, Havarti launched himself at her like a jet-propelled rocket. She dropped her tote and the bouquet on her hallway table, then lifted the little dog into her arms, where he proceeded to lick her face with abandon.

"My goodness," Carly said, setting him down, "you'd think I've been gone for a year."

After a quick washup, she dug out one of her favorite vases from beneath the kitchen sink, filled it with water, and stuck the flowers inside. That done, she escorted Havarti into the backyard for a bathroom break, then led him back inside for dinner. Ari would be arriving soon with Chinese takeout, and she wanted to set the table and open a bottle of wine.

In the bathroom, Carly fluffed her chestnut-colored hair and freshened her face. These days she was wearing her hair a tad longer than the pixie style she'd sported for years. The extra length brought out her soft curls and gave her more styling options. Not that she did much styling, but if a special occasion arose, she could add a little pizzazz to her do.

By the time Ari arrived, her table was set for dinner. He kissed her soundly and wrapped her in a hug, then placed a large paper bag on the counter. Havarti danced at his feet, begging to be noticed.

"Don't worry, I see you." Laughing, Ari gathered the dog in his arms and kissed him on the snout. "Now, be a good boy while we eat, okay?" He set Havarti down. "I hope you're hungry," he said to Carly.

"I am, and it smells delicious." The spicy aroma of soy, ginger, and garlic wafted around her, making her even hungrier.

Ari headed to the bathroom to wash up and returned a minute later. Carly gave Havarti a few doggie treats so he'd leave them in peace to enjoy dinner.

"Good day?" Carly asked Ari, pouring them each a glass of wine.

"Not bad," he said. "I was at the high school gym all day, doing the wiring for the new scoreboard. How about you?"

Carly sat down and took a small sip of her wine. "We had a busy day, always a good thing. I read that the gym is getting major renovations next year."

"It is," Ari confirmed, "and it sure needs it. After that water pipe break this past winter, the floor got pretty damaged. It's usable, but it buckled in places. It definitely needs to be replaced."

They helped themselves to sesame chicken, veggie fried rice, and steamed dumplings. When they were through, they packed up the leftovers and stashed them in the fridge.

"Fortune cookie time?" Ari smiled at Carly, his dark eyes twinkling. Carly thought it was cute that it was his favorite part of Chinese takeout. He passed one over to her, and they opened them simultaneously.

Ari made a face. "A calm demeanor will soothe an angry heart." He tossed the fortune on the table. "Yeah, not always."

Carly read hers. "A challenge arises that will require tact." She stared at it for a beat too long. Ari noticed.

"Uh-oh," Ari said. "I know that look. Anything you want to tell me?"

"Let's go in the living room."

They sank onto the flower-patterned sofa. Havarti plopped onto the cushion between them, assuming his usual role as chaperone. His efforts would ultimately be fruitless, but Carly liked her pup to think he was helping.

"Okay, I'm all ears." Ari tickled Havarti's chin. The dog closed his eyes in bliss.

Carly plunged right in. "Do you know Octavia Gray?"

Ari's mouth collapsed into a frown. "Uh, yes, I do. She is, *was* a customer until I told her I couldn't do the work for her. Not at the deep discount she wanted."

"Ah, now that's interesting. So, you had a bad experience with her?"

Ari looked uncomfortable. "I never like dissing a senior citizen, but Octavia Gray is the most unreasonable, quarrelsome, unbearable woman I've ever met."

His tone surprised Carly. "Wow. I've never heard you say that about anyone. Now *I'm* all ears."

Ari sighed. "It's a long story, so I'll cut to the heart of it. Octavia needed her entire electrical system rewired. Her house was built in the forties, and the wiring was seriously outdated. She still had the two-prong outlets, which needed to be replaced with three-prong grounded outlets. I was also supposed to install dedicated circuits in the service panel to power some of her heavy-duty appliances, like her fancy new fridge."

"I understood only a little of that, but tell me the rest," Carly urged.

Ari went on. "I performed a thorough inspection and explained the extent of the work she needed. She asked for a quote, and I wrote one up. I always try to give seniors a break. A lot of them are on fixed incomes—although word around town is that Octavia's husband left her pretty well-off."

"Hmmm. If that's true, why did she wait so long to upgrade the wiring?"

Ari rubbed Havarti's tummy. "I'm not sure, but she told me she might be looking to sell the place. A broker told her she'd never be able to unload it—her words—if she didn't replace the electrical. Long story short, she went ballistic when she saw my quote, which was more than reasonable for the number of hours I'd have to put in."

"Did she say why she wanted to sell?"

He laughed. "Yeah, she said she was getting too old to take care of a home. She was thinking of moving to a senior community, if she could find one that suited her."

"Interesting. So tell me, did you lower your quote?"

Ari laughed. "Any lower and I'd have been losing money. I took another hundred off, but she still called me a crook and sent me packing. I dodged a proverbial bullet on that one. Working for her would've been a nightmare."

Carly nodded slowly. "I think you're right."

Ari reached over and rubbed Carly's shoulder. "Now it's your turn."

Carly related all the details of Ross's issues with Octavia Gray—the argument he overheard, her accusations, and how he dreaded having to deliver to her.

"Poor Ross." Ari shook his head. "Wrong place wrong time, in his case. So, he had no idea who the guy was that threatened Octavia?"

"No, but he said the man had a nasally voice. Not much to go on."

"Honey, for what it's worth, if Octavia pulls another stunt like that, you're well within your rights to drop her as a customer. She's a bully, pure and simple. Unfortunately, people like that think they can get away with anything. It never occurs to them that one day, they might push someone too far."

A chill skittered down Carly's spine. "You just gave me the willies, but I think you're right. After what Ross overheard, maybe Octavia should be watching her back."

Ari's gaze sparkled over a mischievous grin. "Right now, there's only one back I want to watch." He leaned over the dog and gave Carly a long kiss.

Carly cupped the back of his neck and pulled him closer, all thoughts of Octavia Gray banished from her mind.

CHAPTER 3

BY THE FOLLOWING MORNING, CARLY HAD ALMOST MANAGED TO EXPEL Octavia Gray from her mind. She vowed not to waste any more time worrying about the situation. If a problem arose, she'd deal with it. With any luck, Octavia wouldn't order from Ross today, and they could both enjoy serving customers who appreciated their efforts.

Carly smiled when she heard a tap at the rear door to the restaurant. Though the eatery didn't officially open until eleven, Carly's bestie, Gina Tomasso, arrived every Tuesday at precisely eight thirty to indulge in one of Grant's grilled bacon and cheese breakfast biscuits.

Gina's apartment was located directly over the eatery. Carly had offered her a key to the restaurant's back door, but her friend refused. "I'm not going to take advantage of our friendship, even if I do live one story up," she'd insisted.

Over the past year, Gina had made her cozy space her own, her décor a colorful hodgepodge of knickknacks and artifacts from the 1960s. Gina lost her mom when she was young, leaving a hole in her heart that was never filled despite having a terrific dad. Every item and piece of furniture she owned was purchased with her mom's specific tastes in mind. Gina was positive her mom could see her living quarters and was smiling down with approval.

Grant slid a mug of coffee across the counter to Gina. With a spatula, he removed the grilled biscuit and set it on a plate. Crispy bacon blended with melted cheddar poked out from the edges. "There you go, Miss Gina. So, how are things at the stationery shop these days?" He began buttering another biscuit and placing it on the grill. Several strips of bacon sizzled and popped beneath a weighted grill press.

Gina, who'd just taken a mastodon-sized bite of hers, held up one finger. She chewed for several seconds, swallowed and said, "Busy. Super busy." She tossed back a slug of steaming coffee. "We're right in the heart of wedding season. I'm pretty sure I've been quilling in my sleep."

The shop Grant referred to was What a Card, the store Gina had opened a few years earlier. Her card designs were unique, and she'd made a name for herself perfecting her quilling technique. She was known for creating stunning wedding invitations. Special orders came in nearly every day, keeping Gina working long hours.

Grant grinned at her. "Your cards are becoming famous. Carly, are you skipping your biscuit today?"

"Yup. I'm eating light today, but thanks."

She and Ari had made plans to have dinner out that evening—something they rarely did. Dining at the Balsam Dell Inn was such a treat that she wanted to be good and hungry.

A key turned in the front door. Valerie Wells flounced into the dining room, her topknot rounder and lighter than usual, her lashes tipped with glitter. "Hey, gang! Hi, Gina." She slung her purse off her shoulder and dropped it onto a free stool.

Carly gawked at her. "Um, hi, Val. Did you . . . do something special to your hair?"

Valerie adjusted her topknot, her cheeks pinking. "I wondered if you'd notice. When I got home last night, I added a few highlights. Do you like it?"

"I think you look beautiful," Carly said, still staring at her friend.

"Yeah, you look all . . . sparkly," Gina added.

Valerie beamed. "Sparkly. What a lovely compliment."

Carly and Gina exchanged glances. Something was up with Valerie. Carly suspected it had something to do with Balsam Dell's police chief, but she tactfully buttoned her lip.

"Hey, I gotta run," Gina announced, wiping her lips with a napkin. She started reaching into her purse.

"Don't you dare," Carly admonished. "And don't try hiding it in a coffee mug, like you did last time."

"Carly, you can't keep giving me free food!" Gina threw up her hands.

"I can and I will, because I'm the boss. Now, go to work and whip up more of those gorgeous cards. Maybe we can chat later, okay?"

"Argh. Okay, you win. And don't forget to stop up and see KitCat one of these days. She misses you terribly. After Zach, you're her favorite human."

Earlier in the year, Gina and her boyfriend, Zach Bartlett, had adopted a black rescue cat. Timid at first, KitCat had grown into a lovable bundle of joy with a penchant for licking ankles.

Carly grinned. "Don't worry, I will. I miss her, too."

Gina bade everyone goodbye and left through the back door. The paved lot behind the eatery had space for only two cars—Carly's and Gina's. Seconds later, Carly heard the roar of Gina's old Chrysler—the car Gina inherited from her dad when he went into assisted living. Despite its numerous issues, she was loathe to give it up.

It was Carly's day to clean the bathroom, so she tackled that job first. After that she wiped down the aqua, vinyl-covered booths and sanitized the marbled gray tables. She tidied the faux daisies in the vintage tomato soup cans that graced each of the tables.

In the kitchen, Valerie and Grant began the daily food prep. They all worked together like a well-oiled machine, each one doing their assigned tasks.

By eleven o'clock sharp, they were ready to serve grilled cheese.

• • •

At two minutes past eleven, three online orders came in. The first one was from Ross, who requested his pickup for eleven forty-five. The other two were from local businesses that were picking up their own orders.

Carly glanced over Ross's list and felt a twinge in her stomach. "Octavia Gray strikes again," she murmured to herself.

"Everything okay?" Valerie came over and asked her. "You don't look too happy."

"Ross Baxter had an issue yesterday with one of our customers, Octavia Gray," Carly explained. "She ordered from him again today, and he's dreading it."

Valerie wrinkled her nose. "Poor kid. Can't he just say no?"

Carly shook her head. "He feels obligated to her. I guess his grandmother got a call from Octavia yesterday, complaining about him. It's kind of a long story. I'll tell you and Grant about it later."

Suzanne arrived, and customers began flocking in. Valerie shuttled between the kitchen and dining room, while Carly helped out at the grill or wherever she was needed.

Ross came in at eleven forty, his expression the gloomiest Carly had ever seen. "Hey," he said dully, unzipping his carrier.

Carly grabbed his drink orders from the cooler, then spoke to him quietly. "Ross, if it helps any, I asked Grant to make sure Mrs. Gray's order was perfect. He added a lot of extra chips, and I also stuck a ten-dollar gift card in there. Tell her it's compliments of the eatery."

"Wow. That is so nice of you. I mean, you really wanna give her a gift card?"

"I'm hoping it might bring out her softer side," Carly told him. "Maybe she's so accustomed to everyone disliking her that she's not used to receiving any kindness."

Ross didn't look convinced. "I never thought of it that way, but it's worth a shot."

"Now," Carly explained, "the Hughes order is below that, and the other two at the bottom. Mrs. Hughes lives near Octavia Gray, right?"

"Yeah, she lives in the house behind Mrs. Gray, but on a different street. Too bad Mrs. Gray can't be as nice as Mrs. Hughes," he groused. "That lady has to use a walker to get around, but she always has a big smile and a cold drink ready for me. And sometimes a slice of cake."

"Well, there you go. Customers like that make it all worthwhile, right?" Carly said brightly.

"I guess so," Ross said with a grudging smile. "Wish me luck!" He zipped his carrier, flashed her the peace sign, and swept out the door.

"What was that about?" Suzanne asked, stopping short next to Carly with a fistful of orders.

"A glitch with a customer," Carly told her. "Nothing that can't be resolved."

Suzanne gave Carly an exaggerated wink. "Whatever, but it sounded more like juicy gossip to me. You can give me all the deets later."

It was moments before noon when Carly got the frantic call. At first, she thought it was a prank, until Ross's terrified voice came through the line.

"M-Ms. Hale," he croaked out. "I . . . something awful happened to Mrs. Gray. She . . . she was facedown on the floor, and she wasn't moving. And a big frying pan—one of those cast iron skillets—was on her head!" He sucked in a shaky breath.

"Ross, try to calm down," Carly said, her own thoughts screaming with alarm. "Is she okay now? Did you call for help?"

He gave out a choked sob. "No, she's not okay! And yes, I already called nine-one-one. I'm sitting on the front steps waiting for them. I . . . think I hear the sirens now."

In the distance, Carly heard the faint whine of a siren. *Thank goodness.*

"Listen, Ross," Carly said, keeping her voice even. "You didn't touch anything, did you?"

"Yeah, I had to! I pulled that heavy pan off her head. That . . . that's when I knew—"

Carly pressed her stomach, which was starting to revolt. "All right, listen. The ambulance will be there any moment to take her to the hospital. You just need to tell them exactly how you found her and walk them through everything you did. They'll probably ask a lot of questions, but that's SOP, okay?"

Another sob broke from him. "Okay. But I think it's too late for an ambulance, Ms. Hale. I'm almost positive Mrs. Gray is dead."

CHAPTER 4

VALERIE HOOKED HER FINGERS AROUND CARLY'S ELBOW. "UM, CARLY, WHY is your face the color of flour?" she asked in a quiet voice.

Carly realized she'd been standing there staring at her phone for at least half a minute. Heart pounding, she looked at Valerie and pulled in a long breath. "I—let's go into the kitchen."

The moment they went through the swinging door, Valerie pushed Carly into a chair. She fetched her a glass of ice water and sat down adjacent to her.

Carly took a few gulps of water and set the glass on the table. "Ross Baxter went to Mrs. Gray's house a short while ago to deliver her order. He found her facedown on the floor with a cast iron skillet on her head."

Valerie's gasp was loud enough to be heard in the dining room. "Wait, you mean—? *What?*"

Carly gave her a shortened version of Ross's story. "He was pretty sure Mrs. Gray was already gone. The ambulance must be there by now, or on its way."

"No doubt the police are, too," Valerie said grimly. Her eyes popped wide open. "Carly, I'll bet Fred is there. Should I text him and ask him what happened?"

"If the situation's as serious as I suspect, he's probably already knee-deep in whatever's going on. Maybe we should give him a chance to contact us first. Since it was our food Ross was delivering, I'm guessing it won't be long before we hear from the police."

The thought made Carly's inner workings ripple with dread.

"You're right. Totally." Valerie rubbed Carly's arm soothingly. "Listen, maybe we're jumping to conclusions. We don't have any details yet, and it sounds like Ross was pretty distraught when he called you. Maybe Mrs. Gray just has a concussion and he only thought she was dead."

"I hope you're right, Val."

But something, deep in the pit of her stomach, told her otherwise.

It didn't take long for the banter in the dining room to turn to Octavia Gray. Carly was always amazed at how fast bad news traveled in Balsam Dell. In the eatery, it seemed to move like a rocket ship on a straight course aimed at the moon.

Nearly every stool at the counter was occupied. A cacophony of chatter rose from every booth, words like *murder* and *old bat* seeping through.

At the grill, Grant was flipping sandwiches and slapping orders onto stoneware plates at nearly warp speed. The moment he spotted Carly and Valerie, he waved his spatula to signal *help me!*

Carly quickly began grabbing completed orders and delivering them to the booths, refilling drinks where needed. Valerie scooted behind the counter to help Grant on the grill, who looked as flustered as she'd ever seen him. Suzanne followed at Carly's heels.

"Hey, have you heard the scuttlebutt?" Suzanne shoved a strand of her dark blonde hair behind one ear. "Everyone's saying Octavia Gray was bashed over the head, and the police think Ross Baxter did it!"

No, no, no.

"That's crazy talk. Ross did nothing except attempt to deliver her lunch. We all need to stop—" Her cell jingled in her pocket. The smiling face of Rhonda Hale Clark, Carly's mom, appeared on the screen. Carly held up a finger. "Hold on a sec."

"Carly!" Rhonda screeched into the phone. "What in the name of Howdy Doody's uncle is going on? Did Ross Baxter really attack Octavia Gray with a skillet?"

Carly groaned. Rhonda had known Ross since he was a kid. He'd delivered her paper every day, shoveled her driveway in the winter, and raked her leaves in the fall. Carly reminded her mom of all these things and instructed her to take deep breaths.

"Okay, honey," Rhonda said after she'd calmed down. "I'm sorry for overreacting. I just got swept up in the moment. Are you—"

"Hey, Mom, I've really gotta dash, okay? We're jam-packed with customers and they're getting antsy."

"Do you need my help?"

Carly remembered the last time her mom helped in the restaurant. By noon the first day, Carly had been forced to give her a pink slip.

"Thanks, but we're okay. I'll let you know if it changes."

"All right, but be careful, okay? I know you all too well. If Octavia Gray is truly dead, I wouldn't put it past you to start looking for her ki—"

"Bye, Mom!" Carly disconnected before her mom could finish the word *killer.*

She closed her eyes and took a deep breath. Why was Ross's name already being tossed around? She'd spoken to him barely a half hour ago, yet he was now being linked to Octavia's death.

Clearing her mind as best she could, she focused on her customers. She rang up orders and cleared off tables, keeping both ears perked for any tidbits of intel that might slip through the chatter. Unfortunately, the name that kept popping up was Ross Baxter's.

She was seating a table of three when she heard two men in a nearby booth engaging in a boisterous conversation.

"—probably at the police station now, getting the third degree," said a husky man with a grizzled beard. On the pocket of his blue work shirt, the words *Balsam Dell Fencing* were embroidered.

"Hey, listen," the man seated opposite him quipped, "if the kid really did off her, he should be given a medal, not a jail cell."

They both laughed and went on chowing down their sandwiches. Carly wanted to question them both, but just then Valerie pulled her aside, her face awash with worry. "Hey, I *really* need to talk to you. In the kitchen."

From Valerie's solemn expression, Carly knew it was bad news.

"I got a text from Fred," Valerie said the moment the swinging door closed. "Someone leaked what happened at the crime scene. That's why it got around so fast. Ross is at the police station now, being questioned."

"The crime scene? So that means Octavia is definitely—?"

"Dead. I'm afraid so." Valerie's face looked ready to crumble. She grabbed Carly in a consoling hug.

Carly pulled back. "Who leaked it? Does Fred know?"

"No, but he's furious about it. He said if he finds out it's one of his people, they're in for a world of trouble." She paused. "Um, one other thing. Fred said we are not to discuss Ross with anyone. That was a direct order." Valerie squeezed her shoulder gently. "I . . . think he mostly meant you, Carly."

Of course he did.

"Well, there's nothing we can do at the moment," Carly said, "so let's keep serving customers." She forced a smile, but she knew it came out like a grimace.

"Excellent plan." Valerie squeezed Carly's shoulder again. "Whatever happens, we'll all get through it together, okay?"

Carly nodded, but her heart felt like a block of iron. Her jumbled thoughts melded into one big horrible one.

Another murder in Balsam Dell with direct ties to her restaurant.

• • •

It wasn't long before calls came in from Ross's three other customers, whose grilled cheese lunches hadn't arrived. Carly had been so rattled over Octavia's situation that she'd forgotten about Ross's other orders.

To the first two customers, Carly promised vouchers for free meals and agreed to absorb any delivery fees. The last one, however—Mrs. Imogene Hughes—begged Carly to deliver her order as soon as possible. Carly recalled Ross telling her that Mrs. Hughes lived behind Octavia Gray, but on a different street.

"Grant, Mrs. Hughes is bummed that she won't be getting Ross's delivery today. Can you whip up another grilled cheddar for me and add a large soup? She lives close by, so I'll drive it over to her myself. I won't be gone long, I promise."

"Give me three minutes and I'll get right on it. Maybe you can get the soup ready?"

"You got it."

Less than ten minutes later, Carly pulled into the driveway of a white ranch home with an attached one-car garage, which, according to her GPS, was the Hughes residence. Delivery bag in hand, she exited her car. Red and blue lights flashed from behind the house. If Ross had been correct about the location of the Hughes home, the lights were no doubt coming from emergency vehicles in Octavia Gray's driveway.

Clutching her bag, Carly climbed the front steps and rang the bell. When no one responded after pressing it twice, she peeked through the screen door into a tidy, picture-perfect living room. At the back of the room, a walker rested against the wall next to a doorway.

Carly banged her knuckles on the screen door. "Mrs. Hughes?" she called out. "It's Carly Hale. I have your lunch order."

Several seconds elapsed, and then Carly heard a thump. "Coming! Be right there!" someone called out.

At the sound of a human voice, Carly sagged with relief. After what happened to Octavia, her nerves were as jumpy as fruit flies.

An elderly woman with thinning white hair and a wrinkled face came through the doorway, grabbing her walker on the way.

"Sorry to make you wait," she apologized. "I was trying to get a look-see at all the commotion outside. Come in, come in."

Mrs. Hughes unlocked the screen door, and Carly stepped into the living room. The sofa and chairs were from a much earlier era, but everything looked immaculate. The maple end tables shone with polish. A stack of *Reader's Digest* magazines sat precisely in the center of a gleaming coffee table.

She looked at Carly's bag and grinned. "You can bring that into the kitchen," she said, pushing her walker. "Follow me."

The kitchen was large and as neat as the proverbial pin. Carly set the takeout bag on the sparkling clean counter, in front of a set of colorful canisters. Three boxes of confectioner's sugar sat at the far end.

"Sorry for the wait, Mrs. Hughes," Carly said. "I got over here as soon as I could."

"Not a problem, and please call me Imogene." Resting her walker against the counter, she opened the bag and removed her sandwich and soup containers. Up close, the woman looked even older than Carly had guessed, judging from her voice on the phone.

"I'm so sorry you had to deliver this," Imogene said. "My son, who lives with me, travels a lot on business and I totally ran out of bread. I don't drive anymore myself."

"No worries. I'm glad to help out." Carly lowered her voice. She wasn't sure how much Imogene knew, so she chose her words carefully. "I'm not sure if you heard, but there was an emergency at Mrs. Gray's home. That's why our delivery person was detained."

Imogene's wrinkled jaw dropped. "Is that what all the hubbub's about?" She pushed her walker toward the window and peered outside. Carly went over next to her and looked out into the yard behind Imogene's.

"I wondered why the ambulance was there, and all those flashing lights," Imogene said, going back to the counter. "Did you find out if anyone got hurt?"

"I think so, but I'm not sure how badly," Carly fibbed. "I'm sure we'll know more once it's on the news."

With a twist of her lips, Imogene set her sandwich on a stoneware plate. "I hate to tell tales out of school, but anytime there's trouble in this neighborhood, Octavia Gray is usually at the root of it."

"Oh my, really?" Carly said. "I hadn't heard that about Mrs. Gray, but then I didn't know her. So, you've had issues?"

"Issues galore," Imogene retorted. She opened the soup container and poured its contents into a bowl. "Ah, still nice and hot," she said with a satisfied smile. She fussed with her walker and then said, "Dear, can you bring these over to the table for me?"

Carly immediately grabbed the plate and the bowl and set them on the kitchen table. Painfully aware of the time, she knew she needed to head back to the restaurant.

"I really do have to run, Mrs.—I mean Imogene," Carly said. "For your trouble today, I'd like to deliver another grilled cheese lunch to you tomorrow, if that's okay. Totally on the house, no charge to you."

"Oh, that's so generous of you, dear. Maybe I'll try the one with tuna this time! What a sweet lady you are. Can I call you tomorrow and let you know?"

"Of course. I stuck a paper menu in your bag with our number. And please, may I suggest you lock your door after I leave? After what happened to Mrs. Gray—"

Imogene swerved her head sharply at Carly. "Wait a minute. I thought you said you didn't know what happened."

Carly wanted to slap herself for her blunder.

"Something bad happened to Octavia, didn't it?" Imogene bleated, her voice rising. "Tell me the truth."

Carly gulped. "Um, I'm sorry, Imogene. I'm afraid you're right. Octavia Gray was attacked in her home. I'm afraid she didn't survive."

CHAPTER 5

By around three o'clock, the eatery was sliding into its midday lull. A few of the booths were occupied, but most had cleared out.

Carly wasn't hungry, nor was Valerie. They both skipped lunch.

Grant had said little, but his face was pinched with worry. Carly knew him so well. He was afraid she would put herself in danger again, despite warnings from everyone who loved her—not to mention the chief of police.

She was collecting dishes from a vacated table when she heard a woman's voice in the adjacent booth. "Old witch," the woman said, her tone indignant. "It's a wonder someone didn't do her in sooner. I'd have done it myself if she'd tried to lasso you. Lucky thing you weren't her type."

Attempting to look casual, Carly moved closer to the source of the voice. A seventysomething woman with rouged cheeks and a flowered polyester top sat opposite a thin, balding man—her forefinger aimed at his face.

"Dear, *please*," the man begged. "This isn't the time or the place. Finish your coffee so we can go."

The woman's gaze shifted to Carly, then back to her companion with a smug smile. "Miss, can I have a coffee refill?"

"Of course," Carly said, smiling at the pair. She fetched a pot of coffee and filled the woman's mug. "Did you both enjoy your meal?"

The man's face tightened. "*Mine* was delicious."

"Mine was okay, but next time I'll ask for extra cheese." The woman plopped two creamer packets into her coffee.

"We're always happy to take special requests," Carly said, then lowered her voice. "Um, forgive me for overhearing, but I gather you knew Mrs. Gray?"

The woman's rouged cheeks reddened even further. "Well, no, not personally, but I knew her reputation. Before she retired, she worked in the bank. Everyone knew what a hussy she was. I'm Sally, by the way, and this is my husband, Ralph."

"I'm Carly, and I'm pleased to meet you," Carly said, in a voice so saccharine she feared her teeth might melt.

Ralph nodded politely and Sally went on, her small eyes glittering. "Octavia Gray preyed on other women's husbands. That's a known fact. Thank heaven my Ralph didn't have the money or the looks to be sucked into her web. But some men did, and a few ended up with broken marriages."

Ralph cringed. "Sally, please—"

Carly felt for the guy, but she needed to know more. "Oh my. That's awful. Is there . . . anyone in particular who might have had a grudge against her?"

Sally lifted her mug to her lips with a sly smirk. "Well, that list is about a mile long. Do you know Tara Shepard? The lady who's going to reopen the pocketbook store?" She took a noisy sip of her coffee.

Tara Shepard. Carly recalled her coming into the eatery for takeout a few times. Attractive, auburn-haired, stylishly dressed. She'd been pleasant, but not overly chatty. Her shop, Pugs and Purses, had closed during the pandemic, but she was on track to reopen soon in a different location.

"I've met her, yes. Does . . . did she have a connection to Mrs. Gray?"

Sally set down her mug and folded her arms over her chest. "Yeah, she had a connection. Octavia Gray was Tara Shepard's evil stepmother."

CHAPTER 6

AFTER SALLY AND RALPH PAID THEIR BILL AND SUZANNE HAD GONE HOME, Carly insisted that Grant take a break.

"Why don't you take a sandwich with you and go sit outside on the green," she suggested. "It's cooler out than it was yesterday, so at least you won't be baking alive."

"Nah, I'm good," he said with a shake of his head. He focused on scraping down the grill, which was already spotless.

Carly sighed. "You obviously heard about Mrs. Gray."

He turned and gawked at her. "How could I not have heard? It's all anyone's talked about since it happened!" He set down his scraper and gave her a penitent look. "Geez, I'm sorry I raised my voice. I know none of this is your fault. But doesn't it seem surreal? I mean, another murder in Balsam Dell with a connection to our restaurant?"

Carly winced. "I know, I hear you. But if there's a connection, it's a very loose one. Even though Ross was delivering our food, he's not our employee." She knew she was splitting hairs, but it was all she could think of to say.

Grant wiped his hands on a towel. "You know what I'm worried about, don't you?"

Here it comes.

"You're worried that I'll try to get Ross off the hook for . . . whatever happened."

"Exactly. Which means you'll start asking questions. And when you start poking your nose into other people's business, *some* people don't take kindly to it."

"By some people, you mean the guilty ones."

Grant stared silently at her.

"All right," Carly admitted. "I know that in the past I . . . kind of pushed a few people too far. But the last time it helped save a life. I don't regret that for a second."

"Okay, I get that. But remember, the chief is going to be on your butt to stay out of this one. You know that, right?"

Carly gave him a wry smile. "Ohh, yes. That's a given."

"And didn't he threaten to throw you in a jail cell if you ever interfered with another murder investigation?"

"Well, yes, but that was an idle threat. And don't worry, I'm not going to do anything risky."

"Famous last words. By the way, does Ari know about it yet?"

Ari was on a job out of town, and Carly hadn't heard from him. She knew she should call him, but she was putting it off. As much as she adored talking to him, this was one conversation she was not looking forward to.

"I don't think so. Otherwise, he'd have called me by now. We're supposed to have dinner at the inn this evening, but there's no way I want to go now."

When Valerie first came on board, Grant came up with the idea of taking turns working shorter days. It gave them each a chance to plan evening activities, or just enjoy a few shorter workdays.

For months it had worked out well. On Monday and Saturday, Grant left at four p.m. Valerie's "early" days were Wednesday and Thursday, and Carly's were Tuesday and Friday. But as spring approached and the eatery's business fell back into its busy season, the practice was pretty much abandoned. If one of them wanted to leave early, they simply asked. Carly always granted their requests.

With her and Ari having made dinner plans for that evening, she'd hoped to leave early. That idea bit the dust with the discovery of Octavia Gray's body.

She decided not to put it off any longer. Ari needed to know what happened, and she needed to hear his voice.

"Hey," she said when he answered his cell.

"Hi, honey! I thought you'd call sooner. You looking forward to dinner at the inn?"

Carly swallowed hard, then took a breath and gave him the disturbing news.

Ari was silent for so long Carly thought she'd lost him. "Ari? Are you there?"

"I'm here." He sounded deflated. "Good glory, I can't believe there's been another murder. I swear, it follows you around like a bloodhound. I've been in Bennington all day and didn't hear about it."

His words pierced her like a jagged arrow. It wasn't the first time she'd heard someone link her with the rise in local murders. Coming from Ari, it cut to the quick.

"Oh, honey, I'm sorry. That was a dumb, thoughtless thing to say. I should kick myself square in the pants."

"No worries," she choked out. "I know you didn't mean it."

After a pause Ari said gently, "Carly, are you okay?"

"Not really, but I'm hanging in there. I'm super worried about Ross."

"I'm sure you are, but I'm worried about you. I'll pack up my stuff and head home as soon as I can. Are you closing up early?"

Carly had considered closing at five, but she knew the police—aka Chief Holloway—would want to talk to her before the day was over. Better to do it in the restaurant, where she'd have the moral support of Grant and Valerie.

That decided, they agreed to postpone their dinner at the inn. Instead, they would meet at Carly's apartment at seven thirty—later if she was detained by the chief.

She, Grant, and Valerie managed to get through the supper hour, but it felt as if a veil of darkness had fallen over the dining room. It was one minute before closing time when the visitor Carly dreaded most walked into the restaurant. She locked the door behind him.

For a long moment, the chief stared at Carly. "What are the odds?" he said gruffly with a shake of his head.

"Hi, Chief. It's a pleasure to see you, too."

With a wave at Grant, Holloway removed his hat and ran a hand through his thick gray hair. "Is Val in the kitchen?"

"I'm right here," Valerie warbled, bounding through the swinging door and scooting over to him.

The chief's eyes brightened, and he gave Valerie a quick squeeze. "Hey, are you okay?"

"Of course I am."

"Good. I have some things to discuss with you all. Can we sit at the back?"

Carly grabbed a bottle of the chief's latest fave—a pink lemonade—and they all slid into a booth at the rear.

Holloway uncapped his bottle and took a healthy gulp. "You all heard what happened to Octavia Gray today. There's a lot I can't talk about, but there's a few things I need you all to know. Keep in mind, everything I tell you is strictly confidential. We've already had one serious leak and we can't afford any more."

"Did you figure out the source?" Carly asked him.

The chief blew out a breath. "Unfortunately, one of the EMTs, a young fellow new to the job, texted his girlfriend while en route to the hospital with Mrs. Gray. Said girlfriend then blabbed it to her coworkers at the gym where she works. From there it spread faster than wildfire over dry brush."

Grant looked baffled. "How did the guy not know better?"

Holloway's smile was flat. "Kid was new, first time he was called to a murder scene. He admitted he wanted to impress his new girlfriend, so he sent her that text. Believe me, he's profusely sorry now."

"Too little too late," Valerie said sharply.

"Chief," Carly put in, "I am very sorry about Octavia's death, but right now I'm concerned about Ross. Where is he? Is he okay?"

After a long hesitation, Holloway said, "The young man is okay, but he's badly shaken. The state police—your old pal Lieutenant Granger, to be specific—questioned him for almost three hours."

Carly remembered Granger from her last encounter with murder. The man was a crafty interviewer, a pro at throwing a potential suspect off guard. The thought of Ross being interrogated by him troubled her deeply.

"But then they let him go, right? I mean, seriously, Chief. You know Ross Baxter didn't kill Octavia Gray, right?"

"Carly," Holloway said, his patience sounding strained, "you know how these things work. It doesn't matter what I think. To answer your question, Ross was released to the custody of his grandmother with instructions not to stray outside of Balsam Dell. He's also been ordered to discontinue his food delivery service until further notice."

"But—"

The chief held up a hand. "Obviously, we have a lot more work to do. We've only started to collect evidence. But until we can put all the pieces together, Ross will remain a person of interest."

"Chief, what about fingerprints?" Grant asked him. "Whoever hit Mrs. Gray with the skillet must've left prints."

Holloway nodded. "There are prints on the handle, but we don't have any results in yet. We'll have a better *handle*—no pun intended—on what happened to Mrs. Gray once we identify them."

Inwardly, Carly cringed. Ross told her he lifted the skillet off Octavia's head, so naturally his prints would be found on the handle. She related this to the chief.

"Ross told us the same thing, but thank you for clarifying," he said a bit tartly.

Carly ignored his tone. "How long will it take to search the crime scene?"

The chief tapped his fingertips together. "This is not to be repeated by any of you, but Mrs. Gray was a messy housekeeper. We found piles of stuff all over the place. The kitchen table alone was cluttered with magazines, catalogs, cosmetic doodads. Combing through it is going to take time, and we're not going to take shortcuts. It will take as long as it takes."

It wasn't the response Carly had hoped for. She glanced at Valerie and then at Grant. "Chief, don't scream when I say this, but is there anything I can do to help?"

"I'm so glad you asked. You can go about your normal routine and let the police do their jobs."

Carly started to respond but Holloway held up his hand. "Carly, listen to me. An elderly woman was killed in her home in broad daylight, and not very far from here. This isn't a time for amateur hour. The police will handle the investigation, and the police will arrest the offender. Period."

Amateur hour? After all the help she'd given the police?

Several retorts popped into her mind, but Carly held her tongue.

Grant, on the other hand, looked vastly relieved, but Carly was still concerned about Ross.

"Chief, I'd like to call Ross this evening to see if he's okay." She tried to sound as if she was asking for permission, but she intended to call Ross with or without the chief's consent.

"Be my guest. He's already been cautioned not to discuss the crime scene or the case. With *anyone*." Holloway turned to Valerie and softened his voice. "Val, it's going to be a late night for me, so I won't be able to treat you to tacos like I promised. Will you take a rain check?"

"Of course, Fred. Aunt Flo and I can have her leftover shepherd's pie and enjoy a rousing game of Parcheesi."

He squeezed her hand, and she curled her fingers over his.

Carly raised her own hand to speak, as if she were in fifth grade. "One more question. Did Octavia have a cell phone?"

"Not that we uncovered, but as I said, we've only tapped the surface. Right now I need to head back to the station. I'm afraid it's going to be a long night. Carly, I trust you'll bring Suzanne up to speed on what we just discussed?"

"Consider it done."

Holloway pushed himself up from the bench seat, and Carly saw how tired he looked. His eyelids drooped and his shoulders hunched. She felt a pang of sympathy for him.

He had a tough job, sometimes a terrible one. She didn't envy him the grueling days ahead. Though the state police would take the lead, the chief would play a prominent role in helping them analyze the evidence.

"Chief," Carly said sincerely, "if there's any way I can help other than keeping my restaurant going, I am willing to do so."

He stared at her for several moments and then gave a sharp nod. "I appreciate that. If anything comes to mind, I'll let you know."

CHAPTER 7

WHEN CARLY PULLED INTO HER DRIVEWAY, SHE SAW A FAMILIAR CAR parked behind Ari's pickup. The sight of Rhonda Hale Clark's shiny red sedan put a sudden lump in her chest.

With not much room for her own car, Carly parked her aging Corolla behind Becca Avery's vintage Lincoln. Becca had inherited the rugged old car from her grandmother, who'd passed away while Becca was serving in the armed forces in Afghanistan.

Every light in Carly's apartment was on, and her mom was gawking out the front window.

Carly had just reached the top of the staircase when the door to her apartment flew open. Her mom, a spangled red band keeping her brunette hair at bay, launched herself at Carly as if she'd just returned from years at sea.

"Honey, are you okay?" She ran her hand over Carly's head as if stroking a favorite pet. "You've got Ari worried sick!"

"I'm fine, Mom. Let me inside, okay?"

Ari moved in beside Rhonda and gathered Carly in his arms. Havarti bounced at their feet like a rubber ball. Ari swept up the dog and all three hugged.

"He's already done his business outside, and I gave him supper," Ari said.

A wave of gratitude for all she'd been blessed with washed over Carly. Her throat started to clog, so she excused herself to wash up and fix her face.

"There, I feel human again," she announced when she returned from the bathroom.

Ari went into the kitchen with her. "Your mom brought over a cold cuts platter, complete with rolls and potato salad."

"I would have made a real meal myself," Rhonda explained, "but I could barely think straight after hearing about Octavia Gray." She wrung her hands as she searched for plates to set the table, a pair of enameled bangles jiggling on her wrist.

"This looks great, Mom. Where's Gary?"

Gary Clark, a retired dermatologist, had married her mom several years earlier. A kind man, he was as laid-back as Rhonda was wired. The two were a perfect match.

"Remember I told you? He's on Lake Winnipesaukee in New Hampshire with his fishing buds—a bunch of retired dermys like him."

"Oh, that's right. You did tell me," Carly said. "Hey, if nobody minds, I need to make a quick call to Ross. I want to be sure he's okay."

Ari smiled at her. "Go ahead, honey. You'll probably feel better after you talk to him."

Or not, Carly thought.

She dug her cell from her tote and dropped onto the sofa. Havarti nestled in her lap so he could listen, too.

Ross answered after a few rings. "Hey, Ms. Hale," he said in a droopy voice.

"Ross, I've been worried about you. I know you've had a long day. Are you doing okay?"

"I'm like, I don't know." His voice was odd, flat. "I'm not supposed to talk about anything, and I'm dead tired. Can we talk tomorrow?"

"Sure," Carly said. "But call me if you need to talk, okay?"

"Roger," he said and disconnected.

Ari poured cold drinks for everyone. Rhonda snapped the cover off the tray of deli rolls, cold cuts, cheese, and potato salad. Carly hadn't eaten since morning and was feeling lightheaded. She snagged a slice of Swiss cheese and downed it in two bites.

"That was quick. Did you reach Ross?" Ari asked. He returned a pitcher of lemonade to the fridge.

"Yeah, but . . . he didn't sound like himself. He said he was too tired to talk and that we could talk tomorrow."

"The poor boy is probably exhausted, just like you are," Rhonda soothed. "Don't take it personally."

"I'm not, Mom. But I'm worried about him."

They all sat and filled their plates. Ari gave Havarti a tiny piece of turkey and a sliver of cheddar, with a promise of more after dinner. Havarti knew the drill. After swallowing the snack, he settled under Carly's chair, waiting patiently for his next course.

Carly was hungrier than she realized. She put together a turkey and Swiss sandwich roll and added a heaping mound of potato salad to her plate.

"So, Mom, have you heard from Norah?" Carly asked.

Norah, Carly's older sister, lived in a gorgeous condominium in Balsam Dell with her opera singer boyfriend, Nate Carpenter. She was currently on tour with Nate and his family—all talented opera professionals. Judging from Norah's infrequent texts, she was having the time of her life.

"Norah's fine, and don't try to distract me," Rhonda said after swallowing a mouthful of potato salad. "You know, I remember Octavia Gray from her years at the bank. As I recall, she wasn't too popular with customers. At least not with the *women* customers," she added.

"How long did she work there?" Carly asked.

"Oh, I don't know. Maybe thirteen or fourteen years? After that she retired." Rhonda took a sip of her lemonade. "Have you ever seen a picture of her?"

"Never. I only know her by name. And now, by reputation."

Ari dug his cell out of his pocket and tapped at the screen. "Ah, here's one.

This is kind of a grainy pic, and it goes back a ways, but it was taken at her retirement party." He gave Carly the phone.

Carly enlarged the image. The photo showed a striking blonde wearing dazzling earrings and a matching necklace. She was flanked by a portly man with a toothy grin and a fortysomething woman who looked as if she'd rather be gutting fish. The caption read: *Octavia Gray, personal banking manager at Balsam Dell Savings and Loan, honored for her years of service.*

"Good gravy on a golf cart," Carly squawked. "This was in two thousand eleven, so in this photo she's, what, sixty-five? She barely looks fifty." She handed the cell back to Ari.

"After she retired, she let herself go a bit," Rhonda said, "but her reputation preceded her. She still attracted looks from roving eyes." She rolled her own eyes to convey the meaning.

Carly poked at her potato salad. "I delivered lunch to an Imogene Hughes today—she's Octavia's neighbor. Seems like a pleasant lady, maybe a bit lonely. I guess her son lives with her, but he was away on business and she herself doesn't drive."

Ari frowned. "Why did *you* deliver to her?"

"I felt bad for her. She called us and said Ross was supposed to deliver her lunch but there must've been a mix-up. She kind of begged me on the phone, so I caved."

With a warm smile, Ari reached over and touched her cheek. "You're too kind for your own good sometimes."

Carly squirmed. "Not really. We got talking, and she, um, hinted that Octavia was the neighborhood troublemaker. I . . . sort of promised to deliver lunch to her tomorrow, too." She felt her cheeks flush.

Ari set down his fork, his eyes narrowed. "You want to ask more questions, don't you?"

"I'm sorry, Ari, but yes, I do. A neighbor like that, especially if she's home all the time, might've seen something important. Or at least she might know if Octavia had any enemies in the neighborhood."

Rhonda wiped her lips with a napkin. "Young lady, I forbid you from asking any questions, of *anyone*, about Octavia Gray's murder. I am *not* going to go through this again, worrying about some crazed killer having you in his sights. My heart can't take it." She shoved the end of a ham-stuffed roll into her mouth and tore off a bite.

Carly stifled the urge to dispel her mom's fears with a casual retort. Over the past year, she'd given her mom more than a few moments of angst. It hadn't been intentional, and she'd helped corral a few nasty culprits. But to Rhonda, Carly endangered herself needlessly doing a job the police should be doing.

"I'm not a young lady, Mom. I'm thirty-three, and I can make my own decisions." She reached over and jiggled her mom's wrist playfully. "Stop stressing, okay?"

Rhonda pulled her arm away. "Don't think you can cajole me into accepting all this crazy Nancy Drew stuff again. It is not acceptable. Is it, Ari?" She gave Ari a pointed look.

Ari speared a chunk of potato with his fork. "Honey, you know I would never tell you what to do, although I might try to persuade you one way or the other. But this time I agree with Rhonda. Think about what a violent crime this was. A very up-close-and-personal crime."

Carly couldn't deny anything they were saying. If Octavia had, indeed, been killed by blunt force with a skillet, then her attacker must have acted with sheer rage.

"Listen," she relented, "I hear where you're both coming from. Right now, my only goal is to help Ross. His prints are on that skillet, and that doesn't bode well—even if his explanation is sound."

"That's true," Ari conceded. "But by tomorrow, the police might well have another suspect. I mean, shouldn't the *real* killer's prints be on that skillet?"

"Unless he, or she, wiped them off." Carly took a small sip of her lemonade. "Another thing. The fact that Octavia was attacked with her own skillet tells me this wasn't a premeditated crime. It was an act of rage, yes, but also a crime of passion. The killer used the nearest available weapon, which just happened to be the frying pan."

"I don't see how that helps," Rhonda said sourly.

"I don't either, Mom. But it was my food Ross was delivering, and I feel partly responsible." She paused to switch tactics. "Mom, don't you know Ross's grandmother?"

Rhonda nodded thoughtfully. "Helen was a few years ahead of me in high school. Such a darling girl. The boys all wanted to date her, but she only had eyes for Randall Quigley. They had a fairy-tale marriage. Helen was devastated when he passed."

"Then imagine what she's feeling right now."

Rhonda's face crumpled. "All right, I won't say any more. Just . . . please remember that Ari and I are never more than a phone call away."

"I would never forget that." Carly got up and hugged her mom, and her gaze fell on Ari. What she saw in his expression made her heart twist.

It was a look of impending doom.

CHAPTER 8

By the next day, the gossip in the eatery about the murder had settled down to the occasional murmur.

Carly tried to reach Ross a few different times, but her calls went directly to voicemail.

Late in the morning, several calls came in asking about delivery to seniors. Carly hated giving her customers the bad news that it wouldn't be available until further notice.

A gent named David Parlee, spokesperson for the activities club at Balsam Dell's senior apartment community, sounded especially distressed about Ross. "Miss Hale, we all know that young man and we trust him completely," he told Carly, disgust lacing his tone. "Not one of us believes Ross Baxter harmed that woman. It's patently ridiculous."

"I understand, and I agree," she tried soothing him. "But Ross's delivery service has been suspended for the time being. I wish I could be more helpful. I'll try to find someone else to fill in, but workers are at a premium these days."

Carly started to bid him goodbye when the man said, "Wait. Miss Hale, we're having a birthday party here on Friday for one of our residents. She's turning ninety, and she simply loves grilled cheese, especially yours. We had already worked out the details with Ross. He was going to pick up a birthday cake at Sissy's Bakery, and then place our orders with you for the lunches and deliver everything in time for the party. We have such a wonderful celebration planned for this charming great-grandmother! I'm afraid this throws a huge monkey wrench into the works." He sighed gustily.

Carly felt terrible. She knew Ross would feel the same.

"Sissy's has already agreed to deliver the cake," David Parlee continued. "One of the ladies here offered to do the sandwich pickups, but her eyesight isn't what it used to be, not to mention her driving. Truth be told, she should have turned in her license long ago. I could ride along with her to navigate, but it would be like the blind leading the blind."

"Have you tried other delivery services?"

"We called a few, but the prices they quoted made our heads spin. If need be, we'll use one of them but . . . well, we wondered if you could work something out."

Carly did some mental calculations. "How many sandwich orders will you have?"

"Well, including the birthday girl's—she loves your Party Havarti—it was going to be eleven."

Eleven. That was a lot of business to lose. More important, it was a lot of disappointed seniors.

"Mr. Parlee, can you get those orders to me by the end of the day tomorrow? I can take them over the phone, if that helps."

His voice brightened. "Oh, you bet I can. I can't tell you how much we appreciate this, Miss Hale."

"I'm happy to help. And let me know which order is the birthday girl's. Her lunch will be our treat." Carly gave him her cell number so he could call her directly.

His voice cracking, David Parlee thanked her profusely before disconnecting.

"Who was that?" Suzanne asked, her fingers looped through the handles of two clean mugs. In her other hand she held a pot of fresh brewed coffee.

Carly explained the situation with the seniors.

"I'm glad you offered to deliver," Suzanne said. "But on Fridays we're usually slammed."

"If I have to, I'll hire a delivery service myself and eat the cost. There's no way I'm going to disappoint those folks."

"Aw, you're a softie." Suzanne scurried off to deliver the coffee to one of the booths.

I'm also a bit sneaky, Carly thought.

In a building populated by senior citizens, she was willing to bet at least a few of them had known Octavia Gray.

• • •

Carly was behind the counter helping Grant plate orders when a familiar face entered the eatery. She'd only met the woman a few times, but Carly knew her immediately.

Today Tara Shepard wore her auburn hair pulled back into a high ponytail. Her green eyes held a weary look, and her face was devoid of makeup. Clad in a pink tee and a pair of beige shorts, she slid onto a free stool at the counter.

"Tara, it's nice to see you again," Carly greeted.

Tara gave up a tired smile. "I thought I'd take a break and eat here today. I've been working in my shop since six this morning, plus, I'm sick of eating meals on a step stool with a takeout bag balanced in my lap. Besides, the ambiance in here is charming."

She ordered an Alvin's Panko Perfection—a sandwich recipe created by Grant's dad, Alvin Robinson, when he helped out one day in the eatery. It was essentially a grilled cheese and tomato with a twist—the tomato slices were coated in panko crumbs and grilled until golden before adding them to the sandwich.

Tara declined a cold drink and opted for coffee. "I need all the caffeine I can get. I'm trying to get the shop up and running by the end of the month. I'm loving the new location, but I think I underestimated how much work it was going to be."

"You'll still call it Pugs and Purses, right?" Carly asked, after putting in her order with Grant.

"Yes, and I'm dying to get it up and running again. I've ordered a new sign for the storefront, one that's way more colorful and inviting than the old one. Plus, I've lined up some new vendors, and the purses they're designing for me are out of this world. I'm hoping to have an open house slash grand opening by the first of July. You'll come to it, won't you?"

"Are you kidding? Try and keep me away! I love purses, but I really favor totes. I tend to carry everything but the kitchen sink around with me." She laughed. "Do you have any help with getting everything set up?"

"My older brother Sawyer is here now," Tara said, averting her eyes. "He drove up this morning from Connecticut. He was supposed to be here yesterday, but he called me with some crazy excuse about his prescriptions not being ready at the drugstore."

"At least he got here, though," Carly said. "That's a good thing."

"True, but so far he's done more grumbling than anything. I love him to pieces, but he's always been sort of a complainer. Right now, he's at my condo *resting*"—she put air quotes around the word—"from his trip. He plans to bunk with me for a few weeks until the shop is on its feet."

"Well, it's great to have help."

Tara leaned closer to the counter and lowered her voice. "You probably don't know this, but the woman who was found dead yesterday was my stepmother."

"Oh, Tara, I'm sorry to hear that," Carly said. "I thought someone mentioned that, but I wasn't sure it was true. It must've been a terrible shock when you learned of her death."

With a slight shake of her head, Tara took a tiny sip of her coffee and then set down her mug. "You wouldn't think that if you knew her. Quite frankly, I wasn't the least bit surprised someone did her in."

Taken aback by Tara's bluntness, Carly stared at her for a moment. "Oh, I . . . um—"

"I'm sorry. I know how uncharitable that sounds. But the woman didn't have a kind bone in her body, at least in her later years. If there *is* someone out there who actually liked Octavia, I'd sure as heck like to meet them." She shot a fast glance behind her, as if worried someone might have overheard.

At that moment, Grant dashed over and set Tara's plate in front of her. Fat slices of Roma tomato and oozing cheddar peeked out from between two slices of perfectly grilled bread. "There you go. Enjoy."

Tara grinned at him. "Hey, thank you! Oh, man, this looks yummy."

"Tara, I'll leave you to enjoy your lunch," Carly said, though she was anxious to hear much more. She'd have to find a way to get Tara alone so they could have a private chat.

If Tara's opinion of her stepmother held any truth, then the suspect list for Octavia's killer should be filling up rather quickly.

• • •

The call from Imogene Hughes came in shortly before one o'clock. She asked specifically for Carly, who agreed to deliver a Farmhouse Cheddar Sleeps with the Fishes, this time without the side of soup.

Valerie crossed her arms over her chest. "You're delivering to her *again*? Methinks something fishy is going on," she said with a sly smile. "I don't suppose the fact that the customer's house happens to be directly behind the murdered woman's has anything to do with your good deed of the day."

Carly folded the top of the brown bag in which she'd packed Imogene's lunch. "Okay, so I might want to pick her brain a little. What's wrong with that? Besides, it'll take the place of my lunch break."

Valerie's smile faded to a look of concern. "May I remind you—Fred said we are not to discuss Ross with anyone. He especially meant you."

"I'm not going to discuss Ross." Carly gave her an innocent look. "I won't be long, I promise."

"Famous last words."

"Oh, good glory, you sound like Grant. I'll be back before you know it!"

Before Valerie could object further, Carly hurried out to her car. Minutes later, she was swinging into the driveway of Imogene's ranch home.

After she emerged from her car, Imogene's lunch bag in hand, she paused to take in the neighborhood. The homes along the quiet street were cookie-cutter versions of Imogene's. One-story ranches with attached garages, carefully trimmed lawns and shrubbery. It struck her that on a June day with temps in the high seventies, she didn't see a single soul outside.

With no time to waste, Carly climbed the few shallow steps to Imogene's front door. The elderly woman was peering at her through her screen door with a huge smile.

"Well, look who's here with my lunch!" Imogene trilled, leaning on her walker. She stepped back to let Carly enter, then immediately locked the screen door.

"Hi, Imogene! You look nice today."

Imogene was clad in a gray and pink flowered housedress that brushed her knees. Around her neck was a delicate chain from which a small pendant dangled. Carly wondered if she'd dressed up a bit in anticipation of her visit.

"Come right in," Imogene said. "I already poured iced tea for both of us. Sit with me while I eat my lunch."

"That sounds lovely. I can only stay a short while, though. Duty calls."

The house felt cooler today, no doubt thanks to the milder weather. A window air conditioner sat in one of the front windows, but it wasn't turned on.

Carly followed Imogene into the kitchen, where the table was already set with two tall glasses of iced tea. On the sparkling clean counter, a gold and white metal cake pan sat in front of the canisters. After helping Imogene plate her sandwich, they sat at the table. Carly made sure to face the window so she could peek outside into the backyard, beyond which was Octavia's property.

Imogene's eyes widened at the sight of her sandwich. "I have never seen a tuna melt like this in my life," she declared. "Look how stuffed it is! No wonder your restaurant is so popular." She picked up one half and aimed it at her mouth, then bit off a chunk.

Carly took a small sip of her iced tea. It was overly sweet, but otherwise not bad. She craned her neck to get a better look outside. The iron fence that surrounded Octavia's property partially blocked her view, but the house was visible through the bars. Unlike the ranch homes on the street where Imogene lived, Octavia's was a two-story affair with a red tile roof and a tall chimney. From what she could see of the driveway, no vehicles were parked there.

She waited until Imogene had swallowed before asking, "Have you seen any more activity over at Mrs. Gray's house?"

Imogene shook her head. "That big van from the state police was there early this morning, but it left around ten. It's been quiet since then."

All the more reason to do a drive-by, Carly thought.

Imogene pressed a hand to her bony chest. "That poor boy, Ross Baxter—he's getting blamed for it, isn't he? As if a young man like that would ever hurt an old lady!"

"I totally agree with you, Imogene. I've known Ross for years, and I'm positive he'd never harm anyone. The police did question him, but so far he hasn't been charged with anything."

"Oh, Carly, I'm so nervous. After what happened to Octavia, I'm wondering if anyone in this neighborhood is safe. My son, Mark, called me from London as soon as he heard what happened. He insisted I call a locksmith to install better locks. Mine are old, and they're not dead bolts."

"I can understand his concern. Not to alarm you, but that's a good idea. You said he travels a lot on business?"

Imogene swelled with pride. "Yes, he's a travel consultant for an agency out of Boston. They sponsor tours in different countries. With the pandemic mostly over, Mark visits hotels and tourist sites and helps design the brochures. He's put together some wonderful tours. Some of the places they visit are off the beaten track. Hidden gems, Mark calls them. He's always been such a smart boy."

"Wow. What an interesting job."

Imogene sighed. "Yes, for the most part. It can be tiring, though, traveling so much. Going back and forth through different time zones."

Carly took another sip of her iced tea, her gaze drifting back to the window. She noticed something odd. Along the base of the fence that separated the two yards, the grass looked newer, as if it had recently been seeded. A maple tree hunkered in front of the fence, its leaves lush and green.

Imogene's wrinkled face fell. She'd finished half her sandwich but hadn't touched the other half. "You know, I saw on the news that poor Octavia was hit over the head with a heavy pan, and that's what killed her. It made me feel so horrible. She wasn't a very pleasant woman, but she certainly didn't deserve that." She pulled a tissue from her dress pocket and dabbed at her eyes.

"I agree. It is very sad," Carly said gently. "You mentioned that she wasn't . . . popular with the neighbors. Did anyone in particular dislike her?"

Imogene crumpled the tissue and shoved it back into her pocket. "If you're thinking enemies, Octavia certainly had her share. But if you're asking in particular, yes. Back in the day, there was a woman who worked at the bank with her who thought she was the devil in a skirt. She lived in this neighborhood, in fact, until her husband passed. That was at least fifteen years ago." She wagged a wrinkled finger. "But as I always say, a wronged woman has a long memory."

Carly glanced at her watch. As if on cue, her cell pinged with a text. She excused herself to read it. It was from Valerie: *Are you on your way back? We need you!*

As much as she wanted to question Imogene further, she had to get back to the restaurant.

"Imogene, my coworkers are texting me. I really do have to dash."

She thanked her hostess for the iced tea and hurried out to her car. Abandoning her plan to drive past Octavia's house, she headed back to the eatery.

"Thank heaven you're back," Suzanne griped, blowing a strand of hair out of her eye. "A van full of tourists showed up and we've got orders up the wazoo."

"Well, I'm here now, but I was only gone about twenty-five minutes," she defended.

"Yeah, but it was twenty-five minutes of the lunch crunch." Suzanne sounded annoyed.

"I know. I'm sorry."

In the dining room, nearly every booth was filled with women of a certain age, as her mom would say. Each one wore purple in one form or another. It turned out to be a book club that toured a different Vermont town each week during the summer months.

For the next hour, she, Grant, Valerie, and Suzanne worked like robots. The women customers laughed and joked and gushed over the food. Before they paid their tabs and left, Carly directed them to the used bookstore about a half mile up on the main drag. The inventory there was phenomenal, and she knew they'd enjoy perusing its shelves.

Carly tried to reach Ross several more times, without any luck. Either he was avoiding her calls, or the police had scared him into refusing to talk to anyone.

Instead of taking even a short break, Carly scarfed down a few slices of cheddar to keep her stomach from growling.

Suzanne left at three, but not before pulling Carly aside near the restroom door. "Listen, we all know what you're doing, and we're not happy."

Carly bristled at her tone. "What are you talking about? What do you think I'm doing?"

"You're trying to figure out who killed that old woman," Suzanne said. "Don't deny it. I can tell by the look on your face I'm right."

Carly opened her mouth to defend herself, but she had nothing.

"And if the chief gets wind of it, *which he will*," Suzanne went on, "don't think he won't rip you a new one."

After an awkward pause, Carly lifted her chin. She met Suzanne's hard gaze straight on. "Well, this sounds a bit like mutiny. Is that what I'm dealing with?"

"Oh, get over yourself, Carly. It's not mutiny. It's called caring. We love you and we want you to be safe. And that means letting the police solve crimes. That's what they get paid for."

Carly swallowed. Suzanne had never spoken to her with such raw candor. "Suzanne, I appreciate that you all care—more than you know. But if the police don't dig up another suspect, they're going to focus on Ross. How fair is that?"

"It's not fair," Suzanne shot back. "It's sucky. But that's the way the world works." She retrieved her purse from beneath the counter and went back over to Carly. Her expression softer now, she said, "I'm sorry. I didn't mean to come off like a tyrant. Just . . . think about what I said, okay?"

"I will. I promise. But in return," Carly added, "I ask that you think about how you would feel, right now, if your Josh was in Ross's shoes."

CHAPTER 9

GRANT LEFT A HALF HOUR EARLY TO MEET UP WITH FRIENDS. A GIFTED cellist, he was part of an informal group of string musicians who gathered once a week to practice. Although his first love was having a career as a chef, his second was playing the cello.

Carly and Valerie were preparing to lock up for the day when Carly took one last glance at her phone. She'd been hoping for a call or a text from the chief, but no such luck.

"I'm surprised the chief hasn't been in touch today," she told Valerie. "Can I ask if you've heard from him?"

Valerie hoisted her purse onto her shoulder and toyed with the latch. "I have, but it was only a brief call. Mostly it was about what night he'd be free for our tacos date. We ended up making it for Friday, assuming nothing hits the fan in the meantime."

"Okaay," Carly said carefully, "can I ask if he mentioned Octavia's murder?"

"Only to say the state police are working on it day and night and that they want to close the case quickly."

"That's all?"

Valerie groaned. "Okay, there was one other thing. I'm not supposed to tell you, though."

"But you will, won't you?" Carly urged.

"I can't, Carly. Fred and I are serious about each other, and I'm not going to break my word to him."

"I understand," Carly said evenly. "And I honor your choice, and your loyalty. Just indicate without speaking if the thing you're not supposed to tell is about fingerprints."

Valerie hesitated, then nodded.

"Is it that Ross's prints were the only ones on the murder weapon?"

With a pained look, Valerie nodded again.

Carly sensed she was holding back something, but she didn't want to push it. Somehow, she'd figure out a way to wheedle it out of the chief.

"Thank you," Carly breathed. "If it's any consolation, that's not a surprise. It's exactly what I expected."

"So what does it mean?" Valerie asked.

"It means that, despite the murder being an act of rage, the killer had his wits about him enough to wipe his prints off the skillet before fleeing the house."

Just then Carly's cell rang. She fished it out of her tote and saw a number she didn't recognize. Taking advantage of the distraction, Valerie waggled her fingers and bolted out the door.

"Hello, this is Carly Hale."

A soft voice came through the line. "Carly, I don't know if you remember me, but I'm Ross's grandmother, Helen Quigley."

Heart thumping, Carly moved over to a booth and dropped onto the bench. "Yes, of course I remember you, Mrs. Quigley. What can I do for you? Is Ross okay?"

"Well, I don't know if *okay* is the right word. Ross is managing, but he's very disturbed over this mess with Octavia Gray. I . . . we were wondering, would you have a few minutes to stop at our house on your way home? Ross told me you close at seven. That's why I waited to call."

Carly had spoken to Ari several times that day, but they hadn't made any plans for the evening. He'd offered to help a buddy move a bedroom set to his girlfriend's house, and they were going to grab burgers afterward. He offered to postpone, but Carly insisted he help his friend, assuring him she'd be fine on her own.

"I'll be glad to stop over," Carly told Helen Quigley.

Armed with directions, she shut off the lights, locked up, and jumped into her car. It occurred to her that Valerie hadn't waited for her—a plan they'd put in place months earlier to ensure that no one left the eatery alone after closing.

Before starting her engine, Carly texted Becca and asked if she would check on Havarti. Becca replied with her usual thumbs-up, along with an emoji of a smiling dog.

Helen Quigley lived on one side of a well-kept duplex home on Pine Street. Each side had its own driveway and garage. The landscaping was sparse but well cared for. At the foot of the front steps, a riot of pink petunias bloomed from an old-style wooden tub.

Carly had met Helen only once, when Ross first started his delivery gig. Helen had stopped by the eatery to thank Carly for doing business with her grandson. Carly'd had the feeling that his grandmother worried his fledgling business might fail.

Ross's car was in the driveway. When he answered the door, Carly was taken aback. Dark circles hung beneath his eyes, and his curly hair was mussed, as if he'd just awakened from a nap. In his rumpled tee and baggy cargo shorts, he looked so forlorn that Carly wanted to hug him.

"Hey," he said, holding the door open. "Come on in. Gram's like, putting together some snacks."

She stepped into a living room graced with comfortable, colonial style furniture. The room was slightly warm, but the windows were open. Carly recalled Ross saying that his grandmother didn't like air-conditioning.

"How are you holding up?" Carly asked Ross.

He shrugged. "Okay, I guess. Have a seat."

Carly sank onto a green plaid sofa and rested her tote at her feet. Seconds later, Helen Quigley came into the room. Her gentle face, framed by a cloud of fluffy gray hair, gave her the appearance of an angel. Her kind eyes watered when Carly rose to hug her. She asked Ross to bring in the snacks she'd left in the kitchen.

"Thank you for coming over," she said after he left the room.

"I'm glad you invited me, Mrs. Quigley. I've been worried all day about Ross."

"Please . . . it's Helen." She shook her head. "I'm worried about him, too."

Ross returned with a tray bearing chocolate chip cookies, three glasses of lemonade, and a stack of napkins. He set it on the coffee table, grabbed a glass for himself, and then plopped onto a reclining chair opposite the sofa.

"Please help yourself, Carly," Helen said. "I made those cookies this morning."

"Thank you." Carly snagged a cookie and set it on a napkin, then took a sip from one of the lemonade glasses.

"I know you've been trying to call Ross," Helen said. "We saw all the missed calls on his phone."

"I did call, several times," Carly confirmed. "As the day went on, I got more worried when he didn't answer." She looked over at Ross, who'd dropped his head into his hands.

Helen continued. "Early this morning he started getting all sorts of harassing calls. Most were from reporters, but a few were from awful people accusing him of murder."

"Oh, Ross, I'm so sorry," Carly said. "How did they get your cell number?"

"Easy peasy," Helen answered sourly. "They called his business number, which is the same as his personal cell number."

Ross lifted his head. "It's okay. Like Gram keeps reminding me, they're just trolls who have nothing better to do. Sickos," he added miserably.

Sickos harassing an innocent person, Carly thought angrily.

"Anyway, Ross shut off his phone," Helen continued. "The police have my landline number, so it's not as if they can't reach us."

That explained why Carly couldn't reach Ross all day. She sampled a bite of her cookie. "This is delicious, Helen."

"I'm glad you like them," Helen replied. "They're Ross's favorite."

"Have the police been over here today?" Carly asked.

Helen reached for a glass of lemonade. "No, they've been oddly silent. That's what makes me so nervous. I contacted my attorney, who referred me to someone that does criminal work. She's on notice if we need her, but I'm keeping my fingers crossed that we won't."

"That's wise," Carly said. "It never hurts to be prepared."

Helen reached over and touched Carly's knee. "Carly, I'm not sure how to say this, but you have somewhat of a reputation for being a . . . what was that word you used, Ross?

"Crime-buster," Ross supplied. "She catches bad guys."

Oh boy.

Carly could see where this was headed.

"Helen, I think Ross is giving me way too much credit. Mostly what happened was happenstance. A 'wrong place at a bad time' sort of thing. If the police hadn't been there for me, those encounters would've turned out a whole lot worse."

Helen removed her hand from Carly's knee. "Well, the newspapers reported it a bit differently."

"Yeah," Ross put in. "And didn't you like, save a lady's life?" He sat back and pinned her with a look. A look that Carly clearly read as *please help me*.

"Okay, I admit I helped the police nab a few bad apples." Carly decided to cut to the chase. "What it is you're asking me to do?"

Helen sagged with relief, her eyes alight with hope. "We don't want you to put yourself in any danger, Carly. But someone was in that house before Ross got there. Someone who despised Octavia enough to commit a terrible crime. If you could work with the police—" She broke off, her voice ragged.

Carly reached over and squeezed Helen's thin hand. "For the record, Chief Holloway has promised me a jail cell if I ever poked my nose into another investigation."

A tiny smile escaped Helen's lips. "Well, don't you worry about that. I'll deal with Fred."

Carly chuckled. She had to admire Helen's grit.

"All right," she relented. "Tell me what you know about Octavia Gray. One of her neighbors—Imogene Hughes—claims that back when she worked at the bank, she was a man-chaser of sorts."

"Gram, you remember I told you about Mrs. Hughes, right?" Ross piped in. "She's one of my best customers. A really nice lady, too."

"You did," Helen said, "and I vaguely remember Imogene from church. She's somewhat homebound now, isn't she?"

Carly reached for another cookie. The haphazard snacks she'd managed to snag during the day had caught up with her. She was craving a real meal, but cookies would have to do in the meantime.

"Imogene uses a walker," Carly explained, "but her home is immaculate. She said her son lives with her, but he's away on business a lot." Carly shifted to face Helen. "Helen, from the bits and pieces I've picked up so far, it might be hard to narrow down the names of people who had a grudge against Octavia. Do you know of anyone in particular? Someone you can think of who really had it in for her, to put it bluntly?"

Helen sat back and folded her hands in her lap. "Over the years, there've been so many. The one that comes to mind is Lois Feeney. Mind you, this goes way back. When she and Octavia were working at the bank, Lois's husband got involved with her. I'll say this for Octavia—she kept herself in great shape and always dressed to the nines. Anyway, she and the Feeneys were also neighbors. They lived practically on top of each other. Late at night Lois's husband would sneak out of the house and go over to Octavia's."

"What a lowlife," Carly said.

"One Sunday after church, Lois confided in me. She wanted my advice."

"What did you tell her?" Carly took a bite of her cookie.

Helen sighed. "Quite honestly, I wouldn't have stayed with the man, but it wasn't my place to say so. I suggested she seek counseling, but she said it wouldn't help."

"So how did it all end?"

"Well, late one night Lois saw her husband running across the yard toward Octavia's. She was determined to catch him in the act, so to speak, so she threw on a coat and followed him. Unfortunately, Octavia's bedroom window was a little too high, so Lois stood on a rickety trash barrel to peek inside. Fell and broke her ankle and was never the same."

Carly shook her head. "What a sad story." She recalled Imogene's words. *A wronged woman has a long memory.* Had she been thinking of Lois Feeney when she said that?

"So, what happened with Lois?" Carly asked. "Did she finally leave her husband?"

Helen shook her head. "No, she ended up staying with the cheater. He died of an aneurysm a few years later. She's at the senior living place now, bless her. I heard she kept her old Ford, but I don't think she uses it much anymore."

Carly knew that many seniors resisted giving up their driver's license. Gina had gone through that with her dad before he moved to assisted living.

A breeze rustled the lacy curtain in one of the front windows. It was nearing eight o'clock. Carly had been there longer than she realized.

"Helen, maybe it would be helpful if you searched your memory for anyone else who disliked Octavia. I'm wondering if she'd had a more recent run-in with someone."

"That's a good point," Helen agreed. "Oh, you've been so kind to stay here so long. How about if I put on my thinking cap and get back to you soon?"

"Sounds like a perfect plan," Carly said, glancing over at Ross.

He opened his mouth as if to say something, but then his shoulders dropped. "Yeah, thanks for coming over, Ms. Hale. I'll probably turn on my cell in the morning. If I see your name, I'll definitely answer. I blocked all the creeps who called me today."

Before Carly left, Helen packaged up some cookies for her. Once again, she promised to rack her brain for a list of Octavia's enemies.

Ross held open the door for Carly, his face morphing into a scowl. "That

Octavia woman was so mean, I bet she had plenty of enemies. Remember, Gram, when she chewed you out a few weeks ago? She said you parked too close to her at the market so she couldn't get in her car, and then she keyed your driver's side?"

Helen stared at her grandson, and her jaw dropped. Her face blanched, while Ross's turned tomato red.

Carly quickly said her goodbyes and hurried out to her car, one question filling her mind.

Had Ross just thrown his grandmother under the bus?

CHAPTER 10

THURSDAY WAS AS BUSY AS EVER, EVEN MORE SO THAN USUAL. BY ELEVEN thirty, nearly every booth was filled. A few regulars occupied their usual stools at the counter.

Calls had come in from some of the seniors hoping that delivery had been reinstated. Carly felt bad having to tell them she was still working on it. The fact was, she hadn't had a minute to think about it.

So far that morning, Carly hadn't heard from either Ross or Helen. While she took that as a positive sign, her thoughts kept drifting back to Ross's bombshell as she was leaving their home. Octavia had "keyed" Helen's car for parking too close to hers at the market. For sure, it wasn't a motive for murder, although people had killed for less. But Helen wasn't that kind of person. She was a kind, caring grandmother who doted on Ross.

Carly wasn't surprised when another familiar face strolled through the door. In fact, she'd been expecting Don Frasco sooner.

"Hey," Don called out. He waved at Grant, who raised a spatula in return, and snagged a bottle of root beer from the cooler.

Don was Balsam Dell's local reporter—editor and publisher of his own free weekly paper. He subsisted on ads from local businesses, but he was always on the prowl for a big story.

Carly was fourteen the day she first met Don. He was in grade school, and his mom had asked her to babysit while she went out for a few hours. Thankfully, it was only that one time. An overactive kid with lungs that would shatter glass, he'd had a meltdown when Carly tried to make him a grilled cheese. These days, his ginger-colored hair was more stylish than in past months—short on the sides and back, with a longish wave in the front that curled upward over his forehead.

Don dug a crumpled dollar bill out of his jeans pocket, dropped it on the counter, and slid onto a stool near the cash register.

Carly pushed the dollar back to him. His heartfelt reporting on a local woman several months earlier, which helped save the woman's job, had earned him free root beers forever.

With a grin, Don shoved the dollar back into his pocket and pulled out his cell phone. He uncapped his soda and took a hefty swig, dribbling some down his chin. He swiped it off with his fingers. "So, what's been happening?" he asked Carly, the flicker of his pale lashes saying he knew exactly what'd been happening. "Maybe a little murder on the menu?"

Carly gave him a one-shouldered shrug. "Why, did you hear of one?" She lifted his soda bottle and wiped the counter, then set it down again, hard.

She had to admit that Don had helped her in the past. The first time, he'd nearly gotten himself killed. In his annoying way, he'd supplied information she might otherwise not have learned. But he drove her crazy with his irritating questions, and his insistence that they "partner up" to solve crimes. Plus, the guy hated cheese!

Don tapped his fingers over his cell phone. "I, um, might have been at the crime scene."

"Really?" Carly's pulse pumped out a few extra beats. Aware that a customer was seated two stools over from Don, she pasted on an innocent smile. "So, would you like a bacon and tomato sandwich?"

"Nah, I've got a PBJ in the car. Unless you're treating."

Carly stifled the retort that hovered on her lips. "I'll put in your order."

A few minutes later, while Don was shoveling his sandwich into his mouth, Carly leaned over the counter and murmured, "Call me at three on the dot."

After he left, Suzanne rushed past her in a hurry to retrieve three orders. "So, what's Don up to these days? I'm sure he heard about the you-know-what," she said, balancing plates on both arms.

Suzanne had a soft spot for Don. Several years earlier, she'd worked with him at a local hot dog place, where he'd been a part-time dishwasher. When the owner's son played a mean trick on Don and nearly got him fired, Suzanne gave the owner a hefty piece of her mind and rescued Don's job.

"Oh, he sure did," Carly told her. "We didn't have a chance to talk, though."

Carly pushed through the door into the kitchen. Valerie stood behind the work counter, looking frazzled. Even her topknot was askew. She was sliding a mountain of sliced tomatoes from a cutting board into a container when she blurted, "Oh, good. I need you. Grant needs two pounds of cooked bacon, ASAP. He's running low at the grill."

"I'm on it."

I should have been on it before, Carly chastised herself. *My mind today is everywhere except where it should be.*

Carly pulled two packages of bacon from the fridge, slit them open, and laid the slices on the griddle they kept on the kitchen stove.

Valerie wiped her hands on a dish towel and snapped a cover over the tomatoes. She went over to Carly with a sheepish look. "Hey, um, I got thinking about last night. You know, when we were leaving? I left you to close up alone, and that was totally wrong of me." Her pale cheeks reddened. "I . . . apologize for being a jerk."

"Come on, Val. You were not a jerk. It was a one-time thing, so don't worry about it. I survived, right?" Carly said genially.

"Okay, but I promise it won't happen again."

When the bacon was crisped to perfection, Carly used a set of tongs to set them in a stainless steel container. She returned to the dining room and went behind the counter, tucking the container into a cubby within easy reach of the grill.

"Thanks," Grant said, and then in a lower voice, "Um, there's a guy here who wants to talk to you. A Mark Hughes." He lifted his chin toward the dark-haired man with startling blue eyes who was standing near the cash register.

Mark Hughes. It had to be Imogene's son.

Carly skirted around the counter and went over to him. "Hi there, I'm Carly Hale. What can I help you with?"

Up close, the man was strikingly handsome. His attire was what Carly thought of as business casual—a short-sleeved dress shirt and a navy tie. His eyes were slightly bloodshot, but his broad smile was warm.

"Miss Hale, I'm Mark Hughes, Imogene's son." He held out his hand and Carly gave it a brief squeeze. "I came to thank you for your kindness to my mom while I was away. She told me you delivered lunch to her twice, even after you lost your delivery boy."

"I was happy to do it, Mark. She's been such a good customer. I didn't want to disappoint her."

"Well, it was much appreciated. She gets lonely when I'm away without anyone to talk to. I hope she didn't bend your ear for too long."

"Not at all. I enjoyed chatting with her. Now, can I get you something?"

"No, not today. I'm going straight home for a nice long nap. I flew in from London overnight, landed at Logan early this morning. I was tempted to grab a hotel room at the airport and sleep for a day, but I wanted to get home to Mom as soon as possible so I drove back. Long ride," he said with a tired sigh.

"I can imagine," she sympathized. "How is Imogene today?"

His face clouded. "She's still quite distraught over what happened to Mrs. Gray. Not that they were friends, but it scared her half to death to think of the way the woman . . . passed. Especially since it happened practically in our backyard."

Carly guessed from the edge in his tone that he hadn't been a fan of Octavia's. She wondered if the woman had had a friend in the world.

"The police came over late yesterday and spoke to Mom," Mark went on, "just in case she might have seen something. Unfortunately, she couldn't help them. But having to talk to them got her agitated all over again. I felt terrible I wasn't here when it happened."

"Well, you're here now. I'm sure that's comforting to your mom. How well did you know Octavia?"

His smile was thin. "Let's just say she wasn't the nicest of neighbors. After a dispute we had over our fence line, Mom and I never spoke to her again. Still, she didn't deserve to be killed like that." Mark rubbed one eye with the heel of his hand.

"No, she didn't," Carly agreed. "What was the fence argument about?"

"Nothing worth talking about. Water over the dam, as they say." He pulled out a business card from his shirt pocket. "On a more cheerful note, I don't know if you enjoy traveling, Carly, but I'm putting together a tour of England that's going to be spectacular."

Carly accepted his card. *Mark A. Hughes, Travel Consultant.* His company was a Boston-based travel agency she'd never heard of. With everyone booking their own trips on the internet these days, she marveled that a travel agency stayed in business.

"Believe it or not," she told him, "I've never traveled outside of the country. But it's definitely on my bucket list. Do you have a brochure I could read?"

"Not yet, but I hope to have a mock-up of one put together within a few weeks. This last trip to England was to scout out places that discerning travelers might appreciate. Out-of-the-way places, not the usual tourist traps. I took some incredible photos." His blue eyes sparkled with excitement. "The tour will start in London, and from there it will go on to some charming, even hidden places most tourists have never heard of. And we don't shuttle our travelers around in smelly buses. We only use luxury vans with every imaginable comfort. For those who can afford that kind of travel, it will be the trip of a lifetime."

Clearly designed for the wealthy, Carly thought, but she couldn't help smiling at his enthusiasm. "You love your work, don't you?"

Mark's gaze narrowed, and he looked away. "I do, most of the time. Sometimes I wonder how much longer I can keep up the pace, though." He glanced around. "You do a great business here, and I've already taken up too much of your time. I'll stop in again soon and pick up lunch for me and Mom. Thanks again for taking care of her in my absence."

"Not a problem," she said, noticing two men hovering near the cash register. They waited until Mark left and moved up to pay their tabs. Carly recognized them from earlier in the week. The Balsam Dell Fencing lettering embroidered on their shirt pockets identified them as the pair who'd joked over Octavia's demise.

"Did you enjoy your meals?" she asked sweetly.

"You bet," the bearded one said and handed her a twenty. "I could eat here every day." He lowered his voice. "Hey, um, I heard you talking to Mark Hughes about that nightmare over his neighbor's fence. Did he tell you what happened?"

Carly handed him his change. "He mentioned a fence, but he didn't elaborate." She widened her eyes at his shirt pocket, as if she'd just noticed the company name. "Are you the fellows that did the fencing work?"

"Yeah," the other one grumped. "No way that fence should've been moved. *No way.*"

"We told Hughes to take that bi—witch to court," the bearded one added, "but he didn't want to make trouble. I even gave him a good lawyer's name, but he got ticked at me and told me to drop it. He said a lawsuit would cost more than moving the fence, and to stop bugging him about it."

"You're speaking about Octavia Gray's fence, right?" Carly asked.

"That's the one," the other man said. "Crazy woman wanted her property line moved closer to her house. Can you believe it?"

"That's odd. She didn't want more land?"

"Nah, she wanted less. See, there was a big maple on her side of the property line, and she resented paying someone every fall to rake the leaves. I mean, is that wacko or what?"

His companion continued the story. "So instead of having the tree removed, like a normal person, she decides to force Hughes to have the fence moved—at his expense. She was a freakin' nutcase if you ask me." He glanced at the ceiling and quickly crossed himself. "May she rest in peace."

Something didn't add up. Carly could almost understand Octavia wanting to rid herself of the offending maple. Almost. But why would Mark Hughes give in to her demand to pay for it? Weren't there laws governing property lines? Weren't there boundary markers on the ground?

"Hey, give this to Suzanne, okay?" The bearded man gave Carly a fiver.

"Will do. Hope to see you again soon."

Watching the men leave, Carly got tangled in her thoughts. Every account of Octavia's behavior spoke of a hostile, bad-tempered woman. A woman who enjoyed causing trouble for its own sake. Was there *anyone* she'd gotten along with?

She could think of one person who might have a clue, but she needed to catch her alone.

CHAPTER 11

AT FIVE TO THREE, SUZANNE REMOVED HER APRON IN THE KITCHEN AND tossed it into the laundry bin. "Well, I'm outta here, guys. I think I walked enough steps today to reach the moon, if they could build a roadway to it." She grinned. "Tips were good, though."

"It was extra busy today, wasn't it?" Carly said. "Go home and relax, Suzanne. You definitely earned your keep today."

Valerie, who was rinsing dishes at the sink, called out, "Later, girl!"

After Suzanne left, Carly went over to Valerie. "Do you mind if I take a short break to make a call from my car? I won't be long."

Valerie turned and gave her a puzzled look. "You can't make it from in here?"

"Some things are personal," Carly joked. "You wouldn't want me listening in when you're talking to Fred, would you?"

"Are you accusing me of being an eavesdropper?" Valerie teased, feigning offense.

"Not at all. I just need some privacy."

Valerie flicked a few drops of water at her and smiled. "You know I don't mind. Just remember to record your convo when you get to the juicy stuff, okay? I want to play it back later."

"In your dreams. Back in a few!"

Thanks to the shade of the building, the Corolla's inside temp was almost bearable. Carly powered down her window for some fresh air, inhaling the summer scent of fresh-mown grass.

Vermont, the Green Mountain state, had always been Carly's home. With mountains stretching everywhere the eye could see and glorious foliage in the fall, she couldn't imagine living anywhere else.

Several years earlier, Carly's mom had gone through a "Florida phase" and moved to Vero Beach with her hubby, Gary. But the charm eventually wore off and Rhonda longed to be back home, where she felt she truly belonged. Soon after Carly opened her restaurant, Rhonda and Gary returned to Balsam Dell and never looked back.

Carly glanced at her phone. It was three minutes past three and Don still hadn't called. She was about to tap his number on her cell when someone pounded on her passenger side window. She jumped, and with an irritated sigh released the lock.

Don plunked onto the front seat and slammed the door shut. "I thought it might be better if we talked in person."

"How did you know I'd be in my car?" she asked crossly. "Were you spying on me?"

He shrugged. "Nah. Thought I'd check here first. If you weren't in the car, I was gonna call you from across the street."

Her annoyance level rising, Carly got to the point quickly. "So, tell me what you know about Octavia Gray's murder. How did you happen to be at the crime scene?"

Don scratched at a pimple on his neck. "I was on my way to the printer's that day when I saw two police cars with sirens blasting turn onto Warren Road. That's where she lived, you know."

"I'm aware," Carly said.

"Natch, I followed them. About a mile up the road, an ambulance was sitting in someone's driveway, next to a police car. The cop cars I was following swung in and parked on the lawn. It was obvious something major had gone down. A few cars had pulled over to the side of the road to gawk, so I did the same. I grabbed my phone and hopped out of my car to see what was happening. My luck, I didn't get too far. The cops were setting up crime scene tape and ordering everyone away from the area."

"Did you know whose house it was?"

"Not then, no. I tried talking to one of the uniforms—explained that I was the town reporter—but he told me the area was off limits and to get out of there. He wasn't too polite about it, either."

"So, you really didn't learn anything," Carly pointed out.

Don gave her one of his sly smiles. "Depends on what you mean by anything. On those TV mystery shows, the sleuth is always taking pictures with her phone, right? Even in places she's not supposed to be?"

"I guess," Carly said.

"Well, before that cop made me leave, I got a few shots of the house and all the official cars. But then I got thinking, don't criminals usually return to the scene of the crime?"

"I think that's a myth, Don. Google it, but I'm pretty sure."

"*Whatever*," he said testily. "When the gawkers started to leave—the police were ordering the drivers parked on the roadside to move—I took photos of their cars. Including," he added smugly, "their license plates."

"So, your theory is that one of the looky-loos might have been the killer. And that you might've gotten a pic of his car as he was driving away."

"Or *her* car."

Carly shook her head. "I don't know, Don. That's pretty weak."

"I'll admit it's circumstantial, but it still might be useful as evidence." He pulled his phone out of his shirt pocket and beamed at it. "I love my new cell phone. It takes professional-grade photos. Anyway, I'm thinking that if I go to Chief Holloway with my pics, maybe he'll give me an interview."

Carly stifled a laugh. She doubted it. No one got under the chief's skin the way Don Frasco did.

"Don, are you going to show me the photos, or do I have to sit here until I turn into a baked potato?"

"Geez, it's not that hot." He tapped at his phone and handed it over to her. "Start there."

One by one, Carly swiped through the pics. She had to admit, the photo quality was superb. After looking at seven photos, she said, "You only photographed two cars."

"Yeah, those were the two parked on the side of the road in front of me. But I took them at different angles, see?" He reached over and tapped the last image. "Anything strike you about that one?"

Moving the phone closer, she squinted at the image of a gray SUV with a roof rack. "I can't see much through the tinted windows. There might be something in the back, but it's barely a shadow."

"Look at the tag."

"The . . . oh. You mean the out-of-state plate?"

"Exactly. Tell me, why would an out-of-towner pull over to the side of the road to watch a scene like that?"

Something tickled Carly's brain, but she couldn't put her finger on it.

"Because that's what people do, Don. It's like the so-called train wreck no one can look away from. Besides, maybe it wasn't an out-of-towner. Maybe it was someone who recently moved here and hasn't changed his registration yet."

"Always possible. But wouldn't it be good to know?"

"Maybe. I don't suppose you could text those photos to me so I can go back to work?"

His eyes, nearly the color of his auburn hair, gleamed. "In return for . . ."

"In return for free root beers for life, which you're already getting," Carly said wryly.

"How about a free bacon and tomato sandwich every day until the murder is solved?" he countered.

"Every day?"

"Okay, every other day."

Carly didn't mind making the sandwich deal. It was the murder she cared about. A murder that needed to be solved so that Ross could resume his normal life. And so that an elderly woman, regardless of how despised she was, would have justice.

"Okay, deal." She stuck out her hand.

Don barely skimmed her fingers before he said, "Hey, what are you doing about delivery to the old folks these days? Isn't Ross Baxter out of commission, so to speak?"

"He is, for now. I'm hoping to find another delivery service that does a cash business, but I haven't had time to look into it." Carly pointed at Don's phone. "Send me those pics so I can go back inside, will you?"

Don tapped at his phone. Seconds later, Carly's pinged with a text.

"Thanks, Don. I gotta run, but—"

"Wait!" He slapped his forehead and swiveled toward Carly. "I should've thought of this before. Why don't *I* take over the deliveries? I can always use the extra cash, and it'll give me a chance to chat up your customers. I'm betting a lot of them knew Octavia Gray. And I'll bet they have tales to tell." He wiggled his eyebrows.

Carly hesitated. "Don, I'm not sure that's a good idea," she said, even as she gleaned the possibilities.

"Give me one good reason," he challenged.

In her mind, a part of Carly still saw Don as that whiny little kid who trod over his mom's dining room table in his cowboy boots—a stunt for which Carly got blamed. But deep in her gut, she knew he was no longer that boy. He was a young man who'd matured into a decent reporter, if not a hugely successful one. In some ways, she felt bad for him. Somewhat of a loner, he was always on the lookout for that one big story that would launch his career with a real newspaper.

"You can pay me whatever you paid Ross," he offered, sensing her hesitation.

"Don, I didn't pay Ross. He worked for himself, and he delivered for other businesses, too. If you work for me, we need a different arrangement."

After a few minutes of bargaining, they worked out a deal. Don agreed that it was only in effect until Ross was back in business.

"Above all," Carly warned him, "you have to be discreet. If Chief Holloway thinks I've sent you out there to badger elderly folks, I'll be toast. *Burnt* toast."

He gave her an innocent smile. "Believe me, I can be discreet. No worries there."

"Good. Then you'll start tomorrow."

There was only one delivery job she intended to handle herself.

The following day's delivery to the Balsam Dell senior apartments for the ninetieth birthday celebration.

• • •

Back inside the restaurant, Carly saw that Valerie and Grant were both in the dining room. Two of the booths were occupied by customers lingering over a late lunch. It was a sight that never failed to lift her spirits.

Cell phone in hand, she went into the kitchen. She poured herself a glass of ice water, then sat at the table. She tapped at her phone until Don's photos appeared.

Unfortunately, nothing about them was remarkable. A glut of official vehicles clustered in front of what had to be Octavia's home. In one photo, a uniformed officer was leaning over one of the cars parked along the roadside—

apparently instructing the driver to leave the area.

She remembered that Don had focused on the two "gawker" cars—on their license plates in particular. With her thumb and forefinger, she enlarged the images. The front car, a smallish vehicle painted to resemble a bumblebee, had a Vermont tag. The other one, a gray SUV with a roof rack, had a blue license plate. Carly enlarged it further.

"Connecticut. The Constitution State," she murmured to herself.

That's when it struck her. The day after Octavia's murder, Tara Shepard said her brother had driven up from Connecticut that morning to help her set up the purse shop.

Which meant the car with the Connecticut plate couldn't have been his— not if he'd driven up Wednesday morning. Besides, Connecticut plates weren't exactly rare in Vermont, especially as the summer season kicked into gear.

She tucked her cell into the pocket of her gauzy blue capris and went into the dining room.

Grant was quieter than usual. Aside from his worries over her asking too many questions about Octavia Gray, she wondered if something else was going on.

"Everything okay?" she asked him, stuffing napkins into one of the dispensers on the counter.

He squirted water on the grill, watching it form tiny bubbles as it sizzled. "Same as always," he said with a shrug. He blew out a breath and turned to her with a forlorn expression. "I'm not sure things are going to work out with Izzy."

Izzy. That was Isabella, the young woman who worked as dietary manager at Balsam Dell's elementary school. Together, she and Grant had joined forces to get his healthy snack packets approved by the school board and served in the cafeteria. Although Izzy was about five years older than Grant, who hadn't yet reached his twenty-first birthday, the two had bonded over their love of food.

"I guess the age difference is starting to become an issue," he said glumly. "Every time I try to see her these days, she has something going on with friends. She doesn't even invite me to join them."

"Did she ever say age was an issue?" Carly asked gently.

"No, but I can read between the lines." He pushed his scraper over the grill in slow, steady motions. "I'm not sure whether I'll call her again. If she's interested in seeing me, she'll let me know."

Carly didn't know what to say to ease his pain. Grant was experiencing the age-old angst of losing his first love.

"I know this doesn't help, and it's not what you want to hear," Carly offered, "but before long you'll be in culinary school making all sorts of new friends. You'll have a whole new outlook by then. I promise." She squeezed his shoulder lightly.

He gave her a grudging smile. "Thanks, Carly."

Customers began stopping in for an early supper, many for takeout orders. At around four thirty, David Parlee called Carly on her cell with thirteen orders for Friday's birthday party.

"Wow. You're up to thirteen." Phone to her ear, Carly went into the kitchen and grabbed a sheet of paper and a pen. "That's going to be quite the celebration!"

"I hope that doesn't present a problem," he said, sounding worried. "Two more friends decided to join us."

"Not a problem at all."

Carly hoped she could keep thirteen grilled cheese sandwiches warm by the time the party began. The eatery's compostable takeout containers typically did the trick, but it was best to eat the meals right away once they reached their destination.

They agreed on a delivery time of eleven forty-five, give or take a few minutes. Carly agreed to help set up the table and put out bowls of chips and salad. To make things simpler, the seniors had dispensed with ordering any tomato soups, and they'd be supplying their own beverages.

Armed with the list, Carly returned to the dining room. She explained her plan to Grant.

He studied the list of orders and then nodded slowly. "This is doable, but you and I will need to work together." He looked at her. "After you leave with the food, how long do you think you'll be gone?"

"I'm honestly not sure. These folks have been Ross's good customers, although they've never ordered thirteen sandwiches at once before." She laughed slightly. "I want to be sure everything is shipshape before I leave. Oh, and one more thing."

Carly explained the deal she made with Don Frasco to handle deliveries until Ross was back in action.

"Yikes. I mean, that's good for us. I just hope we can keep up." A trace of worry flickered in Grant's eyes.

"We will," Carly assured him. "Somehow we always do, right?"

The remainder of the workday went without any hitches. Ari called and offered to bring over a pizza around seven thirty. It was an easy supper with almost no cleanup, so she readily accepted. Most of all, she wanted to spend time with him.

The surprise of the day was Ross Baxter. Shortly before closing time, he strode through the front door. Hands stuffed in the pockets of his cargo shorts, his eyes heavy from lack of sleep, he looked more dismal than ever.

Carly quickly went over to him. "Ross, I'm surprised to see you. Is everything okay?"

"Yeah, nothing's really changed. Can I talk to you for a few minutes?" He waved to Grant and Valerie, who both gave him kind smiles.

Carly led him to the rear booth so they could chat privately.

"What's happening?" Carly asked quietly. "Have the police given you any updates?"

"Not really. It's like, we're in a holding pattern. But . . . there's something I want to show you." He slid his cell phone out of his shorts pocket and pulled up his photos. "That day, that awful day when I found Mrs. Gray"—he swallowed hard—"I took a picture."

"A picture? Of . . . the crime scene?"

"Not of Mrs. Gray, no. But even in my horrified state, I thought something looked weird." He gave her his phone. "That's the kitchen table you're looking at. Mrs. Gray was lying on the floor about a foot away from it."

Carly studied the picture. The table, which appeared to be pine, was covered with so many odds and ends it was impossible to see any one object clearly. Enlarging the picture helped slightly, but it was obvious that tidiness had not been Octavia's strong suit. The bulk of the mess looked like unopened mail. With the exception of two neat stacks of envelopes, the mail sat in disorderly mounds that had toppled from their own weight.

"Looks like she never opened her mail," Carly noted. "Maybe she was starting to organize it all when she was surprised by the killer. See these two stacks here?"

"Yeah, I saw that." His eyes twitched. "There's something else that bugged me, except that I can't prove it. Every time I delivered to Mrs. Gray, she always, and I mean *always* took the money out of a fancy purse that hung over the kitchen chair. When I got home that day, after the cops let me go, I took a close look at this picture. That purse wasn't there. I know it doesn't sound like anything, but it bothered me, you know?"

Carly gave Ross his phone. "It could've been in a different room, or the killer might have stolen it. That's the more likely scenario. Did you mention it to the police?"

"Nah. I figured they'd think I was crazy, or that I stole it myself." He groaned.

"But you didn't have it on you, and they searched your car, right?"

"Yeah, totally. They like, turned everything upside down! Plus, they took my food carrier with all the food orders still inside."

"I'd forgotten about those." Carly wondered what happened to the carrier's contents. "Ross, can you text me that pic? It doesn't tell us much, but maybe I can examine it under a better light."

"Yeah, sure." He tapped away at his phone.

"About the purse," Carly said, "was there anything distinctive about it?"

"That's what I wanted to tell you. The handle was like a chain, and the purse had these elaborate pictures on it, like a lady lounging on a sofa and all sorts of flowers around it. It was sort of like, what's that called . . . tapestry?"

Using her own cell, Carly located images of vintage needlepoint purses. She showed them to Ross. "Like these?"

"Hey, yeah. Almost exactly!"

Carly tucked the information into a mental file, but she didn't see how it helped. "If I can ever get the chief to talk to me, I'll mention it to him." She hesitated, then said, "Ross, I never heard back from your grandmother, and frankly, I'm worried about both of you."

His face fell. "Yeah, you and me both. Gram's hanging in there, I guess. Until this happened, I was doing really well saving money for textbooks. I have a partial scholarship and a student loan, but the books are gonna cost a fortune. Without a summer job, I'll have to tap Gram for some coin."

The clock had crept past seven. Grant and Valerie were shooting anxious looks at her. And then, like an electric jolt, an idea sparked in her head.

Carly tapped the table. "Ross, excuse me for a few seconds. I'll be right back."

She slid out of the booth and gathered Valerie and Grant for a confab. When she returned to her seat, she was smiling.

"Listen, Ross, we could seriously use some help in the kitchen. It's not glamorous, but it's honest work. If you're willing, you can start tomorrow."

His face brightened. "Really? What would I do?"

"Load the dishwasher, scrub pans, chop veggies, shred cheese. Fun stuff like that," she added with a grin. "I'll pay you minimum wage, plus all the food you can eat."

"But . . . what about the police?"

"They told you to stick around Balsam Dell, right?" Carly said mischievously.

A slow smile emerged on Ross's face. "I'll do it. And I promise I'll be the most hardworking dishwasher, scrubber, chopper, and shredder you ever saw."

CHAPTER 12

On Friday morning, Carly left home an hour earlier than usual. At the drive-up window of her favorite donut shop, she picked up two steaming coffees and five blueberry muffins.

Tara Shepard's soon-to-be purse shop was located two blocks past Carly's eatery, in a meticulously restored brick building graced by green-and-white-striped awnings.

Carly swung her car into the paved lot adjacent to the building. *Lucky Tara, she has customer parking,* she thought with a twinge of envy. Carly's own customers had to park either on the street or in the town lot on the opposite side of the main road.

Only one car was in the lot—a sporty sedan with red metallic paint that sparkled in the early morning sun. Carly crossed her fingers that it was Tara's. If not, she'd have to scrap her mission—for the time being, anyway.

Clutching the goodies with both hands—she didn't want to spill the coffees—she walked around to the sidewalk in front of the shop. She noticed that the rental space adjacent to Tara's was empty. A large sign advertising the space for rent was taped to the inside window.

When she peered through Tara's glass front door, she saw that the overhead lights were on. At least a dozen cardboard boxes rested in short stacks in the middle of the room. Garbed in a yellow tee and cutoff denim shorts, Tara was moving a large box from one stack to another.

Carly freed one hand and knocked hard on the glass. Tara whirled around to the source of the sound, almost losing her balance in the process. Carly held up her coffee and muffins.

With an easy grin, Tara loped over and unlocked the door. Her auburn hair twisted into a messy bun, she relieved Carly of the cardboard coffee holder. "Hey, what are you doing here at the crack of dawn?"

"I thought you might like a pick-me-up to start the day," Carly told her. "I'm guessing you've been putting in some long hours setting up shop, and I know from experience how exhausting that is."

"So, you're a mind reader *and* a grilled cheese diva," Tara joked, her green eyes beaming. "Come on, we'll go into the back room, which eventually will be my office. I finally brought in a card table and some folding chairs so I don't have to eat takeout from a step stool anymore. Plus, my brother whined all day yesterday about the lack of seating. I love him to death, but he's a major pill." She rubbed her hands together over the goodies bag. "I can't wait to dive into those breakfast treats, whatever they are."

"Blueberry muffins."

Tara clutched her chest. "God love you."

The back room was an L-shaped space with beige filing cabinets lining one wall. A fluffy pink dog bed and a water bowl occupied one corner. Tara and Carly sat kitty-corner to one another at the card table. Tara reached into the bag for a muffin.

"Do you have a dog?" Carly asked her.

"Yeah, my little pug, Paisley. I used to think I wanted kids, but now I'm glad I don't have any. Dogs, especially pugs, fill the bill quite nicely—and with a lot less trouble."

"Hence the shop name Pugs and Purses," Carly said with a laugh. "I have a Morkie named Havarti. Maybe someday they should have a playdate."

"Oh, that would be fun," Tara agreed. "I'll warn you, though—Paisley is a bundle of mischief. My brother Sawyer's bringing her in this morning, if he ever gets here. He's supposed to help me paint the walls today. He doesn't have pets of his own and he absolutely dotes on her."

"Sounds like a good brother."

"Yeah, well, most of the time." Tara broke off a chunk of her muffin. "Actually, I feel kind of sorry for him. Before the pandemic hit, he owned a kitchen accessories store in Connecticut. It was doing pretty well, but the virus changed everything. He ended up having to shut down for good."

"I'm sorry to hear that," Carly said. She'd heard similar stories, and they always made her feel bad. "Do you think he wants to start it up again?"

Tara shrugged. "Sometimes he says he misses it and might like to reopen. But he gave up the leased space, so he'd be starting from scratch. Plus, he'd have to get a commercial loan to start up again. Which, frankly, I don't think is possible."

An interesting tidbit, Carly thought. If she understood his situation, Sawyer Gray might well be in need of some cash.

"I'm excited about my new carpeting," Tara said, switching topics. "If the stars are in alignment, it'll be installed next week. It's so gorgeous, Carly. It's pale green with a leaf pattern, and so easy to care for." She popped the chunk of muffin into her mouth and jiggled the bag at Carly. "Have one!"

Carly helped herself to a muffin and cracked the lid off her coffee cup. She needed to ask Tara about her stepmother, but wanted it to sound natural, not as if it was her sole mission. "I'm anxious to see it all when it's done. What kinds of purses are you going to sell?"

Tara swallowed her muffin and grinned. "Oh, I'm so glad you asked. Mostly I'll be buying from local crafters. The talent that's out there is amazing. Quilted handbags are super popular, especially in a quaint town like ours. And there's a group of women in town who make felted purses. They donate most of their earnings to charity, so that'll be a good selling point. So many others, it's hard to describe them all."

"Sounds awesome," Carly said. "What about designer purses? Are you into those?"

Tara shook her head. "No, not so much. But"—she held up a finger—"I've discovered that *vintage* designer bags are in great demand, so I'm going to create a special display for those. Since they're so pricey, I'll probably take them in on consignment. I've studied them a bit, so I know how to recognize a knockoff, in case someone tries to pull a fast one. Carly, you would not believe what people will pay for the old designer bags. I recently saw a Dior from the seventies advertised for two thousand dollars."

"Wow. Now I really can't wait for your shop to open." Carly pushed her muffin to one side. "Tara, I had kind of an ulterior motive for coming here."

After a pause that felt endless, Tara said, "I had a feeling. I've read a few things about you. You're quite the detective, aren't you?"

If there was any sarcasm in Tara's words, Carly didn't sense it. "Not really, but I'm worried about Ross Baxter."

"Ross Baxter. Isn't he the poor kid who found my stepmother's body?" Tara took a slow sip of her coffee.

"Yes, and he's sick with worry over it—as is his grandmother. The police questioned him for hours that day, but they let him go. Until Mrs. Gray's death is resolved, his life is on hold." Carly took a sip of her coffee.

"I feel for him. I really do. How can I help?"

Carly's nerves relaxed slightly, though she knew Chief Holloway would be furious if he knew where she was.

"I'm glad to hear you say that. At the risk of sounding nosy, may I ask what your relationship with Mrs. Gray was like?"

"Wow. That's a loaded question. Gosh, where to start."

"At the beginning?"

"As good a place as any, I guess. I was eleven when I lost my real mom. It was an awful time for me, and for my dad."

Carly had lost her dad when she was seven and had only vague memories of Paul Hale. Her sister Norah, who was nine at the time, had been far more bonded with him. "You must have been crushed," she said.

Tara's gaze clouded. "That's putting it mildly. Sawyer was twenty-two when Mom passed. By that time he'd moved out of state. My poor dad floundered for a long time, and then he met Octavia. At the time I was thrilled. She was kind to me, and I desperately missed my mom." She took a long sip of steaming coffee.

"After a seven-month courtship, as Dad called it, they got married. My God, he was such a gentleman. He wouldn't even let her spend the night in our home until they tied the knot." She shook her head. "Over time, that knot became an ever-tightening noose. Everything had to be done her way—from decorating, to meals, to cars. There was never any compromise."

"She was inflexible," Carly said.

"Completely. But here's the funny thing. Back then I had a little pug named

Ziggy. He was getting old and had tons of health issues, but he was sweet and gentle. What was strange is that Octavia really loved that dog. She'd never struck me as the animal-loving type, but she doted on that sweet little guy. When I saw how she adored him and spoiled him, I started to develop a stronger bond with her. To an extent, I grew to love her."

"So your relationship with her was positive?"

Tara's expression turned stony, as if the wheels of her memory were scrolling backward. "It was, until she committed the ultimate sin. I came home from school one day to find she'd taken Ziggy to the vet and had him put down."

Carly reached over and touched her wrist. "Oh, Tara, that's terrible. Why would she do that?"

Tara blinked. "I should clarify. We knew it was only a matter of weeks for Ziggy—he was ailing from kidney failure—but we'd planned to do it during my school vacation, so I would have the week to mourn the loss." Her mouth twisted.

"I'm so sorry."

"Octavia claimed she did it to spare me the pain of going through it. And maybe she did, who knows? The thing was, even though I knew Ziggy had passed peacefully, I wanted my face to be the last one he saw before he crossed that rainbow bridge."

"She deprived you of those last moments with him."

Tara blinked again. "You know what's weird? I think she truly believed she did that for my benefit, to save me the agony of going through it. But at the time I didn't see it that way. When I ranted at her over what she'd done—and I used some choice words—she looked as if I'd punched her. My anger literally shocked her. After that, things went on a downhill slide."

What a sad experience, Carly thought.

Tara shook herself and waved a hand. "I don't even know why I'm telling you all this. It was a thousand years ago. Anyway, after that I pretty much stopped speaking to her, except when I had to. I couldn't wait to go to college to get away from her. Luckily, Dad had set up a savings account for my tuition, and she couldn't touch it. I was a junior in college when Dad died after a long bout with heart disease. When I went back home for the funeral, I discovered that Octavia had cleaned out all my mother's belongings, including the handbags she'd treasured. Told me they were old and stodgy, and that she donated most of them to the church. The good ones, the nicer ones, she kept for herself. Claimed that Dad told her she deserved them for taking such good care of him."

Carly was appalled. "Did that sound like something your dad would do?"

"Yeah, it did. He was such a great guy. At the end he was so weak, not as sharp as he'd been in the past. She probably told him she deserved them for all the care she'd given him, and he went along with it."

"Still, she should have asked you first if you wanted them."

"Well, she didn't." Tara mimed washing her hands. "That was it for me. I wanted nothing more to do with her after that. The house was in her name and there was nothing Sawyer or I could do. He'd already moved to Connecticut, and by then I was engaged."

"I should have guessed you were married from your name," Carly said.

"*Was* married," Tara corrected. "Twice. Neither of them stuck." She gave a wry chuckle.

"Tara," Carly said, "I know your stepmother wasn't exactly well-liked, but do you know of anyone in particular who had a serious grudge against her?"

Tara gave a harsh laugh. "Another loaded question. Like I said, I kicked her out of my life after Dad died. After that I moved to Arizona with my first husband, and to New York with my second. I only moved back to Balsam Dell five years ago to open my shop. The pandemic and the remnants of a messy divorce shut me down for a solid three years. I'm hoping I can make a go of it for good this time. But that doesn't really answer your question, does it?"

Carly smiled. "Not really. Have you always loved purses?"

Tara's eyes took on a dreamy look. "Always. I inherited the trait from Mom, I guess. She loved unusual handbags and was always collecting them from different places. When I finally woke up to the fact that marriage wasn't for me, I decided to honor her memory by opening the shop."

The sound of the front door opening and closing again drew Carly's attention. Seconds later, an adorable ball of fawn-colored energy wearing a pink paisley collar burst into the back room.

"Oh, what a sweetie. Look at that face!" Carly reached down to pat the dog, but the little pug raced around the women's legs and refused to stay still.

"Settle down, Paisley," Tara chided in a singsong voice.

After sniffing Carly's legs for at least a full minute, Paisley chuffed with approval and pawed at her knees. Carly lifted the dog onto her lap and accepted her exuberant kisses.

"Hey."

Carly turned to see a heavyset sixtysomething man wearing a blue polo shirt and baggy jeans filling the doorway. Clutched in one hand was a pink pet carrier trimmed in paisley fleece with a matching blanket inside. He set it down next to the dog bed, his gaze homing in on Carly.

"Sawyer, this is Carly Hale, from the grilled cheese restaurant," Tara introduced. "Carly, my big brother, Sawyer Gray."

The man shook Carly's hand warmly. "Glad to meet you." He gave his sister a quizzical look.

"I'm . . . very sorry about your stepmom," Carly told him quietly.

His lips parted slightly and he stared at her, as if he was mulling over his response. Then he cleared his throat and said, "Well, thank you, Carly. Tara and I weren't close to her, but it's still been very distressing. Dealing with the police and all that." His fleshy face reddened.

"I brought some blueberry muffins, so help yourself," Carly offered.

Sawyer reached into the white bag and extracted a muffin. "Thanks. Don't mind if I do."

"Use a napkin, Sawyer," Tara instructed. "Did you pick up the drop cloths?"

"Yes, Tara," he said with mock sarcasm. "I always do what you tell me."

The obvious tension between the two made Carly squirm. Did they always speak to each other this way?

Tara drained her paper coffee cup and her demeanor shifted. "Carly, I really appreciate you coming over this morning. To answer your question about Octavia, I can't name anyone specifically who hated her. She had an issue with her neighbor over the fence line, but that was resolved. Anyway, that Mark Hughes is such a sweetheart of a guy. I know for sure he wouldn't swat a fly." Her creamy cheeks turned slightly pink.

An odd response, Carly thought. Why would Tara even mention Mark Hughes if she was so sure he was innocent?

There was so much more Carly wanted to ask, but it was obvious that Sawyer's sudden appearance had changed the direction of the conversation. She also had to get to work. Ross would be starting his job in the kitchen soon, and she wanted to show him the ropes.

After making a vague promise to arrange a playdate for their dogs, the women exchanged cell numbers and Carly departed.

The sun was climbing and the day was growing warmer. A soft breeze caressed Carly's skin as she hustled toward her car. She stopped short when she noticed another vehicle parked beside her own.

It was a gray SUV with a roof rack and a Connecticut license plate.

Carly took a quick photo with her cell and dropped the phone back into her tote.

Unless she was wrong, and she didn't think she was, it was the same car Don Frasco had photographed at the scene of Octavia's murder.

CHAPTER 13

Ross Baxter turned out to be a dream employee.

"I don't know why you call this hard work," he told Carly, feeding chunks of sharp cheddar into the food processor. "It's like, so easy!"

"Well, I'm glad you're enjoying it. After you finish shredding, can you wash the pans in the sink? There's a pair of rubber gloves you can use."

"You got it," he said. "I aim to please."

Valerie peeked in from the dining room and crooked a finger at Carly. "Got a sec?"

"You bet."

Carly followed her to the back of the restaurant where they could speak privately. "Um, I told Fred about us hiring Ross as a temp."

"That's fine, Val. I didn't intend to keep it a secret from him."

Valerie made a face. "I know, but . . . well, he's not exactly thrilled."

"I didn't expect him to be thrilled. But we need help desperately, and I have that senior birthday party today—not to mention Don taking on deliveries. With Ross in the kitchen, you'll be able to help out more in the dining room. It's a win-win for all of us."

Valerie blew out a sigh. "I know, but that's not all. Early this morning he saw your car parked next to where Tara Shepard's new store is going in. Why didn't you tell me you went there?"

A sliver of irritation shot through Carly. Leave it to Chief Holloway to spot her car at Tara's purse shop. She couldn't help wondering if he was spying on her.

"Val, none of us has had a free minute to chat since we got here this morning. Right now, I'm more concerned with getting those thirteen sandwich orders ready for the senior party, and making sure Don gets his delivery instructions."

Valerie squeezed her arm lightly. "I know, I know. I just wanted to give you a heads-up about Fred." Her eyes lit up. "I . . . oh, never mind. Let's get back to work."

"Wait. What were you going to say?"

"It's . . . well, lately Fred's been acting different, and I don't mean because of the murder. There's something simmering beneath the surface. Something I can't quite pin down."

"Simmering in a good way?" Carly asked, her curiosity piqued.

"I think so, unless he's acting. Maybe he's gearing up to dump me, so he's trying to be extra nice."

Carly hoped that wasn't the case. "That doesn't sound like the chief. He's a no-nonsense kind of guy."

"You're right. I'm being silly." She gave Carly a quick hug. "Thanks for listening. But be prepared for a lecture the next time you see Fred."

Forewarned is forearmed, Carly thought.

True to his word, Ross washed, scrubbed, chopped, and shredded as if he'd worked in a restaurant all his life. "You're an old pro at this, aren't you?" Carly teased him.

"Yeah, well, Gram taught me well. Every holiday she used to make these unbelievable meals for all of us. My mom would make a pie, but that was about it. So, guess who got stuck with all the grunt work?" He grinned and aimed a thumb at his chest.

"Good training," Carly noted. "Speaking of moms, have you heard from your folks this week?"

Ross's mom and dad had made a permanent move to North Carolina when Ross was a young teen. A passionate skier and snowboarder, Ross told them he'd rather live with his grandmother than leave Vermont. A deal was struck, and his folks reluctantly agreed. Aside from that, Carly knew nothing about their current relationship.

"Yeah, I talked to both Mom and Dad last night. They're like, super bummed about the mess I got myself into. That's how they put it. They said if I'd moved to North Carolina with them like a good son should have, none of it would've happened."

"I'm sorry, Ross." Carly didn't know what else to say. She only wished they'd been more supportive.

"The thing is," he said, snapping a lid over the container of shredded cheddar, "ever since they moved away, I've always spent one of the summer months with them. But this year, with me going to college in the fall, I really wanted to earn some cash for books. I guess I could've gotten a job down there, but everyone knows me here, you know? And Gram came up with that great idea about the food deliveries to seniors."

"It sounds like a tough situation, but right now your folks must be really frustrated. I'm sure they only want what's best for you."

He shrugged. "Yeah, I know. Hey, I got pans to scrub, remember?" He scooted over to the sink.

Carly took the hint. *Conversation over.*

On the assumption that seniors would be calling in for delivery service, Valerie had agreed to coordinate with Don Frasco to set up his schedule. Don, in turn, had repeated his promise to use discretion if and when he delivered to Carly's customers.

Shortly after eleven, Carly and Grant joined forces to prepare thirteen grilled cheese orders. She'd expected some pushback from him over her leaving the eatery during the lunch crunch, but he didn't mention it. She sensed he was distracted by thoughts of losing Izzy, but it was something he needed to work out on his own.

After Grant wrapped each sandwich and secured it in a takeout box, Carly scribbled the customer's name on the outside. By eleven thirty, she was stacking the boxes into her insulated carrier. Grant carried a brown bag holding salad and chips out to Carly's car and set it on the floor in the back. "Good luck, Carly. I hope they all enjoy themselves."

"Thanks, Grant." She waved, but he'd already gone back inside.

• • •

David Parlee, a silver-haired gent with hazel eyes and a ready smile, rubbed his hands with delight as Carly came into the lobby with her carrier and brown bag.

"Miss Hale, how wonderful to finally meet you. Let me help you with those." He immediately relieved her of the brown bag.

"Thanks, Mr. Parlee, and please call me Carly."

"Only if you'll call me David."

"Deal."

David led her down the wide front hallway and into the recreation room. Carly's smile widened at the sight of the dozen or so eager faces that greeted her. A few were using walkers, and one woman leaned on a cane.

"She's here!" someone called out.

Carly felt like a movie star as the seniors gathered around her, introducing themselves and thanking her for making their party special.

The birthday girl, Edith Winston, used neither a walker nor a cane. She clasped Carly's hands in both of hers and held them for several seconds. Despite her snow-white hair and deeply wrinkled face, she was bright-eyed behind her tortoiseshell eyeglasses. "I can't thank you enough for doing this," she said in a papery voice. "Please, stay with us and have some of David's special punch."

"I'd be honored to," Carly said, giving her a gentle hug.

Glancing around, Carly was impressed at how much effort had been put into the decorations. Across one wall, a colorful streamer had been hung. Its message—Happy 90th Birthday, Edith—was spelled out in huge, bright pink block letters.

"We made that ourselves," David said proudly. "So much better than those cheap ones in the discount store, don't you agree?"

"I certainly do. It's fantastic."

The room's long rectangular table was covered with a pink paper tablecloth. Plates, napkins, and plastic flatware rested at one end, next to a cut-glass bowl filled with cherry-red punch. David and a woman named Thelma, whose straight hair was tinted purple, were removing the sandwiches from the carrier and setting out bowls of chips and salad.

"Oh, look, David, the sandwiches are labeled with our names!" Thelma gazed at Carly with sheer admiration.

The woman's gratitude over such a simple thing brought a lump to Carly's throat. A shard of guilt pierced her. She'd come here with the hope of gaining some insight into Octavia's life, and she was being treated like a queen.

David poured punch into a paper cup and gave it to Carly. "My special formula," he said with a wink. "Hope you like it."

Carly slid into a chair next to the birthday girl, who sat at the head of the table. The punch was tart but tasty, with a touch of something she couldn't quite place.

She looked around the table, watching everyone enjoy their grilled cheese sandwiches. Of the thirteen, four were men and the rest were women. Was Lois Feeney, the woman Octavia had wronged, among the partygoers? Carly didn't recall a Lois having introduced herself.

From across the table, a petite woman with curly salt-and-pepper hair stared at Carly. Each time Carly tried to make eye contact, the woman quickly looked down at her sandwich.

When lunch was over, David and Thelma collected the used containers and sorted the trash into the proper receptacles.

"I hope you all saved room for birthday cake," David announced to the group.

Everyone clapped, and then a balding man with a napkin tucked into his shirt wheeled a metal table into the room. Cheers went up, and everyone gasped at the stunning creation.

The cake was rectangular, encased in lavender fondant and designed to look like a wrapped gift. In front of a huge white bow, also fondant, a frosting tag read "Happy Birthday, Edith."

Tears of joy brimmed in Edith's eyes as the revelers sang an enthusiastic round of "Happy Birthday" in her honor. After everyone finished clapping and hooting, Thelma began cutting the cake.

The woman who'd been staring at Carly came over to her, one hand leaning on a cane. "Miss Hale," she said quietly, "my name is Lois Feeney. I want to thank you personally for helping us out today."

Lois Feeney. Exactly who Carly hoped to talk to.

"I'm happy to meet you, Lois, and you don't need to thank me. I'm grateful I was able to do it."

"The thing is," Lois said fretfully, "we had this party planned for three weeks, right down to the last detail. Sissy's Bakery delivered the cake, but when we found out that nice young Ross couldn't deliver our sandwiches, we weren't sure what to do. I offered to drive to pick up the orders, but deep down I was terrified. I haven't driven in a while, and my reflexes aren't so good anymore. David offered to ride shotgun, as he put it, but since your restaurant doesn't have parking, I wasn't sure how that would help."

"It all worked out fine," Carly assured her with a smile. "Edith is a lovely person, isn't she?"

"She's a darling. As for poor Ross," Lois went on, lowering her voice, "we all know he didn't harm that . . . that *woman*. It's a disgrace the police won't let him continue his delivery business."

"I'm sure the police will find the real culprit soon," Carly said softly. "Lois, you sound as if you knew Mrs. Gray."

"Oh, I knew her all right." Lois's eyes shone with fury. "I know it's wrong to speak ill of the dead, but that harlot is the reason I'm walking with a cane."

Carly recalled the story Helen Quigley related about Lois spying through Octavia's window and falling off the trash can.

"I'm so sorry. You obviously had a bad experience with her."

"Darn right I did. Before my husband died, Octavia seduced him into having an affair with her. I wanted to catch them in the act, so I climbed onto a barrel outside that hussy's bedroom window." She paused.

"And you fell?"

"No, she—"

"Lois, perhaps we shouldn't be discussing that right now." David Parlee had come around silently from behind Carly. "We're here to celebrate Edith's milestone birthday, and Carly is our guest. Thelma cut a slice of cake for you. Why don't you go and enjoy it?"

"I'm sorry," Lois choked out. She grasped Carly's hand with her free one. "Thank you again." With that she turned and went back to her chair.

David shook his head. He guided Carly away from everyone's earshot. "I'm sorry you had to hear that. Even after all these years, Lois hasn't been able to let it go."

"That's okay, I felt bad for her."

"So," he said jovially, "have you guessed my special ingredient in the punch?"

"I might be wrong," Carly said, "but I tasted a hint of raspberry."

David's smile lit up his face. "Right you are! I added a cup of raspberry juice, which isn't easy to find, by the way. Your taste buds are right on target."

"Thanks for the tip. It was delicious. Everyone here has been so gracious, David. I'm happy you invited me to join you all."

"You're welcome back anytime," he said.

"Um, David, I have to be honest about something. Someone else told me that same story, about Lois falling off the trash can while she was looking through Octavia's window."

His eyebrows shot upward. "Falling off the trash can? Oh, no, my dear. The way Lois tells it, Octavia opened the window and pushed her off."

CHAPTER 14

AT THE EATERY, BUSINESS WAS BUSTLING. CARLY WAS PLEASED TO SEE THAT every booth was filled. Three of her regulars occupied counter seats. Suzanne was joking with two couples seated in one of the booths, and they all burst into laughter.

Carly's head was still reeling from David Parlee's disclosure about Lois and the trash can. Did Octavia Gray *really* push Lois off that barrel? Or had Lois embellished the story to gain more sympathy? Only one living person knew the truth—Lois herself.

Carly headed into the kitchen to see how Ross was faring. She found him standing at the worktable, an apron tied around his waist. Using a set of salad tongs, he was tossing field greens in a large bowl. He grinned when he saw her.

"Hey, Ms. Hale!" Ross dumped a cup of dried cranberries into the bowl. "I'm using Grant's recipe to make another batch of salad. How did the party go?"

"It went very well, thank you." Carly tucked her tote under the table. "Everyone had a great time. Thanks to you helping us out today, I felt a lot less guilty about staying away so long. Also, a lot of the seniors asked about you. They miss you, and they're concerned about you."

His broad shoulders drooped. "Yeah, well, I miss all my customers. Gotta tell you, though, I'm getting to like doing kitchen work. I mean, I know I'm only doing menial stuff, but something about it makes me feel like I'm contributing."

"No honest job is menial, Ross."

He shrugged. "Yeah, I guess."

From inside her tote, Carly's cell pinged with a text. It was her mom again, checking on her for about the tenth time since Octavia's murder. Carly texted her back with a perky response—complete with exclamation points and smiley faces—assuring her that all was well. She didn't know if her mom was buying it, but it was the best she could do.

Valerie pushed through the swinging door carrying a tub of dirty dishes. "Hey, party girl, how did everything go?" She set the tub on the counter next to the sink.

Carly gave her and Ross a condensed version of her visit to the senior apartment community. She omitted any reference to Lois Feeney.

"I'm glad you did that, Carly," Valerie said. "You made a lot of new friends—friends who'll be loyal customers. And the birthday girl must have been thrilled."

"She was." Carly poured herself a glass of ice water from the fridge. "They're all such nice folks. I enjoyed getting to chat with a few of them. David

Parlee is such a gentleman. From what I saw, he keeps everything running smoothly in the activities department."

"Um, Carly, I hate to interrupt," Valerie said, "and I do want to tell you about Don. But first, Fred asked me to tell you to stick around this afternoon. He has a few questions for you. He said he'll stop in between three and four."

"Oh happy day. Well, I guess it's better to get it over with. Besides, I haven't done anything wrong. I can't think of one thing he can fault me on."

Valerie raised an eyebrow but said nothing. "Okay, about Don. We ended up with three calls from seniors who Ross used to deliver for. One guy asked about the sub shop, but I told him Don's deliveries were strictly from our restaurant. He ended up putting in four sandwich orders for him, his wife, and his in-laws!"

"Oh, that's terrific. What about the other two?"

"A woman, a friend of Ross's grandmother, ordered lunch for herself and a sick neighbor. The other one was a friend of Imogene Hughes. She said you came highly recommended. She was hoping you'd handle her delivery yourself." Valerie winked at Ross. "You're getting to be quite popular in your own right, Miss Carly Hale."

"Don't be silly. They only want me for my cheese," Carly said with a dramatic sweep of her hand.

"I kind of miss delivering to Mrs. Hughes," Ross piped in. "Sometimes she gave me a piece of cake."

"See? I never got cake."

Valerie laughed and tapped the table. "Time to get back to work. Can you help Grant in the dining room while I take a quick break?"

"Sure can."

Carly bustled around the dining room, pitching in where needed. Her mind kept traveling to David's parting words about Octavia pushing Lois off the trash barrel. Something occurred to Carly. If Lois's version was true, then she was more than a wronged woman.

She was a woman who sustained a permanent injury thanks to her husband's thoughtless lover.

• • •

True to his word, Chief Holloway came into the eatery at quarter past three. Carly spied him from behind the counter, where she was finishing up a takeout order. Valerie greeted him with a smile and a pink lemonade and led him to a booth near the rear.

Carly came over and slid onto the bench opposite him. "Grant's on a break and Suzanne left for the day, so this isn't the best time, Chief."

Holloway's glare was intense. "I'm doing you a favor, Carly. My first inclination was to bring you in to the station to talk. I came here out of respect for your time. Especially since you've been doing so many personal deliveries lately. Now, is there a reason we can't talk in the kitchen?"

Carly blinked at the verbal slap. "Well, as you know, the Board of Health has rules about—"

"Cut the act, Carly. I know Ross Baxter is working for you, and that's why you don't want me in there. I only have two questions, so I'll try to make this quick. First of all, what made you think hiring Ross was a good idea? Do you understand he's a person of interest in Octavia Gray's death?"

"I do understand that, but I also know that Ross is innocent. Didn't the police tell him to stick around Balsam Dell?" She lifted her chin. "As it happens, that's exactly where my restaurant is located."

"Very amusing. *Not,*" he said. "Second question, what were you doing at Tara Shepard's yet-to-be-open shop early this morning?"

Carly was prepared for this. "I wanted to pay a condolence call, so I picked up coffee and muffins. I knew she'd been working long hours getting her shop set up, and I figured she might appreciate a treat. Turned out I was right."

"So, you're friends now?" He folded his hands on the table.

"You could say that. As women business owners, we have a lot in common. Tara's brother Sawyer showed up with her little dog, but I left shortly after that. You might be interested to know that a car with a Connecticut tag was parked next to mine when I left. I assumed it was Sawyer Gray's car."

"Why is that of interest?"

"Because Tara told me that her brother arrived in town the day after the murder. Yet Don Frasco took a photo of his car on the day Octavia's body was found. It was parked on the street behind another car. The police were ordering all the gawkers away, but Don managed to get a few pics first. I can share them with you, if you'd like." A tiny surge of triumph swept through her.

Holloway pressed his lips together and looked away. Carly pictured the wheels of his mind doing mental calculations. "Why was Frasco there in the first place?"

"He followed a couple of squad cars with sirens blasting and they led him right to the crime scene. You know Don, always chasing down a story!"

"All right, I'll speak to Frasco myself. He should've come to me, not to you. And yes, I'd appreciate seeing those photos."

"Done. For the record, Don tried getting an interview with you, but he said you kept putting him off. One more thing, Chief, and don't go ballistic when I tell you this. When Ross found Octavia's body that day, he thought something looked out of place. He took a picture of the kitchen table—"

"I've seen the picture. Your point?"

"He remembered that Octavia's purse always hung on a kitchen chair. Ross remembered it because it was distinctive-looking—a tapestry bag with a chain handle. Every time Octavia paid him, she'd take the cash out of it. But the day of the murder, the purse wasn't there."

"The absence of something is not evidence. Why didn't Ross bring this up during his interview?"

"He said he couldn't prove it was ever there, so he didn't think the police would believe him."

The chief stared hard at her. "This is my last warning, Carly. Your involvement in investigating Mrs. Gray's death ends now. You're already too close to some of the players, and I don't want history repeating itself. Is that clear?"

Carly sighed. "Yes, Chief, crystal clear. But unless I'm breaking the law, I'm not sure you have the authority to—"

"I have the authority and the duty to protect the citizens of this town," he said in a clipped voice. "And this time, I'll do whatever it takes. I suggest you think about that." He rose from his seat. "And now, I need to get ready for a date with the most wonderful woman in the world. You don't have any problem with Valerie leaving early, do you?"

Blindsided.

Carly smiled. "Not at all, Chief. You both have my blessing."

After he left, Carly felt she could breathe again. Valerie hugged her for letting her leave early. "You're the best, Carly. Toodles!"

• • •

With Ross tidying up the kitchen as he worked, nearly every surface was spotless by six thirty. Before leaving, he thanked Carly repeatedly for giving him a job and promised to be there early on Saturday. She reminded him that she was hoping to hear from his grandmother and asked him to pass along the message.

In spite of the chief's admonitions, Carly couldn't get Octavia's death out of her mind. So many faces bobbed into her thoughts—Tara's, Sawyer's, and Lois's for starters.

Carly knew who she needed to talk to—Gina. She missed their long, leisurely chats, something they rarely had time to indulge in anymore. If there was one person Carly could count on not to lecture her about interfering with a police investigation, it was Gina.

Instead of texting, Carly called her friend.

"Hey, I've been thinking about you," Gina said. "Hold on a minute." She excused herself to assist a customer, then, "Can you stop up after work? KitCat and I want desperately to see you. I have raspberry squares from Sissy's."

"You and Zach don't have plans?"

"Nope. He took his mom for a colonoscopy today, and she's insisting he spend the night at her place just in case she has aftereffects."

"Way more than I needed to know. I'll be there right after seven. See you then!"

On Fridays, Ari typically came over to Carly's for a relaxing evening of TV and takeout. She texted him to let him know she'd be delayed, and he texted back with:

No problem. I'll chill with Havarti till you get home, followed by a double heart emoji.

CHAPTER 15

GINA HAD SET HER FORMICA TABLE WITH HER MOM'S 1960S-STYLE earthenware. The pattern was white with blue and brown polka dots, and she had tall drinking glasses to match.

A furry black cat purring in her lap, Carly sipped a glass of minty iced tea. Her gaze drifted up to the kitchen wall next to the fridge, where a wooden shelf painted pastel green boasted a dozen or so vintage Nancy Drew books. "I swear, every time I come in here you've added something new."

Gina nodded over a mouthful of her raspberry square, then swallowed. "Zach and I are still going through the boxes in storage."

The year before, after Gina's dad had gone into assisted living, she'd packed up decades of treasured memories and rented a storage unit for them.

"How's it coming along?" Carly asked softly.

"We try to tackle a few boxes every week, depending on our schedules. When I found Mom's old Nancy Drew books, I nearly fainted. I'd totally forgotten about them! Zach picked up that shelf at a flea market. Isn't it perfect?"

"It is, and those books are in mint condition." Carly scratched KitCat between her ears, eliciting a revved-up purr.

"So, tell me about your latest investigation," Gina said. "And don't tell me you're not looking into Octavia Gray's murder."

"I won't tell you that, since you know me too well. But mainly I'm trying to get Ross off the hook. His life is pretty much in a holding pattern right now."

Gina gave her a *yeah, right* look and urged her to spill everything.

Carly gave her friend a detailed summary of the events of the past week, ending with the chief's stern warning. With so many moving parts to the story, she'd skipped a few and had to backtrack.

"Wow, that's all so unreal." Gina tapped her fingers on the table, and her dark brown eyes gleamed. "Octavia had so many enemies, how are we going to narrow them down?"

"We?"

Gina laughed and grabbed her laptop off the counter. "Let's see, who shall we google first?"

"Shouldn't we make a list of suspects first?"

"Good point. I'll pull up a blank document." She tapped her fingers over the keyboard.

"I'd start with Octavia's stepchildren," Carly suggested. "Sawyer Gray and Tara Gray Shepard."

"Done. Who else?"

Carly broke off a chunk of her raspberry square. "I hate to say this, but I'm afraid Lois Feeney will have to go on the list. Not only did her husband have an affair with Octavia, but according to David Parlee, Octavia pushed Lois off that trash barrel and caused her permanent injury." She popped the chunk of pastry into her mouth.

"Aw, poor woman. But you said she never drives anymore."

Carly swallowed. "Hardly ever," she corrected. "And I only have her word for that."

"I still can't imagine her somehow getting into Octavia's house and bopping her with a frying pan," Gina said doubtfully. "Okay, anyone else?"

"Yeah, there's something odd about Mark Hughes. He comes off as a seasoned traveler and businessman, but he also seemed a little edgy. And that battle with Octavia over their common fence line cost him some serious money. Which would've been okay if it was justified, but I'm almost sure it wasn't."

"Wait a minute." Gina slapped her hand on the table. "OMG, could something be buried under that tree?"

KitCat lifted her head at the sound and Carly stroked her back. "Shoot. I never thought of that. That's an excellent observation, Miss Marple."

"Much obliged. Before we get around to motives, is there anyone else?" She wiggled her fingers in preparation.

Carly winced. "Another name I hate to add, but have to, is Helen Quigley."

Gina looked horrified. "Ross's grandmother? Tell me you're not serious."

"Unfortunately, I am."

"Okay, let's start with motives then. What could possibly make that lovely, kind, generous woman want to kill someone, even someone she didn't like?"

"Gina, you didn't see her face when Ross spilled that story about Octavia keying Helen's car. I thought she was going to pass out. And poor Ross, he got this panicky look on his face."

"I still say no way. You don't kill someone for keying your car."

Carly lifted KitCat onto her shoulder and cupped her gently for support. "I know that, but Octavia had been giving Ross a terrible time. She accused him of spying on her and stealing her potato chips. Maybe Helen was seething inside and decided to do something about it."

Gina shook her head. "I'll never believe it. I'll add her name, but only because you twisted my arm. Anyone else?"

"Not that I'm aware of. Might as well start with what we have. We can always add on later."

Gina gulped down a mouthful of iced tea. "Okay, the stepkids. What do we know about them so far?"

"I'll start with Tara," Carly said. "She's smart, savvy, personable. But it seems she never got over Octavia having her ailing dog euthanized without telling her first."

"That was despicable." Gina spat the words. "But why would Tara wait all this time to get revenge?"

"I can't think of a reason, unless something triggered it. It was weird when she proclaimed Mark Hughes's innocence out of the blue. I wonder if they have something going on."

Gina tapped away at her laptop. "Okay, Tara's definitely a possible. Let's move on to her brother."

"Well, we know Sawyer Gray was in town on the day of the murder. And that his sister believed he'd driven up the *following* day."

"Or did she?" Gina said slowly. "Maybe Tara only told everyone that to cover for him."

KitCat took a sudden leap off Carly's shoulder.

Gina laughed. "Hey, was that a sign that I was right?"

The cat meandered over to her food bowl and began snacking on her kibble. "Nah, I think she's just hungry," Carly said. "But one thing's for sure. I need to have another chat with Tara. How do I manage that without the chief finding out?"

"We'll think of something," Gina said. "More iced tea?"

"Half a glass." Carly held up hers.

Gina freshened their glasses and sat down again. "Let's tackle Mark Hughes next." She typed his name in the search box and squinted at her laptop. "Uh-oh. There's a ton of links to that name. I need to narrow it down. Let's see . . . Mark Hughes, Balsam Dell, Vermont. Ah, I found him. Ooh, he's a good-looking dude, isn't he?"

"I guess," Carly said airily. "If you like that type." She didn't like admitting that anyone might be better-looking than Ari.

"Well, there's a lot to look at. He travels a lot, that's for sure," Gina said.

"Social media?"

Gina tapped away. "There's an Instagram account for his business. I'm not finding a personal one, though."

"Any photos of him with a woman?"

"Um . . . not so far. All professional stuff, from what I'm seeing. I'm going to text you some of these links so you can look at them later," Gina said. "I know Ari's waiting for you. I certainly wouldn't want to interfere with any romantic notions you two might be entertaining." She wiggled her eyebrows suggestively.

"Oh, get real," Carly said, knowing full well it was true. "Can I bring him a raspberry square?"

"You bet."

Gina was stuffing a handful of pastries into a container when she stopped short. "Do you know if Octavia had a will?"

"Now that, my friend, is a good question," Carly said. "How can we find out?"

Gina went back to her laptop. A minute or so later, she read from the screen. "In Vermont, a will has to be filed with the county probate division within thirty days of death. The person who has custody of the will is responsible for the filing."

"It's only been three days," Carly noted. "And we don't even know if she had one. Plus, it's Friday, so the courts won't be open till Monday."

"Another reason for you to chat up Tara again," Gina pointed out. "Too bad her store's not open yet. We could go there shopping for new purses." She chewed on a thumbnail, then her expression morphed into a slow, mischievous smile. "Didn't you say Tara plans to sell vintage designer bags in her shop?"

"On consignment, yes."

"So, what if I found my mom's vintage Prada or Hermès bag or whatever, when I was going through the storage boxes? And what if I wanted to find out if it's worth anything?"

"Did you?" Carly squealed.

"No, of course not. But when my Aunt Lil was still working, she used to buy them cheap from some of the salon's clients. Like when they got tired of them, or thought they were out of style, they'd sell them for a song."

Aunt Lil was Gina's elderly aunt, a sweet, quirky woman who'd worked for years as a hair washer at the Happy Clipper. Only recently, she traded in her sprayer for a volunteer job at the animal shelter—a position she found far more rewarding. It resulted in her adopting two dogs and a cat, but that was another story.

"Okay, listen," Gina went on. "I'll ask Aunt Lil to lend me one of her old designer bags. If I can somehow get Tara to let me in the shop, I'll make up some story about wanting to know the bag's value. I'm a pretty good actor when I want to be." Gina's eyes glittered.

Carly laughed. Gina had played minor roles in two high school productions. And she *had* been pretty darn good.

"Great idea, except for one thing," Carly warned her. "She'll know for sure that I talked to you."

"Don't worry, I won't let on about the other stuff."

Carly thought about what could go wrong. Tara was a smart woman, not one to be fooled. If Gina showed up on her own, even on a pretext, Tara might think Carly sent her there to put her under the hot lights.

The other thing, the *big* thing that bothered Carly, was that she genuinely liked Tara. Without a murder hanging over their heads, she could easily see them becoming friends.

Still, Carly couldn't deny that Tara had carried an intense grudge against Octavia. And what about Sawyer? Did he feel the same? And did Tara know his car was seen in town on the day of the murder?

Carly shook her head. "No, Gina. I need to go with you. Tara's no dummy. If she suspects you're there to question her, she might never talk to me again. I don't want to lose that connection." She tapped a finger to her lips. "I have Tara's cell number, so I can send her a text and let her know we want her opinion on something. If she's not receptive, at least we'll know."

Gina finished packing up the raspberry squares. "Works for me. Let me know what happens. We didn't really get to finish our motives list," she grumbled.

"I know. We need another confab."

Carly lifted KitCat into her arms, kissed her furry forehead, and then set her down again. Armed with pastries and a promise to see Gina again soon, she bounded down the stairs and outside to her car.

Waiting for her at home: the man she loved and the dog she loved.

It didn't get any better than that.

CHAPTER 16

THE MOMENT CARLY STEPPED INSIDE HER APARTMENT A MOUTHWATERING aroma wrapped itself around her. She hugged Havarti and Ari—in that order—and was escorted by both into the kitchen.

"Sit down, my good lady," Ari said gallantly, "and allow me to serve you."

"Can I wash up real quick first?"

"Of course you can." He kissed her cheek.

When she returned to the kitchen, Ari was removing a covered bowl from the oven. The sight of him wearing her dog-themed oven mitts made her heart skip. He set the bowl on a wicker pad in the center of the table, next to a basket of rolls and a tub of butter.

Carly inhaled deeply and grinned. "Ari, what is this? It smells wonderful."

He pulled out her chair. "Remember we wanted to try that new healthy place—Canoodle the Noodle? Well, tonight we're having one of their most popular dishes—cauliflower penne with basil pesto. The rolls are made with whole wheat flour and Greek yogurt."

"Ah. No wonder it all smells so heavenly. I love basil."

Carly sat down, and Ari poured each of them a goblet of wine. He removed the glass cover from the bowl, revealing the steaming pasta entrée. With a serving spoon, he stirred the pasta carefully, then handed her the spoon. "There's extra pesto if we need it. I bought a whole container."

They each helped themselves, and Carly dove into her meal. "This is unbelievable," she said after swallowing a huge mouthful. "The blend of the pasta and pesto is phenomenal. Why didn't we try this place before?" She lifted her wineglass.

Ari buttered a roll. "I guess we got set in our ways, like most people. Same old same old, week after week."

Carly froze. Something in his tone put her antennae on high alert. She set down her glass without taking a sip.

"Is that how you see us, Ari? Set in our ways? Same old same old?"

For a long moment he was silent, then, "Honey, I didn't mean it quite that way, but maybe we should talk about it after dinner. Let's enjoy our meal first."

Enjoy our meal. Like that was possible after his oddball remark.

Carly's appetite went quickly on a downhill slide. What started out as a relaxing, romantic evening turned as sour as week-old cabbage. Was she overreacting? Probably, but his words still bothered her.

She'd planned to tell Ari about her busy day—her chat with Tara and then her visit to the senior apartments. Not to mention her not-so-fun convo with Chief Holloway. But if Carly was reading his signals correctly, they had more important things to discuss.

Over bits of small talk and long stretches of silence, they poked at their food for another ten minutes or so. The delicious pasta felt heavy, like an anchor dropping into her stomach.

When she couldn't force another bite, Carly insisted on cleaning up the table alone. With a worried expression, Ari nodded and went into the living room. Havarti trailed at his feet.

Carly fought back a lump in her throat as she put away everything and cleaned up the dishes. She stored the leftover pasta in a sealed container.

When her hands were dry, she fetched her tote from the hallway table. She pulled out the container of raspberry squares, then plunked down beside Ari on the sofa. Havarti scooched in between them, his brown-eyed gaze going from one to the other. No doubt the little dog sensed the tension. He seemed unsure of where to curl up.

Carly handed Ari the container. "Gina sent these. Raspberry squares."

Ari smiled but avoided eye contact. "Thanks, honey. Listen, I'm sorry for the way I spoke earlier. After I said it, I realized how harsh it must've sounded." He set the unopened container on the end table beside him.

"I felt . . . I don't know," she said in a shaky voice. "As if you thought we were getting bored with each other. Or you were getting bored with me."

Ari looked stricken. "Bored? How could you even think that? That's the farthest thing from the truth." He reached over the dog and took her hand in his. She squeezed his fingers but then pulled away.

"Ari," she pushed on, "is it, I mean, are you upset because we haven't officially moved in together?"

It was something they'd talked about but never really decided on. Carly had only visited Ari's small house four or five times. To her it looked more like a colorless "man cave" than a home. Yet her own cozy home—the apartment she loved—wasn't large enough for the two of them to live in comfortably.

"There's no 'officially' about it, honey," Ari pointed out. "I mean, I'm here all the time, but at the end of the day I still live someplace else."

She nodded and felt her eyes water. "You love your home, and I love mine. But that doesn't mean—"

"Wait a minute." Ari's jaw dropped. "You think I love my house? That drab slab of wood my sister and I inherited when Mom passed?"

It was Carly's turn to be shocked. "I just assumed you did. Are you saying you don't?"

His laugh came out like a bark. "No, I don't. I stayed there because it held memories of my mother, and it was a lot easier than moving." He rubbed one eye with his fingers. "And then I met you, and my whole world shifted. Now, every minute I spend there only reminds me that I'm not with you."

In the pit of her heart, Carly knew what the real problem was—her hesitation in making their relationship permanent.

79

That past winter, after Carly had survived a harrowing brush with a killer, Ari had given her a stone paperweight as a gift. Engraved on it were the words *Grow old along with me, the best is yet to be.* Looking back, she knew it was Ari's quiet way of asking her to marry him.

She'd never given him an answer.

"I'm not sure where we go from here," she murmured, her voice wobbling.

"What would you like to do?" Ari asked her.

Havarti whined. Carly smiled and ruffled his fur. "I was going to tell you all about my day, but I'm not sure now is the best time. Maybe it's time we talked about moving in together."

It would be a huge step, but it wouldn't resolve the issue of whether marriage was in their future.

Ari's eyes searched her face, and he touched her cheek with his fingers. "Okay, it's a start."

Carly knew what he was thinking.

It's a start. But it's still not enough.

• • •

The following morning, over a breakfast of oatmeal and fresh berries, Carly gave Ari a recap of her exploits the day before. He listened carefully, his gaze fastened on hers. When she was through, he set down his coffee mug and shook his head.

"Honey, I know you're doing what comes naturally to you. Helping people is in your DNA. I get that. But except for hiring Ross, this time I have to agree with Holloway. You're getting too close to some of the players."

With a smile she hoped was reassuring, Carly reached over and squeezed his arm. "I can see why you think that," she acknowledged. "But you can't seriously think someone like Lois Feeney or Helen Quigley would be a danger to me, right?"

"I don't know about those two, but the stepkids and the neighbor, Mark Hughes? Now, they worry me." He sat back and crossed his muscular arms over his chest.

The evening before, over raspberry squares and wine, they'd talked well past midnight about where they were headed as a couple. They both agreed that moving in together was a positive step forward, but it wouldn't be easy. First they needed to find a home, or even a condo, that they both loved.

If and when that happened, Ari would sell his house and use the proceeds toward their new digs. Investment-wise, Carly had far less to offer. Since she didn't own a home, she wouldn't have a chunk of cash to contribute. Most of her disposable income went back into her business.

As for the subject of marriage, they'd tiptoed around it as if it were broken glass. It left Carly feeling adrift, but she blamed herself. After all, she was the one who was on the fence. If she had to explain why, she couldn't.

But there it was.

Together they cleared off the table and rinsed the dishes. "So, we're agreed on our plans for Sunday, right?" she asked him.

Ari grinned. "Totally. I'm so psyched about us going house hunting." He pulled her into a close hug. "And we also agreed there'd be no—"

"Talk of murder," she finished. "Got it. So, what's on your agenda today?"

"I've got a few projects to tinker with at the shop. Since I've started doing small appliance repair, a lot of my customers have been showing up with stuff for me to work on. Not my favorite thing, but it adds a little more cash to the till."

Ari's shop, Mitchell Electric, was located on a side street opposite the town green. Although he used it as a base for his business, most of his jobs were done in private homes or on commercial sites.

"And makes you a hero to your customers." Carly teased. "Don't deny it. I know you've done plenty of those repairs for free."

He laughed. "Got me there."

"Shoot," Carly yelped. "It's almost eight. I have to get to work."

"You go. I'll bring Havarti into the yard for a bit, then I'll take off. Pizza and a movie tonight?"

"You betcha."

Carly left feeling more settled than she had the night before. As for her plans for house hunting with Ari, she'd share them with Gina but with no one else. Gina had a lot of contacts in town. She might know of a few folks planning to sell their homes—folks who might appreciate an offer before putting their homes on the market.

At this stage, Carly would take any help she could get.

CHAPTER 17

"HEY, CARLY," GRANT SAID, FLIPPING BISCUITS ON THE GRILL. "YOU WON'T believe what our favorite sisters added to their grilled cheese sandwiches yesterday."

Carly was relieved to see him looking more like his old self. His bright smile was natural instead of forced, and his eyes had reclaimed their usual sparkle. Even his dreads looked perkier.

The sisters he referred to were Maybelle and Estelle, the ninetysomething identical twins who frequented the eatery. Carly adored them. Both women favored neon bright colors. On occasion they sported clashing outfits that made Carly want to slip her sunglasses on.

"Wait a minute," Carly said. "Added? As in, brought their own food from home?"

"Yup." He laughed. "Their niece's homemade raspberry jam. They opened up their Sweddar Weathers and slathered the jam inside. God love 'em, they polished off every last crumb of those sandwiches. They asked if I wanted to keep the jam for our other customers. I thanked them and politely declined."

Carly liked the idea of the raspberry jam. Especially now that fresh raspberries were in season, fruit-minded customers would gobble it up.

"Grant, I think the jam is a great idea. Let's brainstorm and come up with our own version. We can call it something like *a berry cheesy delight.*"

"Or maybe," he suggested, *"I'm only razzing you."*

They both laughed. "Okay, the name definitely needs tweaking, but it's the sandwich that counts. Maybe we can work on it when we both get a few free minutes."

"Sounds good, if we don't get *berried* in customers today."

Carly smiled. "You seem a bit more cheerful today. Have you worked things out with Isabella?"

"No, but I had a long chat with my dad, who's the smartest person I know. Izzy was a bright spot in my life, but she's moved on and I will too. Yeah, it still hurts like the devil, but that's part of life, right?" He flipped one of the cheesy biscuits onto a plate. "If you're heading into the kitchen, would you give this to Ross? Val is skipping today. You want one?"

"Thanks, but I ate breakfast at home. And your dad is a very wise man." She took the plate and went through the swinging door.

In the kitchen, Ross and Valerie were busy prepping for the day. She caught them mid-discussion about the chances of the Red Sox beating the Yankees in the upcoming series. Carly couldn't help chuckling to herself. It was a sign that the two were getting along in the workplace.

Ross's eyes and smile both widened at the sight of the biscuit. "Aw, man, thanks, Ms. Hale. I could smell the bacon from in here."

"Why don't you sit and have it with your coffee," Carly said. "Val, I didn't know you were such a baseball fan."

She shrugged and flashed a grin. "Fred's a bigger fan than I am, but we love watching the games together." A hint of pink colored her cheeks. "By the way, he wanted me to thank you for texting him those photos of Don's."

After Carly left Gina's the night before, she'd remembered her promise to text Chief Holloway Don's pictures from the day of the murder. The chief hadn't acknowledged her text, but Carly was sure he'd received it.

"Glad he got it," was all she said.

Around midmorning, Don Frasco texted Carly with an update: *No luck getting intel yesterday,* followed by an emoji of a frowning face. He agreed to take on more deliveries if needed, and she texted him a thumbs-up sign.

The rest of the morning flew by without any drama.

Across the street, Balsam Dell's town green was a hotbed of activity. Every summer, beginning on the third Saturday in June, area vendors set up tables and booths on the green and peddled their wares—everything from hand-crafted goods to cotton candy to fried dough. In one corner of the green, music students from the local college set a makeshift stage. Throughout the day, they entertained the crowd with a blend of classical, country, and rock songs.

Carly still remembered the day, after she'd first opened for business, that Gina captured a video of Grant playing the cello with two other string musicians. Carly had nearly wept at the beauty of the sound. Until that moment, she'd had no idea that her grill cook was also a gifted cellist.

It had taken a while, but Grant's folks—both classical musicians and professors at the local college—had finally given their blessing to his pursuing a culinary career. Although music was his passion, it was the dream of becoming a chef that rocked Grant's world.

Carly peered across the street at the hustle and bustle of the merchants setting up their booths. "Before the day ends," she announced, unlocking the door for business, "I have got to go over there and buy some cotton candy. I haven't had any since last year!"

Suzanne had arrived and was busy fussing with the faux flowers in the booths. "You'll probably see Jake and Josh over there. They can't wait to eat some of those deep-fried snack cakes with the gooey stuff inside." She wrinkled her nose. "Even I can't get my head around that. Too much sugar."

Jake was Suzanne's husband. Only the year before, he came close to being her ex-husband. His gambling addiction had led to a serious rift in their relationship. Luckily, and with help, they worked out their issues and saved their marriage.

By noon the mercury had crept into the mid-eighties, with the sun blazing down from a near cloudless sky. Despite the attraction of the outdoor food vendors, Carly's restaurant did a brisk business. She attributed some of that to air-conditioning—one of the best inventions of the twentieth century, in her opinion. Notwithstanding the enticing aromas drifting from the town green, she knew it was her delicious grilled cheese sandwiches that brought customers into her eatery.

That, and the best staff a restaurateur could ask for.

No one called for delivery, a blessing Carly was thankful for. Around two thirty, after business had quieted down, she took a break and dashed across the street.

The soft twang of a country song drifted from the far corner of the green. Over the ambient noise of the crowd, it was barely audible.

Carly wove her way among the displays, stopping here and there to admire the work of local crafters. At one booth, a young woman with beads woven through her long black hair was selling handsewn backpacks. Made from sturdy canvas, the designs were spectacular. Carly wondered if Tara planned to offer bags like these in her shop.

When she spotted the cotton candy vendor, she made a beeline for it. She smiled at the sugary confection swirling inside the machine. The color was the turquoise blue of a robin's egg. She didn't want to think about what made that shade of blue, but decided it wasn't worth worrying about. It wasn't as if she ate cotton candy every day.

After a short wait in line, she walked away with a cloud of fluffy blue cotton wrapped around a paper cone, a tiny napkin crunched in her hand. She'd taken one sugary bite when she heard someone call, "Carly Hale, what a nice surprise!"

She turned on her heel. After a quick glance around, she saw Mark Hughes waving at her from about a dozen feet away. A huge smile on his tanned face, he looked stylish in beige shorts and a short-sleeved patterned shirt the color of fresh celery.

He ambled toward her, his smile broadening with every step. "Hey, I was hoping I'd see you here. Great day, isn't it?"

"Yes, um, it sure is. It's good to see you too." She patted her mouth with her napkin, praying she didn't have blue sugar stuck to her lips. "How's your mom doing?"

"She's . . . doing okay. Fusses over me when I'm home. Always making me one of her special cakes." He patted his flat abdomen.

No excess cake there, Carly thought wryly.

"Mom actually has a little business going. She bakes cakes using her old grandma's recipe and ships them to people. The business happened kind of by accident. She shipped a cake to a friend who lost her husband. From there it was word of mouth."

"That's great," Carly said. "Does she advertise?"

"Oh, no. She could never keep up if she did. On average she does one or two a week. It keeps her mind off other things, and she loves baking. Since the cakes are so delicious, she can charge quite a bit."

"I'm sure," Carly said. "I hope she's not still stressing over what happened this past week."

His smile faltered. "Sadly, she is. When I'm not working, I try to take her mind off it by watching TV with her or playing gin rummy. But she still can't help worrying that there's a crazed killer out there picking off old people in our neighborhood. She even asked me to buy her a taser."

That was interesting. Hadn't Imogene said whenever there was trouble in the neighborhood, Octavia was at the root of it? Maybe now she was seeing things in a different light.

"I'm sorry to hear she's still worried. Have the police talked to you at all?"

Mark's blue eyes flickered. "They have. Mostly because of the brouhaha we had over moving the fence. Obviously, I couldn't tell them much since I was overseas when the . . . incident happened. Funny thing, though. I wasn't supposed to be away that week. My trip had been planned for a few weeks earlier."

"What made you postpone?" Carly asked him.

He gave a slight laugh. "I got hit with the worst summer cold ever. Looking back, though, I'm grateful for it. If I'd been stateside when Octavia was killed, the police might think I did it over that silly fence dispute." He rolled his eyes as if to emphasize how ridiculous that was.

A group of young kids, joking and laughing with each other, jostled Carly's arm. Mark frowned. With a hand barely skimming the small of her back he led her to one side. His touch felt strange, the implications even stranger.

His gaze seemed to grip hers and hold it in a vise. "Carly, I know this isn't exactly the ideal place to ask this, but I wondered if you would have dinner with me some evening. That is, if you're not currently seeing anyone."

Carly nearly choked at the bluntness of the question. She coughed and then wiped her lips with her crumpled napkin. "Mark, I—forgive me, I wasn't expecting that. I'm flattered that you would ask. But yes, I'm in a serious relationship."

Maintaining his smile, he pointed at her left hand. "That's fine, and I'm happy for you. I only took a chance because I noticed you're not wearing a ring."

"Oh, well, I know, but—"

He interrupted her with a chuckle. "I'm sorry. I wasn't asking for an explanation, and I didn't mean to put you on the spot. On a different note, I've been working on that brochure I told you about. The one for the tour of England? Once I have the mock-up done, I'll drop one off to you. Maybe one day you and your . . . partner might be interested in booking a tour?"

"Um, yes. Maybe one day we will. It sure sounds like a dream vacation." She swiped her lips again with her napkin. "Well, I'd better get back to the restaurant. My customers await!"

It was a lame goodbye, but he told her to "take care" and strolled off in the opposite direction.

Carly threaded her way through the crowd, her thoughts stuck on the odd encounter. On the surface, there'd been nothing threatening, or even suspicious, about her conversation with Mark Hughes. Still, something in his manner made her wonder about his agenda.

Had he truly only wanted to have dinner with her? Or was he sniffing for information about Octavia's murder? He mentioned that he'd talked at length to the police. Did that mean he was a person of interest for the crime?

But no, that wasn't possible. Mark had been out of the country when Octavia was murdered. Surely the police would've verified that by now.

Carly had to accept the obvious. Mark had wanted a dinner date with her, pure and simple.

She finished eating her cotton candy, then tossed the paper cone and napkin in a trash receptacle. She started toward the edge of the green, where the fire department had set up a raffle table for one of its fundraisers. She bought two tickets and was starting to cross the street when she noticed someone on the sidewalk glaring at her.

Arms crossed over her chest, her auburn hair scooped into a neat ponytail, Tara Shepard was shooting daggers at Carly with her stunning green eyes.

CHAPTER 18

TAKEN ABACK BY TARA'S SEVERE EXPRESSION, CARLY STOPPED SHORT. Then, as if a light switch had flicked on, Tara grinned and strode toward her as if she'd just that moment spotted her.

Garbed in a gauzy, halter-style sundress with a jungle pattern that accentuated her eyes, Tara reached out and gave Carly a one-armed hug. "Hey, I was going to drop by your restaurant and say hello to you! I guess now I can do it here."

"Hey, Tara. Long time no see," Carly joked. "For a second there I thought you were mad at me. I wondered if you were upset that I invaded your privacy yesterday."

Tara's eyes popped open wide. "Invaded my privacy? Carly, you did no such thing! And let me tell you, my brother polished off the rest of those muffins like there was no tomorrow. We both enjoyed your visit."

Something in her tone was a bit too perky, but Carly pretended not to notice. "Did you finish your painting yesterday?"

Tara rolled her eyes. "Almost. One wall left to go, but Sawyer promised to do it this afternoon." Her gaze shot past Carly. She seemed to be searching for something, or someone, on the town green.

"If you're here to browse," Carly said, "there's a woman in one of the booths selling her handmade backpacks. She has some awesome designs. It occurred to me that they might be a good fit for your shop."

"You must be a mind reader." Tara laughed. "She's exactly the person I'm here to see."

"Oh, then . . . good luck," Carly said. "And before I forget, there's something I wanted to ask you. I was talking to my friend Gina last night. She's been going through her mom's things. They're packed away in boxes, and she's trying to clean out the storage facility."

Tara's face softened. "When did she lose her mom?"

"Quite a while ago," Carly said. "When we were still in middle school. Anyway, she found an old purse that her mom used to love. It's a designer bag—a Coach or a Hermès maybe?—and she wondered if it had any value. Since we were talking yesterday about vintage bags, I wanted to ask your opinion."

Tara rubbed her arms, as if a chill had swept over her. "I could certainly look at it. Or she could google it to see if any similar bags are for sale. But even if it's worth a few thou, she wouldn't want to sell her mom's handbag, would she?"

"Oh, no, I'm sure she wouldn't," Carly replied. "She was just curious about it. Actually, I think you'd like Gina. She owns the card shop one street over from my restaurant, and she designs most of the cards herself."

"I'd love to meet her." Tara smiled brightly and touched Carly's arm. "Hey, can we have a girls' night out one day next week? You can bring your friend, and we can dish about all sorts of girly stuff."

Tara's suggestion was perfect. Instead of dragging Gina to Tara's shop on a pretext, they could meet during a casual evening out.

"You know what? That's a super idea. I'll check with Gina and we'll suggest a date, if that works for you."

"Any day's good for me. Except for being tethered to my shop, I'm free as a bird," Tara said with a tinkling laugh. She shot a look across the green. "Quick question. Did I see you talking to Mark Hughes earlier?"

The sudden switch in topics gave Carly a jolt. "You probably did. I was eating my cotton candy when he came over to say hello. I'd only met him once, but I met his mom a few times. Sweet lady. I guess your stepmom's death has her worried, big-time, since their homes are so close to each other."

Carly knew she was babbling, but something in Tara's voice had touched a nerve. One thing was certain. She had no intention of telling Tara that Mark had asked her for a date.

Misgivings aside, Tara's suggestion to have a girls' night out had been perfectly timed. It gave Carly an excuse to learn more about the purse purveyor—and her brother Sawyer. Gina would be there too, and they'd be in a public place.

After agreeing with Tara to firm up a date, Carly returned to the eatery. Grant had taken a break, and Valerie was managing the grill. In a prior life, the one before Valerie's longtime boyfriend dumped her and ran their country store into the ground, she'd managed a busy lunch counter. It was a job she'd loved, so filling in for Grant was a no-brainer.

Which still didn't explain the enigmatic smile hovering on her lips.

In the kitchen, Ross was rinsing dishes in the sink. Carly sat at the table and made a quick call to Gina.

"Hey, are you interested in having a girls' night out with Tara Shepard and me?"

Gina squeaked. "Are you *kidding* me?"

"Nope. I'm deadly serious. But first you have to get one of those old designer bags from your Aunt Lil. I told Tara you wanted her opinion on the value of your mom's vintage bag."

"You sneaky little devil."

Carly laughed. "*I'm* sneaky? You're the one who thought of it. Anyway, can we try for Monday?"

"You bet," Gina said, sounding excited. "Hey, let's try that new wine bar. The one on Dalton Avenue. I heard they serve hors d'oeuvres that'll blow your taste buds away."

"Perfect. I'll suggest it to Tara, but she told me she's free any night."

Tentative plans agreed on, Carly told her friend about Mark Hughes asking her to dinner.

For a long moment Gina was silent. Then, "Are you going to tell Ari?"

"Of course I am. That's not something I'd keep secret. And speaking of Ari . . ." Carly related their plans to go house hunting on Sunday.

"So, you're taking the next step," Gina murmured. "Does that mean . . ." She trailed off, waiting for Carly to fill in the rest.

"No, we are not engaged, and this info is for your ears only. I don't want my mom getting wind of it. Before I know it, she'd have me shopping for wedding gowns."

"I hear you there," Gina said with a chuckle. "Don't worry. My lips are sealed."

They disconnected and Carly sat for a minute, staring at her phone. After mulling over their girls' night out plans, she realized what was bothering her.

She'd fibbed to Tara about the vintage purse.

She'd tricked a woman who might well become a friend. A woman who most likely was innocent of murder.

But there it was. *Most likely.*

Carly had to be sure.

• • •

"Um, Ms. Hale?" Ross set down a glass of iced tea in front of her. "You look like you could use this."

Carly looked up and smiled at him. "You read my mind, Ross. Thank you."

"You're welcome. Um, I have a question. I know I said I'd work all the hours you want me to, but I was wondering if I could leave at five thirty today. There's like, an outdoor concert in Bennington, and I want to take my girlfriend. If we don't get there early, all the good spots will be taken."

"Ross, of course you can. You've been working hard all day, and I've never seen anyone leave a kitchen so spic-and-span." She grinned. "I didn't know you had a girlfriend."

"Yeah, well, her dad hasn't let me see her all week because of the, you know. But since I haven't been arrested yet, he figures the cops don't suspect me anymore."

If only that were true, Carly thought soberly.

"Why don't you leave at five and get a head start," Carly suggested.

"That would be great! Thanks, Ms. Hale. And, um, just so you know, I didn't hear any of your phone conversation. When I saw you making a call, I stuck my headphones in." With a sheepish grin he went back to the sink and continued rinsing dishes.

What a great kid, Carly thought, then corrected herself. He was a young man, with a bright future ahead of him.

If the taint of being a murder suspect didn't ruin it for him.

Frustrated with the lack of progress on the part of the police, she tapped at her cell. She enlarged each of Don's pictures from the day of the murder. Nothing caught her eye that she hadn't already seen. With a sigh, she moved to the pic Ross had taken after he discovered Octavia's body. Except for one section where envelopes of all sizes had been neatly stacked, the rest of the table was an avalanche of paper.

Then she saw something—the tip of a small silver tube. With her thumb and forefinger, she enlarged the photo as far as it would go.

Lipstick. That's what the tube was, but there was something else underneath. It appeared to be a container of breath mints. Beneath that were a few loose coins.

Ross had been sure that Octavia's purse was not where it should have been that day—hanging on the back of the chair. Did someone steal it and dump out its contents? If so, what were they looking for and why was the purse missing?

A familiar laugh coming from the dining room gave Carly a start.

Chief Holloway.

She drew in a calming breath, shoved her cell into her pocket, and went through the swinging door.

Only two booths were occupied. At the counter, on the stool closest to the cash register, the chief was enjoying a Smoky Steals the Bacon, one of his favorites. Valerie was at the grill. She wore the same cheery smile that seemed to be a permanent fixture on her lovely face these days.

"Hey, Chief." Carly went over and slid onto the stool beside him. She'd caught him mid-chew, so he didn't respond right away.

"Hello, Carly," he said after he swallowed.

She swung her stool around to face him. "After you finish your lunch, I'd like to talk to you about something, if that's okay."

"If it's about the topic we discussed before, then no, it's not okay." He took another bite of his sandwich.

Again, she waited. "It's actually an easy question. Kind of a yes or no thing." When the chief remained silent, she forged ahead, keeping her voice low. "I wanted to ask if the police verified that Mark Hughes was outside of the United States when the . . . *you know what* happened."

Holloway turned to stare at her, his eyebrows tilting toward his nose. "And why would you want to know that?"

Carly scrambled for an answer he'd go for. "The thing is, his mom, Imogene, has become one of our good customers. She has some physical challenges, and the . . . incident with her neighbor really upset her. I'd like to know that she doesn't have to worry about her son, too, poor woman."

Behind the counter, Valerie's smile had collapsed into a sulk. She scraped at the grill as if it were coated in tar—a sure sign of anxiety.

"Why would you think she might?" Holloway said.

He was not going to make this easy.

Carly cleared her throat. "I heard there was a dispute over a fence, that's all. Sometimes neighborly spats can turn into, you know, bad blood."

Holloway turned to face Carly. In a voice dangerously soft he said, "I'll say this only one more time. You are not to speak to any of those people. Not to the neighbors, not to the relatives, not to anyone connected to Octavia Gray. If you do, I promise you there will be consequences."

Inwardly Carly fumed at his tone, but she kept her cool. "Chief, I'm sorry, but I don't think you can tell me who I can or cannot talk to. I haven't done anything wrong. I run a business, and I speak to people all the time. If they come in here, I can't simply ignore them."

She'd hoped to ask him if Octavia had left a will, but that ship had long since sailed. Before he could continue his reprimand, she slid off her stool. "Have a great day, Chief. Your meal is on the house."

The customers in one of the booths ambled up to the cash register to settle their tabs. Carly accepted their payments and thanked them for their business. After the way the chief had spoken to her, she felt as if she were back in tenth grade, when she'd been given detention for talking in class.

She cleaned up the vacated booth and carried a tub of dirty dishes into the kitchen.

Grant returned and took over the grill, after which Valerie came through the swinging door. Her face pale, her lips pressed into a firm line, she walked straight up to Carly.

"Carly, I have to say this," she said in a shaky voice. "What you did to Fred really upset me. I know you're my boss and I'm probably risking my job telling you this, but I don't think you appreciate what he's trying to do."

Carly felt her jaw drop. Until that moment, she had no idea how her actions were affecting Valerie. "My gosh, Val, I didn't mean to upset you. I . . . had a question I thought the chief could answer for me, that's all."

Valerie blinked back tears. "For pity's sake, don't you get it, Carly? I haven't said it before because I try not to interfere, but I'm really worried about you. Remember what happened last winter?"

As if Carly could forget being trapped with a desperate killer.

"I know, but that's over," she soothed. "Long over."

Valerie shook her head and covered her eyes, now leaking with tears. "My God, you really don't get it, do you? With you, it's never over."

Carly wrapped her friend in a hug and patted her back. She'd never intended to hurt her, and now she felt like a monster.

Over Valerie's shoulder, Carly saw Ross staring at them, his face the image of despair.

"This is all my fault," he said, his voice raw. "You guys are friends, and now because of me you're fighting. I can't take it anymore, what I did to you."

"No, Ross, it's not—" Carly began.

He threw up his arms. "If I hadn't started my stupid business, none of this would've happened. My folks were right—I should have spent the summer with them." He removed his apron and tossed it in the laundry bin. "Look at all the trouble I caused."

"Please, Ross," Valerie begged. "You didn't do anything wrong."

"Maybe not, but it's still my fault. Ms. Hale, please don't pay me for today, okay? The dishes are ready to be washed, and I wiped down all the shelves."

Carly's throat burned. *This can't be happening.*

"I'll expect to see you here Monday morning, okay?" she tried.

Ross shook his head. "I don't think so. Not unless the police have a magic way of nailing Mrs. Gray's killer by tomorrow."

CHAPTER 19

BY THE TIME CARLY ARRIVED HOME, ARI HAD SET THE TABLE FOR WINE AND pizza. The sight of his dark brown gaze and jaunty smile gave her heart the flutter it always did. Tonight, however, she needed something more to lift her spirits—if that was possible after the afternoon she'd had.

She hugged him hard, drinking in the fresh scent of the botanical soap he used. For whatever reason, it made her feel safe. As if nothing bad could happen in the world as long as they were together.

Ari stood back and touched her cheek, his face creased with concern. "Honey, is everything okay? Did something happen?"

"I'm just happy to be home," she said wearily. "Truth be told, I had kind of a crappy afternoon. Valerie's ticked at me, and Ross says he's quitting if the police don't find the killer by Monday. It feels like everything's falling apart around me." She let her tote slide off her shoulder and onto the floor.

Ari scooped it up and set it on the hallway table.

Havarti trotted out from the kitchen and leaped at Carly's knees. "Hey, I wondered what happened to my faithful companion," she teased. "You didn't come to the door to greet me." She lifted the dog into her arms and kissed his snout.

"That was my fault." Ari chuckled. "I just gave him his favorite food—the chicken chunks in gravy—so I think he was torn."

Or he was sensing my gloomy mood? Carly wondered. She set Havarti on the floor and said, "Did you order the pizza yet?"

"Not yet. I waited to see what you were in the mood for. Do you want to talk first? I can pour us some wine and you can tell me what happened."

Despite the way her workday had ended, her stomach felt stirrings of hunger. The last thing she'd eaten was the sticky cotton candy. Not exactly a meal to be proud of.

"Sounds good to me. Are you okay with a margherita pizza? Maybe we can order it for an hour from now."

She settled on the sofa while Ari poured the wine and called for pizza delivery.

"All set," he said. "It'll be here by eight thirty."

Wineglass in hand, Ari snuggled next to Carly on the sofa. Havarti tried to squeeze in, but eventually opted to curl up on Carly's lap.

Ari listened in silence as Carly recounted the events of her day. When she was through, he set down his wineglass and took her hand in his.

"Honey, I feel terrible that your day ended on such a sour note," he said. "I want to help you, but I don't know where to begin. I'm definitely not happy with the way Holloway's been treating you. I get that he's worried about your safety, but he's usually not so harsh."

Carly nodded. "I know. The thing is, he and Val have such a nice relationship, but Val is my friend, too. I feel as if I'm coming between them, and that's the last thing I want."

"Let's think about this," he offered. "Tomorrow's everyone's day off, right? They'll all have a chance to chill. I bet things will look different by Monday. Time has a way of softening things we thought were unfixable."

"I hope so." She gave him a grudging smile and squeezed his fingers. "I'm still worried about Ross, though. He seemed content, almost happy, working in the kitchen for those few days. I think it took his mind off his issues with the police."

"Why don't you give him a call tomorrow, maybe later in the day," Ari suggested. "You might find him in a different frame of mind."

Carly leaned over and kissed his cheek. "You've already cheered me up. You're not bummed that Mark Hughes asked me for a dinner date?"

Ari blew out a breath. "I'm not thrilled, but I'm also not surprised. You do know you're adorable, don't you?"

She laughed and rested her head on his shoulder. "Only in your eyes. It was my question about Hughes's whereabouts on the day Octavia died that triggered the chief's dire warning. He ordered me, *ordered* me not to talk to anyone connected to her!"

Ari rested his empty wineglass on the end table and pulled Carly closer. "Okay, I have to play devil's advocate here. Holloway is undoubtedly remembering the other scary stuff that happened to you. Not just scary—dangerous. Despite his brusque manner, he truly is concerned for your safety. *As am I.*"

"I know. Mom's been texting me every day. I keep having to tell her how busy I am at work so she won't think I'm sleuthing."

"Except she probably sees through that." Ari's expression grew serious. He closed his eyes and tilted his head toward the ceiling. "You know who I think the wild card is? Tara Shepard. She's the one who gives me the jitters."

Carly sat up straight and stared at him. "Tara? Why her?"

"I'll tell you why—motive. She admitted to you that she hated her stepmother."

Carly had been struggling with the same thought, but she'd tucked it into the back of her mind. Ari voicing it made it seem more possible. And disturbing.

"But . . . why would she risk killing Octavia when she's finally getting her new business up and running again? According to her, reopening that shop has been her dream for a few years. I can't see her taking a chance like that—even if she did despise her stepmom."

"People don't always do what's logical," Ari reasoned. "Maybe the anger was building inside of her for so long that she"—he shrugged—"did the unthinkable. Remember, a cast iron frying pan isn't a weapon you carry with you. It was the weapon of choice because it was there. If Tara's the killer, I don't think she went there with the intent to murder. Maybe she and her stepmom got into a huge fight, and Tara hit her with the pan out of rage."

Carly groaned. "I know, I get it. But I truly hope you're wrong. Gina and I are going to suggest Monday night for our 'girls' night.' You're okay with that, right?"

"Again, not thrilled. But you and Gina together should be safe, especially with people all around you. A buddy of mine's been in that wine bar. He said it's pretty cool. A great place to relax after a long day."

She leaned over and kissed him. "I feel better now. Let's not talk about murder for the rest of the evening. Deal?"

"Deal." He waggled his eyebrows. "Have any better ideas?"

"Well, we could eat our pizza when it gets here, and then you can show me pictures of those homes you thought were possibles."

Ari had spent much of his afternoon searching online for homes for sale in the area. Most were beyond their price range, but he'd saved links to three he thought might be a good fit. He'd texted Carly with his progress report, but at the time she'd been too rattled over Valerie and Ross to think about house hunting.

And, she had to admit, there was still a stubborn part of her that was loathe to give up her cozy apartment.

As if the pizza gods had read her mind, the delivery person arrived. Ari paid for the pizza, and they settled at the kitchen table. The savory scent of basil and spicy tomato sauce wafting from the pie revved up Carly's hunger pangs.

After they'd stuffed themselves with three slices each and polished off the bottle of wine, Ari brought up three links he'd saved on his phone.

"Can you forward those to my laptop?" Carly said after they cleaned up the table. "It'll be easier to see them on a bigger screen."

They sat together at the table so they could both get a better view.

The first house was on a small lot in an older subdivision. It reminded Carly of the neighborhood where Imogene Hughes lived. They scrolled through pics of the rooms, and Carly noted how small they were. The sole bathroom was outdated, and not in a charming, vintage way.

Carly closed the link and moved to the next one. A lovely, bungalow-style home painted gray with red trim popped onto the screen. "This is sort of cute. I like the wide columns in front, and that porch is adorable."

"One and a half baths," Ari added. "And it has a basement."

"I like it better than the first one," Carly said after they'd swiped through the photos.

Ari grinned. "I saved the best for last. I think this is more your style."

The third home was a two-story affair located on a picturesque lot. Flower beds bloomed in profusion along the front walkway, and the driveway had room for four cars. The kitchen was huge, a feature Carly liked, and the appliances looked new. With two full baths, both recently remodeled, the house was the best of the three.

"I had a feeling you'd like that one," Ari said. "Remember, anything that needs an electrical upgrade can be done by yours truly."

"Hmmm, but can we afford his rates?" she said with mock concern.

His warm smile made her heart tumble in her chest. "Oh, I'm pretty sure we can work something out."

CHAPTER 20

SUNDAY MORNING COULDN'T HAVE BEEN MORE PERFECT. HIGH SEVENTIES, sunny skies, a light breeze rustling the lush green trees. Carly threw on a pink crop top and a pair of lightweight red capris. She was ready for a day, or at least an afternoon of house shopping.

She and Ari ate breakfast first and then perused the Sunday paper. Ari went directly to the sports section, while Carly devoured the book reviews.

By midmorning, they were ready to look at houses. Instead of using Ari's truck, they drove Carly's aging Corolla. They both decided against viewing the first home on Ari's list. After looking again at the photos, they saw that it was more like a fixer-upper, something neither of them wanted to deal with.

The other two houses were listed with the same Realtor—a local woman named Penelope Primrose—who agreed to meet them at her office at eleven thirty.

Ari drove, and they took their time. Carly loved Sundays—the one day she didn't have to rush through every activity.

"Need another caffeine fix?" Ari asked her, seeing their favorite donut shop up ahead.

"I'd love an iced coffee. Can you swing through the drive-up?"

They each ordered an iced mocha coffee, and Ari bought a bag of donut holes in case they wanted to munch.

Traffic was busy. Sundays in Balsam Dell attracted tourists galore, especially with the kids out of school. At every intersection, they waited while people crossed the street in clusters, mostly families with young kids. Carly couldn't help wondering if that would be her and Ari one day—shuttling a kid or two from one place to another. Having a family was a subject they'd touched upon but never really discussed. How could they? They weren't even engaged.

A few miles from the downtown area, churchgoers were pulling out of the parking lot next to St. Sebastian's church. The white-steepled church, with its towering windows that sparkled in the sun, was often featured on postcards of southern Vermont. Carly herself didn't belong to any particular church. She tried to lead a spiritual life, which felt more important to her than observing a specific religion.

An old blue Ford driving in front of them turned abruptly into the church parking lot without using its blinker. The Ford came close to sideswiping a shiny white Lexus, the driver of which blasted his horn. After that, the Ford wove its way slowly toward the back of the lot, scraped the curb, and parked crookedly near the church's side entrance.

Frowning, Ari flicked on his signal and swung onto the side street adjacent to the church lot. "I'm wondering if that driver is okay," he said. "I just want to check it out."

"I was thinking the same thing," Carly agreed.

He turned into the back entrance to the church parking lot and pulled up alongside the Ford. When the Ford's driver's-side door opened, Carly was shocked to see its occupant. Lois Feeney, her cane grasped in one hand, was struggling to inch herself out of her front seat.

"Ari, that's Lois Feeney. The woman I met at the birthday party Friday."

They both hopped out of the Corolla and hurried over to help the elder woman. Carly slid her arm through Lois's and eased her to her feet. Once she was steadied, Ari closed the car door behind her.

"Oh my, it's you," Lois said when she recognized Carly. "I should have guessed. You always seem to come to my rescue." She chuckled, but her eyes filled with tears. With her free hand she adjusted the black chapel veil perched on her salt-and-pepper hair.

"Are you okay?" Carly asked her.

"No, not really. I'm . . . a terrible person, Carly. That's why I'm here. I asked Pastor Anderson if I could talk to him, to tell him what I did. He said I could come by after the last service was over. I'm a bit early, but I don't mind waiting for him." Her watery gaze drifted to Ari, as if she'd just noticed that Carly wasn't alone. "Are you Carly's beau?" she inquired.

Ari smiled and took Lois's hand. "Yes, I'm Ari Mitchell, and I'm pleased to meet you. Can we help you into the church?"

"Thank you, yes. How kind of you to offer. My legs aren't so steady these days." Clutching her cane, she tilted her chin toward the side entrance to the church. "I'm supposed to meet him in the vestibule on the parking lot side."

Ari took her free arm and guided her up the short walkway. Once inside the vestibule, Lois hooked her cane over the back of a wooden bench and Ari helped her get seated. Carly sat down next to her, inhaling the sweet aroma of incense and flowers. It reminded her of a fragrance she recalled from the past— at a place she'd visited with her mother. Though she couldn't recall where, she was surprised at the sense of tranquility it gave her.

Lois pulled out a tissue from the pocket of her charcoal gray dress. "I hope Pastor Anderson will grant me absolution," she said, dabbing at her eyes. "But after the horrible thing I did, I'm afraid he'll say I'll be joining the devil where all the bad people go!"

With that declaration, Lois broke down, her loud sobs echoing in the vestibule. Carly slipped a comforting arm around the petite woman's shoulder, but Lois continued to quake uncontrollably.

Eventually, the flood of tears subsided to a few snuffles. Lois mashed her tissue against her eyes. "Thank you both for being so kind to an old lady. It's been weighing on my mind so much, I guess it all came out at once."

Carly exchanged glances with Ari, whose expression was unreadable. "Lois,

I know the pastor will be here soon," she said softly, "but if you want to talk about it, Ari and I are pretty good listeners. Whatever you did, I'm sure it's not as bad as you think."

Lois flapped her hands around her face. "But it is, Carly, it is. If it wasn't for me, Octavia Gray would still be alive!"

CHAPTER 21

CARLY FELT HER STOMACH FLIP, AND SHE SAW ARI'S JAW DROP. SHE squeezed Lois's shoulder lightly but said nothing, a silent encouragement to continue.

After a long pause, Lois hitched in a breath. "About a month ago, I went into the lobby of my apartment building to read the activities board. I nearly fainted when I saw Octavia standing there, reading the same board. I couldn't imagine why she was there. To me, she was the enemy, and she was invading *my* territory." Her mouth pinched into a fierce scowl, and she blotted her eyes again.

"What happened then?" Carly prompted.

"When she saw me, she said, 'Hello, Lois, how are you?' I tell you, in that moment I came close to raising my cane and smacking that phony face of hers all the way to the moon. It took every ounce of restraint to stop myself."

"So how did you respond?" Carly asked her.

"I demanded to know why she was there. She said she was thinking of selling her house and renting an apartment in the building. I told her she'd move into my building over my dead body—either mine or hers, and if I had anything to say about it, it would be hers. I warned her that if she even tried to move there, I would make her life a living nightmare. And then"—her voice cracked—"and then I said I would pray that God would strike her dead so she could never darken my life again!"

With that, the tears flowed again, and her small frame trembled. Carly looked at Ari, who was shaking his head in dismay.

Finally, Lois lifted her head, her eyes swollen and red-rimmed. "Don't you see? I invoked God's name to wish her dead, and now . . . and now she *is* dead, and it's all my fault."

Carly spoke quietly. "Lois, it's not your fault. You had a normal human reaction to someone who wronged you and you lashed out, that's all. Wishing someone dead doesn't make it happen. Someone else was angry enough to go to Octavia's home and attack her, but that wasn't you, was it?"

Lois's eyes narrowed, and then she shook her head. "No, it wasn't."

Carly gave her a sideways hug. "You know what? I think you're being way too hard on yourself. I'm sure you'll feel much better after you talk to Pastor Anderson."

"I hope so. You've already eased my mind, a little." Lois looked up at Ari. "Thank you, both of you, for being so kind to a crazy old lady."

"You're far from crazy," Carly said with a smile.

The inner door from the nave into the vestibule opened, and Pastor Anderson came in. A slight sixtyish man wearing rimless glasses, he greeted them all warmly. Judging from his tranquil demeanor, Carly felt sure he'd be able to put Lois's worries to rest.

She and Ari said their goodbyes and went out to their car. Ari started the engine and flipped on the AC, then turned and stared at Carly. "You are amazing, you know that?"

Carly gave him a puzzled look. "I am?"

"I totally get it now, why you're so good at this. You have a way of getting people to open up to you. You know exactly what to say."

"Not always, but I felt so bad for Lois." She snapped her seat belt into place. "She hesitated for a split second when I asked if she'd gone into Octavia's home. But I've decided I'm taking her off my suspect list. She's far too frail to have committed that crime."

Ari's face creased with concern. "I tend to agree, but I wouldn't take her off the list. It's surprising what people are capable of when they're motivated."

"Maybe you're right." Carly sighed. "I guess I can't take anyone off the list until the killer is safely behind bars."

CHAPTER 22

PENELOPE PRIMROSE WAS A BUBBLY WOMAN WITH A BRIGHT SMILE AND A low, throaty voice. Somewhere in her thirties, she wore her streaked blonde hair in a wavy bob that accentuated her pink-tinted cheekbones.

"*So* delighted to meet you both and please call me Pen," she said, thrusting one gorgeously manicured hand into Carly's. She moved her hand to Ari's, gripped it firmly, then ushered them into her plush office.

"My partner is off today," she said, dropping onto her leather chair, "but I love working on Sundays. You said you wanted to see the two-story on Greenridge Avenue first?"

After discussing it in the car, Carly and Ari decided to view the house they'd chosen as their favorite of the three first.

"We do," Carly confirmed. "And any others you think might fit our needs— and our price range."

Pen shoved a sheaf of papers into her briefcase and grabbed her car keys. "Then let's go! I do the driving."

Slipping on her designer sunglasses, she escorted them into her shiny white Nissan, the inside of which was immaculate. Within minutes, Pen pulled into the driveway of the two-story home. In person, it was even more appealing than on the computer screen. The front walk was lined with bright pink petunias, and the wide porch boasted hanging planters overflowing with red and white impatiens.

Pen walked them through the house, pointing out all the modernized features.

The large kitchen had all new stainless-steel appliances. Pen assured them that the plumbing was in prime condition. Walking through the rooms, Carly couldn't help comparing them to her own cozy apartment, which felt more like a home than this one. She knew she was biased, and maybe a bit unreasonable, but she couldn't deny her feelings. She also noticed that the backyard didn't have a fence, which meant they'd have to install one before Havarti could run free.

Reading her expression, Ari slid an arm around her waist. "No worries. Let's see the next one."

The next house was the bungalow with the red trim. The moment they stepped inside, Carly knew it wasn't for her. Despite its open concept, the rooms felt claustrophobic. The aroma of stale cigarette smoke clung to the walls. The basement smelled damp, which she took as a bad sign.

Pen showed them two other homes, both of which tipped the scale on what they'd hoped to pay.

A smile slid across the broker's lips. "I have one more to show you, a brand-new listing with a highly motivated seller. I have a feeling they'll accept an offer far below the asking price, but first let's see if it tickles your fancy."

They all hopped back into Pen's car, and the broker headed toward the other side of town. The moment she turned onto Warren Road, Carly suspected she knew why the seller was so "highly motivated."

It was on the same street as Octavia Gray's home.

Pen softened her voice to a reverent tone. "You probably heard that a murder took place on this street this past week. In fact, that's the *murder* house up ahead."

But Carly already knew which house was Octavia's. Between Don Frasco's photos and the view she'd gotten through Imogene's kitchen window, she recognized it immediately.

Her heart thudded as they drove past Octavia's.

"Yes, we both heard about the murder," Ari told the broker. "Is that why your seller suddenly decided to sell their home?"

Pen blew out a dramatic sigh. "Partly, but they'd been thinking about doing it for a long time. Both are in their eighties and can't maintain a home any longer. After they heard about the murder, it solidified their decision. They want out of this neighborhood, ASAP, and into assisted living."

Carly thought that strange. "Have there been other problems in this area?"

"Not at all," Pen said firmly. "But they're old and a little paranoid, so they decided to bail." She smiled. "It might work out perfectly for you, though. Their home's been meticulously maintained. I think you'll be pleasantly surprised."

The home was, indeed, in pristine condition. The landscaped yard was neatly mown, and the shrubs trimmed to perfection. Since the owners were away with family for the weekend, Pen didn't need to notify them of their visit.

The inside was even more startling. The gleaming oak floors were graced with area rugs in shades of muted yellow and tan. The papered walls complemented the rugs with a delicate leafy pattern, giving the feeling of a warm summer day. In the massive kitchen, the high-end appliances were set into the wall, leaving room for a marble-top island the size of a dance floor. The bathrooms were even more luxurious, and each of the three bedrooms had its own color scheme.

Carly felt a lump forming in her stomach. *The house was perfect.*

But surely the sale price was far more than they were able to pay.

Pen handed them a sheet with the specs and the asking price. It was high, more than they could afford. But if the broker was right about the seller being motivated, they might be able to work out an offer.

Ari's eyes looked animated. Carly could see that he loved the house but had the same concerns about the cost.

"Can we talk about it this evening and get back to you?" he said to Pen. "It's a lot to think about."

"Absolutely! I haven't even put out my sign yet—that's how fast it went on the market. But tomorrow's Monday, so I'll add it to my listings. Anyone looking for a home in Balsam Dell will see it on the internet. Just so you know, this beauty is likely to get grabbed up pretty quickly."

It might have been a ploy, but Carly suspected she was right.

With a promise to call the broker the following day, they headed home. Carly rested her head back in her seat, her mind spinning from house-shopping overload. "I think we should make an offer," she said as they were pulling into their driveway.

Ari smiled. "Then let's sit down tonight with a notebook and figure out our finances. If we make an offer they can't accept, then it wasn't meant to be, right?"

She reached over and squeezed his arm. "Right."

Through the windshield, she waved at the two women sitting in wicker chairs on the front porch. On the small metal table in front of the pair was a pitcher and two tall glasses. Joyce's walker rested beside her chair.

"Ari, maybe we should tell Joyce about our plans. When I move, she'll have to find a new tenant. I don't want her to be blindsided." Carly unsnapped her seat belt.

"I think that's a good idea. She's going to hate losing you."

"Hey, you two," Joyce chirped, her springy gray curls tied back with a loose scrunchie. "Been out enjoying this bright summer day?"

"Kind of," Carly said, climbing the porch steps.

Becca jumped up. "I'll get more glasses. Grab a couple chairs, you guys. You need lemonade and cookies!"

Ari pulled over two chairs and set them around the metal table. Moments later, Becca returned with a tray that held two empty glasses and a plate of daisy-shaped sugar cookies coated with yellow sprinkles. She poured each of them a glass of lemonade. "Try these cookies. They're awesome."

"So, what's happening with you?" Joyce asked pointedly, her razor-sharp gaze homing in on Carly. "Lately we're like ships passing in the night."

"I know. Work has been busy." She took a small sip of lemonade. "You no doubt heard about the murder."

"Oh, we sure did," Joyce said. "I figured by now you were up to your ears in trying to solve it. Am I right?"

"Not . . . totally," Carly hedged. "But I do want to help get Ross Baxter off the hook. Poor guy, he was only doing his job when he found Octavia Gray's body. And it was my restaurant's food he was delivering."

Joyce looked incensed. "The police have their heads up the wrong chute if they think that young man had anything to do with Octavia's death."

"I'm not sure how strong a suspect he is, but he's been ordered to suspend his business and stay in town." Carly picked up a cookie and broke off a petal. "The more I ask around, the more I'm learning how many people in town had grudges against Octavia." She popped the cookie petal into her mouth.

Becca, who'd been silent until then, shot her a worried look. In her mid-twenties and an Army veteran, she was acutely aware of Carly's run-ins with murder. Only a year before, when Becca was homeless and living out of her grandmother's old Lincoln, it was her quick action that helped rescue Carly from the clutches of a dangerous killer. In her opinion, Carly took far too many chances with her safety.

"Listen, Carly," Becca lectured, "you know I'm always here for you. But I can't monitor you twenty-four-seven. It makes me sick to think how close you came to—" She broke off when she caught Ari's alarmed expression.

After an uneasy pause, Ari spoke. "Becca's right, honey. I know we agreed we wouldn't talk about murder today, but we can't deny anything she's saying."

Carly blinked back tears. These were her dear friends. Ari was the man who loved her—the man who would give up his life for her. They all cared so much that it made her heart twist into one big lumpy knot.

She managed a smile. "Then let's not talk about it. We have other news to share, don't we?" She looked at Ari, and he gave her a nod. "Ari and I have decided to look for a home together. Much as I love my apartment and adore having you both as neighbors, it's not roomy enough for the two of us."

"And since you want to move in together, you need to find a different place." Becca lifted the pitcher and topped off their lemonade glasses.

Carly let out the breath that was trapped in her chest. She looked at the kind woman who'd been her landlady and friend for close to two years. "Exactly. Joyce, I wanted to give you as much notice as possible. Ari and I went house hunting today, and we found one we might make an offer on. Budget-wise it's probably stretching it, even if our offer is accepted. But the other places we looked at weren't right for us. If this one doesn't work out, we'll have to keep looking."

Joyce sat back in her chair, her bony fingers gripping the wicker arms. After what seemed like half an eternity, an enigmatic smile stretched her lips. Becca smiled too, as if a secret passed between them. "I have a better idea," Joyce said. "Why don't you two buy this house?"

CHAPTER 23

CARLY GAWKED AT JOYCE. "WAIT A MINUTE. *WHAT?*"

"I'm saying you and Ari should buy this house. Having Becca as my caretaker and dear, dear friend has been a godsend. She gave me a whole new lease on life, as they say." Joyce's eyes grew moist, and Becca reached over and squeezed her arm. "But she'll be getting her LNA certification soon, and she'll want to pursue her career."

"We found a place in Woodford that's perfect," Becca said, her voice hoarse. "Joyce will have daily attention to the extent she needs it, along with all her meals. They have yoga and other wellness programs that fit every individual."

"It's in a beautiful spot on a private pond," Joyce added, pressing her palms together. "Reminds me of where my mom and pop used to take me as a kid during summers. Oh, and you should see the library! I swear, it would knock your bloomers off."

Becca laughed. "Tell her the other part."

"I don't know if you realize it, but at one time this house was a one-family. About thirty years ago, my folks converted it to a two-family so I'd have a steady income in my golden years. They hired a contractor to close off the staircase and install a kitchen upstairs. The bathroom was already there. I still have all the architectural plans. It would take a bit of work to convert it back to a one-family, but it can be done."

Speechless, Carly looked over at Ari. He hadn't uttered a word, but for the first time all day, his dark brown eyes sparkled with genuine enthusiasm.

"Joyce, I'm . . . I'm totally blown away by your offer," Carly finally said. "I'm not sure we can afford it, though, and—"

"Stop right there," Joyce interrupted with a big smile. "I assure you—you can afford it. I don't need to make a fortune selling the house. I'm more interested in knowing that its future owners will love and care for it as I always have, and as my mom and pop did."

Carly took that to mean Joyce was willing to sell to them for less than the house was worth. "But . . . won't you need the money to pay for your new place?" Carly asked her. From the description, she knew it had to be pricey.

"Let me explain something," Joyce said. "My parents were very frugal people. Generous when they needed to be, but otherwise they watched their pennies. They didn't travel to faraway lands. They weren't big on having what other people call luxuries. What they did, however, was invest their money wisely. I assure you, Carly—financially I'm in solid shape. The money from selling the house will be gravy."

Carly sat back. She felt a bit dazed.

"I can't help thinking," Ari put in gently, "that you've been contemplating this for some time, Joyce."

Joyce gave out a rich cackle. "Listen, I've known for a while that this day would come. Heck, I knew from the get-go that you two were meant for each other. I also know how much Carly loves this place." Her gaze shifted to Carly. "If you accept my offer, you'll be inconvenienced for a few months, if not longer. And you'll have to get permits from the town. But once the work is done, you'll have a home you'll be proud to raise a family in."

A family. Was that ever going to happen?

As for buying Joyce's home, Carly loved the idea. She could easily imagine it transformed back to a one-family. With both an upstairs and a downstairs, they would have plenty of room for storage and for all of their treasured belongings. And if they ever did have a family, the extra space would be a blessing.

She shot a look at Ari. "Joyce, can Ari and I have some time to talk it over first?"

"You sure can. Take all the time you need."

"Thank you, Joyce," Ari said. "It's such a generous offer. If we decide to buy the house, I know just the person to do the renovations. He's a buddy of mine, and his work is impeccable." He flashed a grin.

Joyce pushed herself off her chair and went around the table. Then she leaned over and gave Carly a noisy kiss on the cheek.

Carly squeezed Joyce's thin hand. "I will miss you so much. Both of you."

Joyce went back to her chair. "You'll be less than an hour away, and I'll be expecting regular visits from the both of you."

Carly started to respond when something struck her. "Joyce, you didn't use your walker just now."

"Darn right I didn't. I've been practicing taking small steps without it. Besides, the silly thing's always in the way," she said with a pout.

"We've been working on it," Becca said, "but she still needs to go slow. I don't allow any broken bones on my watch."

Joyce waved a hand at her. "Now, with all that settled, what would you like to know about Octavia Gray?"

Carly's ears perked. "You really want to talk about her?"

"Only if you want to. I know you and Ari are giving *murder* a day off, but we don't need to talk about that." She folded her hands on her lap. "I thought you might want some insight into who she was. Who she *really* was."

"Sounds like you knew her pretty well," Ari commented.

"Not so well these days. But I remember her from school days—she was a few years ahead of me." Joyce's face softened. "Even when I was a kid, what I saw broke my heart. Octavia's parents were harsh people, real disciplinarian types—especially the father. Never any leeway with those two." Her eyes dimmed.

"They sound awful," Carly said.

"She was barely out of high school when they pressured her to marry a man *they* approved of. He was not a good man. Treated her like a servant instead of a wife. Her parents were useless. They blamed everything on Octavia. She lucked out when the fool decided he didn't want her anymore. She couldn't get divorced fast enough."

"Poor woman," Ari said. "She didn't have a very good start in life, did she?"

"No, but once she got the courage to stand up for herself—watch out. She was a force to be reckoned with. After she was free of her husband, she gave her parents the heave-ho, too. Told them they could pound sand because she was done with them." Joyce rubbed her palms in a handwashing gesture.

"How did she support herself?" Carly said. "She must have gotten a job."

"Started working as a bank teller, then rose through the ranks quickly. Changed jobs a few times, but always worked in a bank. She was a nice-looking woman, which didn't hurt any," Joyce added tartly. "But despite her grating personality, she was smart and competent. Sadly, her severe upbringing and marriage to that idiot made her bitter as bile. She would set her sights on a man and go after him like a cheetah. Single or married, it didn't matter to her. She'd finish with one and move on to the next. Far as I knew, she had zero women friends."

Carly mulled over all of this in her head. Starting with her father, Octavia's experiences with men had been far from positive. No doubt it affected her outlook on life—and her view of people in general.

"What about Tara Shepard's dad? She married him, so maybe that was a turning point?"

Joyce gave up a cheerless smile. "Oliver Gray. One of the nicest men I've ever known. I can't say if Octavia loved him or not. But if you believe the local gossip chain, she ruled their household with an iron fist. Much as she despised her own parents, she took on some of their least desirable traits."

Tara had said as much a few days earlier, except that her relationship with Octavia hadn't soured until the death of her beloved dog.

It occurred to Carly that Joyce, who'd lived her entire life in Balsam Dell, knew a lot of things about a lot of people. "Have you heard the story about Lois Feeney and Octavia?"

"Oh, I sure did." Joyce clasped her hands in her lap. "Poor Lois. She was never the same after that fall."

"I heard from a friend of Lois's that Octavia *pushed* her off that barrel," Carly added.

Joyce shrugged. "Only Lois knows the real truth, but at this point, does it matter? The result was the same."

It matters if it was a motive for murder, Carly thought grimly.

"Carly, I only shared this with you because I truly believe no one is all bad,"

Joyce said. "Octavia wasn't well-liked for sure, but she had her good points."

Carly bit her lip absently, wishing she knew of one. Maybe when she and Gina joined Tara Shepard for cocktails the following evening, she could glean a deeper peek into Octavia's psyche.

They finished drinking their lemonade, and Becca packed up some cookies for her and Ari to enjoy later.

"We'll let you know soon about the house," Carly said, hugging them both.

But I already know the answer.

CHAPTER 24

ON MONDAY, CARLY SKIPPED HER MORNING WALK WITH HAVARTI AND LEFT for work earlier than usual. Ari subbed as dogwalker for the day. When the little dog saw Ari holding his leash, he leaped into the air to signal his approval.

The night before, Carly and Ari had sat at the kitchen table working out the numbers. It was a huge relief to Carly that he was as excited about buying Joyce's home as she was. Armed with the architectural plans from the decades-ago renovation, she was already imagining what the house might look like with the staircase opened up. They agreed to let the idea marinate for a few more days, after which they would give Joyce their answer.

But they both knew the answer. It was definitely a "go."

Carly arrived at the eatery a bit past seven thirty. She flipped on the lights and turned on the AC, then fired up the coffee maker. She loved this place so much—it was the restaurant she'd always dreamed of. Would it be the same without Grant? Would he be as easy to replace as he'd assured Carly he would?

Her gaze flitted over the dining room, pausing along the way to admire the decor. As always, she felt a surge of pride in what she'd created. What had once been a fading ice cream parlor was now a warm, inviting eatery. The comfy booths, upholstered in muted aqua vinyl, complemented the chrome-edged counter area with its eight vinyl-covered stools. She was especially proud of the vintage tomato soup cans that graced each table. Each was artfully arranged with seasonal faux flowers. The overhead pendant lights, which Ari had installed, resembled lamps hanging in an old barn. She blessed the day she hired him to do the electrical fix-ups. It was how they first met.

Enough dream-weaving, she scolded herself.

Her thoughts jumped to Valerie, who'd become such a treasured friend. After the words they exchanged on Saturday, was their friendship still intact?

"Hey." Grant came through the front door and went over to the counter. He looked surprised to see Carly. "You beat me in today. I could sure use some of that coffee I smell."

Again this morning, he looked refreshed and rested.

"It's just about ready. Good day yesterday?" Carly said casually.

"Yeah, pretty good. Got together with a few of my buds and did some hiking on Peebles Island. We even saw a great blue heron. So cool. How about you? Do anything special?"

"Nothing in particular," Carly said, circling the question. "Ari and I had a nice visit with Joyce and Becca. Even though they live right below me, I don't see them often enough."

Grant opened his backpack and pulled out a jar. "Hey, my folks had a new jar of raspberry preserves in the cupboard. I thought we could play with some recipes today."

"Ach. You stole their jam?"

He smiled. "Trust me, they don't mind." His smile fading, he moved closer to Carly and said, "Um, have you talked to Val since Saturday?"

Carly poured them each a mug of coffee and slid onto a stool. "No. I'm terrified she's going to quit, though. She was well and truly furious with me when she left here on Saturday."

"She's not going to quit," Grant soothed. "But you two need to talk. Want a biscuit?"

"Not today, thanks. My stomach already feels like knotted rope."

Carly carried her mug and her tote into the kitchen. Still worried about how she'd left things with Valerie, she removed the container of pesto she'd brought with her and set it on the worktable. She silently thanked Ari for buying extra pesto at Canoodle the Noodle. It gave her an idea she wanted to try.

She was keeping her fingers crossed that Ross might show up. She'd texted him Sunday evening, begging him to return to work on Monday. He responded by saying he was "on the fence" but that he'd miss the job if he bailed on her. He'd sounded guilty at the thought of abandoning the job. Maybe it would work in her favor.

Carly shoved her tote in the closet and stashed the pesto in the commercial fridge. First task of the day: call Don Frasco. With everything she wanted to tell him, a phone call would be more efficient.

"I knew you'd be calling," Don said, his grin obvious in his tone.

"Great. I have one question and one assignment," Carly told him. "Can you—"

"Before you tell me," he interrupted, "how many bacon and tomato sandwiches do you owe me?"

Eek. She'd forgotten. "Two, I think, but you can have more if you do me a favor."

"Deliveries? I'm on it. So what's the favor?"

Carly lowered her voice. "I need you to do some digging at the probate court. You'll have to go to Bennington. I want to know if anyone filed a will for you-know-who."

"Are her initials O.G.?" Don loved playing games.

"You know perfectly well they are. If a will's been filed, try to get a copy. It would be public record, so it shouldn't be a problem. I hope."

"Do we know if she even had a will?" Don sounded doubtful.

"No, and that's where you come in. You're an investigative reporter, aren't you?" She knew that would pump his ego.

"You betcha. I'll check in with you later."

She was tying on a crisp apron when Valerie came in. Paler than usual, she avoided eye contact with Carly as she stowed her handbag in the closet.

"Hi, Val." Carly swallowed back a lump of nerves. "How was your Sunday?"

Valerie shook her head. "Not very good. I worried myself into a dither over the things I said to you. I was so . . . so *awful*," she blurted, and then the tears flowed.

Carly went over and enfolded her friend in a hug. It was starting to feel like a ritual. "Come on, Val, stop it now. Everything you said came from the heart. That's what's important. Besides, sometimes I need a good talking-to, don't I?" she teased.

Valerie stood back and swiped her eyes with the heel of her hand. "You sure?"

"Totally sure."

"Will you promise to be extra careful? And stop hanging around with murderers?"

Carly smiled at her friend. "I don't intentionally hang around with murderers, but I will use every precaution. Nothing bad will happen to me."

With that, they began their day as usual. It was Valerie's turn to clean the bathroom, and she scrubbed the fixtures until they sparkled. Carly took a short break to text Tara Shepard. Tara happily agreed to meet Carly and Gina at eight o'clock that evening at Balsam Vino. She added a wine bottle emoji and a red heart at the end of her text.

At a little past ten, Ross Baxter strode into the kitchen.

"Ross!" Valerie rushed over and hugged him as if he'd been lost in the woods for a month. "I knew you couldn't stay away."

Carly laughed at the pair and thanked him for showing up. With a sheepish smile, Ross donned an apron and said, "I'm glad I showed up, too. It wasn't fair to ditch you guys with no notice. So like, what should I do first?"

After assigning him his duties, Carly left him to rinse and slice tomatoes—enough to get them through the lunch crunch. With the outside temperature creeping above ninety, Carly anticipated a busy day.

Suzanne came in a few minutes early and spruced up all the booths. Shortly before noon, the eatery received two calls for deliveries. Surprisingly, one was from Imogene Hughes. Carly wondered why she needed delivery with her son back in town. But business was business, and Don was available. More important, Imogene's home being so close to Octavia's meant that she might know more than she realized about who'd wanted her neighbor dead.

As Carly was juggling a container of sliced tomatoes and a large jar of pickles on her way from the kitchen, the eatery's landline rang. Valerie, who was closest to the phone, picked it up. "Carly's Grilled Cheese Eatery. How may I help you?" she warbled. After listening for half a minute, she asked the caller to hold and then signaled to Carly.

Carly set down her containers next to the grill. "You need me?"

Valerie cupped her hand over the receiver. "There's a woman on the phone named Nina Cyr. She wants to know if she can stop by today with samples of her hand-crafted cookies."

Carly liked the idea of adding something sweet to her menu. She also liked working with local vendors, and specialty cookies might be a perfect fit for her eatery.

"Sounds enticing, but today isn't a good day. Ask if she can stop back in a day or two, sometime in the afternoon."

Valerie relayed the message, and everyone went into worker bee mode.

At around twelve thirty, Don came in to pick up his orders, his freckled face flushed from the heat. As Carly packed the insulated carrier Ross had lent him, she quietly said, "When you deliver to Mrs. Hughes, keep your eyes and ears open for any mention or sign of her son Mark. Don't be obvious, just . . . be aware, okay? If you find an excuse to linger, all the better."

He gave her a flat smile. "Don't worry, I'll be discreet as always. After that I'm heading to Bennington," he added with an obvious wink.

He'd make a terrible spy, Carly thought.

It occurred to her that Mark's passport would show the date he left London. Most likely he wouldn't leave it lying around, though. He'd probably already tucked it away in a safe place.

As Carly predicted, people swarmed into the eatery for lunch. Having Ross helping out in the kitchen made a huge difference.

When they all got the chance to take a break, Grant directed his coworkers to a rear booth and surprised them with his latest creation. Ross opted to eat his in the kitchen, away from the "public eye," as he termed it.

"So simple it's sinful," Grant said with a wicked grin. He'd made them each a grilled cheese on sourdough bread—bulging with raspberry jam and oozing melted Brie.

"This is an experiment," he cautioned. "I still want to try it with different breads and cheeses, like maybe multigrain and cream cheese. First, I want to know how you guys like this version."

They each grabbed a sandwich and began taste testing.

"Oh. My. Goodness," Valerie said after swallowing her first bite. "I want one of these every day!"

Suzanne nodded in agreement. "This needs to go on the menu. It's a total home run."

Carly smiled at all their faces. Moments like these made her world a happy place. "This is a winning combo, Grant. But I would like to test it with multigrain and cream cheese."

"Have you decided what to call it?" Valerie asked Grant.

"That's up to Carly, but I think we should wait until we decide which cheese to use."

After they all finished, Grant gathered up their dishes.

"Grant, I have another ingredient I'd like to experiment with," Carly said as he carried the plates into the kitchen. She told him about the yummy pesto Ari had brought home from Canoodle the Noodle.

"Aw, man, I love pesto. But only if it's super fresh and top quality."

"Test it yourself. It's in the fridge."

A quick taste of the pesto brought a huge smile to Grant's face. "This is perfect. Pretty much how I would have made it except with a touch more garlic. Let me work on some ideas, okay?"

"You got it."

Shortly after three, Suzanne was bidding them all goodbye for the day when Carly got a text from Don. *Lots of good intel. Make me a B & T sammy and I'll be there in a flash.*

True to his word, Don sailed through the front door barely ten minutes later. Grant had prepared his sandwich and had set it down in an empty booth at the back, along with a bottle of root beer.

Carly slid into the booth opposite Don, moments after he'd taken a ridiculously large mouthful of his sandwich. His cheeks bulging, he was taking forever to swallow it all down.

"You act as if you haven't eaten in a week," Carly noted with a touch of annoyance.

Don shrugged and wiped his mouth with a napkin. "Sorry. I'm hungry." He took a few seconds to wipe his fingers, then opened his padded notebook. From the slot on the left-hand side, he pulled out a document and passed it over to Carly.

"Last Will and Testament," Carly read, her pulse doing a high jump. She looked at Don, who gave her a satisfied smile.

"It was filed on Friday by a lawyer in Bennington," Don explained. "It's pretty straightforward. No charitable bequests. But wait till you see who she left all her worldly belongings to."

Carly read through the document, skimming much of the legalese until she got to the mother lode. "I hereby bequeath all my worldly goods, including any bank accounts, cash, jewelry, furnishings, real estate, and all other possessions owned by me at the time of my death, to my stepdaughter, Tara Gray Shepard."

CHAPTER 25

FOR A MOMENT CARLY WAS SPEECHLESS. SHE REREAD THE CLAUSE, JUST IN case she'd misread it the first time. But there it was, plain as vanilla pudding. Tara was the sole beneficiary of Octavia Gray's estate. Not a single mention of Sawyer.

"Can I keep this?" she asked Don, still stunned by the revelation.

He nodded over a mouthful of bacon and tomato. Then he swallowed and said, "I took pics with my phone, so it's all yours. But there's something else." Once again, Don wiped his fingers. This time he slid his cell out of his shirt pocket, along with a neon yellow stylus pen.

"Does that pen glow in the dark?" Carly asked him.

"Yeah, that's why I like it. I lose about fifty pens a week." After a few taps on his cell phone with the stylus, he handed her the phone.

"Mrs. Hughes left the kitchen for a few minutes to get her change purse from her bedroom. She wanted to add to my tip but didn't have enough in her wallet. So, while she was gone, I took the opportunity to take pictures of everything in the kitchen. I was hoping to find something about her son Mark, but no such luck." He laughed. "I almost got caught. She got back faster than I thought she would."

Carly scanned the photos. There were at least eight, taken from different angles around the kitchen. Meticulously neat, everything looked as immaculate as it had been on Carly's visits there. On the counter was a tall cake resting on a wire rack. To Carly it looked like a sponge cake. She remembered Mark telling her about his mom's home business.

The other pics showed nothing of interest, until she got to the last one. At one end of the kitchen table was a short stack of mail. A message was stamped in oversized letters on the top envelope. Using her fingers, Carly enlarged the pic. The words *Past Due* jumped into her vision. It was a bill from the gas company—an apparently overdue bill.

Whoa. Was Imogene Hughes having money troubles? Was that the reason for her side business? Or did she forget to pay one bill, and this was only a reminder? Since Imogene lived with her son, who had a successful career in travel, she couldn't help wondering if the overdue bill was simply an oversight.

"Did you see what I saw?" Don took a swig from his root beer bottle.

"Yeah," Carly said. "A past due notice from the gas company. I'm not sure it means much, though. I mean, how would it relate to Octavia? By the way, did you get your extra tip?"

"Yeah. It was all quarters, but it came to three extra bucks. I guess she was happy with my service." He stuck out his skinny chest like a proud five-year-old. "I was hoping she'd offer me a piece of cake, but no such luck."

"Hmm," Carly said absently. "Can you text me those photos?"

"Yup." Don texted the photos to Carly and then finished his sandwich. "Let me know if you need anything else. Otherwise, I'll check in with you tomorrow."

"Thanks for your help today, Don." Carly folded the copy of the will in half. "Wait. When you delivered to Mrs. Hughes, did you notice any activity over at Octavia's house?"

"Nope. Still as a tomb over there."

Carly groaned.

"Sorry. My bad."

After Don left, Carly scrolled through the pics again. Something had caught her eye the first time around, but now she couldn't remember what it was.

The front door opened and a gaggle of teens flooded in. Almost instantly they filled two booths, their young voices sending laughter across the dining room. Carly quickly folded the will again and tucked it inside her pocket.

Valerie, who'd heard the commotion from the kitchen, was instantly at the ready with her pad. She joked with the kids as she scribbled down their orders. Each table placed two orders of the eatery's cheesy dippers, a snack made by grilling habanero cheddar between slices of asiago bread and then cutting it into half-inch wedges. Served with a bowl of tangy tomato soup for dipping, they were a popular finger food.

Carly went behind the counter to help Grant on the grill.

One thing—no, two things continued to gnaw at her. She still didn't know what day Mark Hughes had returned from his trip to England. She knew what he claimed, but she'd never been able to confirm it.

The other wild card was Sawyer Gray. Don had supplied evidence to the chief that Sawyer had been in town the day Octavia was murdered. Shouldn't the police be focusing on him, questioning him as to why his car had been parked on the street shortly after his stepmother's body had been found?

There was a time when Chief Holloway could be coaxed into sharing information with her. Sadly, those days were gone. Her bond with him had changed, and not in a good way.

There was no way she could prod Valerie for the information—not after what happened on Saturday. But nearly a week had passed since Octavia's murder, and progress appeared to be at a standstill.

Or was it?

After the dining room had nearly emptied out, Carly snagged Ross in the kitchen. "Ross, have the police talked to you lately?"

He nodded miserably. "They came over like, yesterday morning and questioned me and Gram again. It's so stupid, and it really upset my gram. They keep asking me the same questions, like what time I got to Mrs. Gray's house that day and how I got inside. They asked Gram at least three times if she had any recent arguments with Mrs. Gray."

"How did your gram respond?" Carly asked.

Ross's shoulders slumped. "She finally told them about Mrs. Gray keying her car, but I wish she didn't. I think she was trying to distract the cops so they'd stop badgering me. But since she didn't tell them about it before, it made her look suspicious. It's all so dumb. I mean, who'd kill someone over a scratched car!"

"No one." Carly touched his forearm lightly. "Ross, last week your gram said she'd let me know if she thought of anyone who had a grudge against Octavia. But from what I've been hearing, that's nearly everyone who came in contact with her."

"Yeah, for sure," Ross said acidly. "I'll mention it to Gram again, just in case she did think of someone. She hasn't said anything to me."

"Thanks. And try to keep your spirits up, okay? I know it's not easy, but everyone in here is on your side."

He still looked troubled. "It's just . . . I don't like Chief Holloway throwing shade at you like he did the other day. That was like, so unfair, you know?"

Carly frowned. "You heard that?"

"No, but I heard what Val said to you afterward. It wasn't hard to put two and two together. Plus, I know the chief's been on your case about you looking for Mrs. Gray's killer."

"Okay, the chief did lecture me, but he had his reasons." Not that Carly agreed with his reasons, but she didn't want Ross to stress over it. "Come on, let's start doing some cleanup and we can all go home a little early."

The remainder of the workday went smoothly. By seven, with everything shut down and the eatery locked up, Carly grabbed some things from her car and headed upstairs to Gina's.

• • •

"Hey, nice threads," Gina said, seeing the hanger draped over Carly's arm. Carly had brought along a pair of loose-fitting floral capris with a white, open-necked blouse, and a pair of strappy sandals.

"Thanks. I didn't want to be too dressy, but I also didn't want to look like I just came from work." She smiled at her friend. "You don't look too shabby yourself."

In her short, crocheted skirt and psychedelic top, Gina could easily pass for a recent college grad. "I'm thinking of getting a blue streak in my hair," she told Carly. "What do you think?"

"I think it would look adorbs, especially with your dark hair," Carly said, heading into Gina's bedroom to change. When she came out, Gina was holding up a dark red purse Carly had never seen before.

"Is that—"

"Yup. One of Aunt Lil's vintage bags—an Hermès Kelly Thirty-Two. Since you already told Tara about it, I wanted to back up your story. Carly, I priced this thing online. Aunt Lil could easily get four or five thou for it. If not more."

"Are you serious?"

"Totally serious. When I give it back to her, I'm going to insist she sell it. She's been wanting to build an addition to her porch so she can take in foster kittens from the shelter. This bag will go a long way toward paying for it."

Carly was aghast. "I should think so. Are you going to ask Tara about it?"

Gina gave a sly grin. "Yeah, but first I want to see if she recognizes what it is. If she's really an expert, she will."

Ari had happily agreed to dog-sit Havarti, so Carly didn't have to worry about rushing home. He made her promise to call him if she sensed anything off, but Carly was sure she and Gina would be fine in a public place. In case the chief had feelers out spying on Carly, Gina had agreed to drive. Carly knew she was being paranoid, but at this stage she wouldn't put anything past him.

In the car, Carly told Gina about her and Ari's plans to buy Joyce's home. "Yay! Does that mean—"

"It means," Carly said firmly, "that we are going to be living together. We haven't talked about anything beyond that. And you're the only one who knows about it, so keep it on the down-low, okay?"

For a moment Gina was silent, and then in a serious tone, "Are you ever going to say yes, Carly?"

Carly stared through the windshield at the peaceful June evening. In the distance, shards of pink stretched above the jagged tree line. It was one of those nights Carly could gaze at the sky forever.

"Let's not talk about it now, okay?" Carly finally said, annoyed by Gina's question. "There's something else I need to tell you before we meet Tara."

Carly told her friend about the contents of Octavia's will.

"So, Tara gets everything?" Gina said with a gasp.

"That's how I read it. The question is, does Tara know? And if she does, did she know about it before Octavia died?"

Up ahead, a lighted sign that read *Balsam Vino* told them they'd arrived. Gina pulled into the parking lot, which was about two-thirds full. She parked as close as possible to the front of the building, although it was still a few rows back.

While the façade of the wine bar was a simple storefront, the inside was impressive. One entire wall consisted of wooden cubbies behind a glass panel, each nook featuring a different bottle of wine. Sleek wooden tables with plush leather chairs were set comfortably apart from one another to allow for privacy. A soft jazz number played from an invisible speaker.

A young woman wearing a clingy black dress greeted them at the door. "Welcome to Balsam Vino," she cooed. "Just the two of you?"

"Actually, we're meeting someone here," Gina explained, bouncing her gaze around the room.

The host grabbed her wrist. "Gina? Gina Tomasso?"

Gina swerved her head back to the host, and then her eyes widened. "Melody Walker, is that you?"

The woman laughed and hugged Gina. "It's been so long. How's your dad doing?"

"Pretty well. He's in assisted living now." She rested a hand on Carly's shoulder. "Melody, this is my friend Carly Hale. Carly, Melody was the home health care provider who gave Dad such wonderful care after his wrist surgery. Did you switch jobs, Melanie?"

"No, I still do home health care," Melody said, "but I work here two evenings a week. It's enjoyable, and I get to glam up a bit. Give your dad my love, okay? It's nice to meet you, Carly. Did you say you're meeting someone?"

"Yes, we—"

"Carly!"

Tara Shepard breezed through the door, her red hair swept into a loose bun, her lovely eyes made up to perfection. She wore a summery frock imprinted with pale blue flowers, with chunky sandals made from the same fabric.

Introductions were quickly made, and Melanie escorted them to a circular booth in a corner. Gina set her purse beside her on the leather seat.

A young server came over and offered wine suggestions. "Most of our wines come from Vermont vineyards," he explained, "but we also offer some select California vintages."

After each of them chose a glass of wine—Carly opted for a dessert wine made with blueberries—they ordered a charcuterie board loaded with local cheeses, olives, fruits, and spiced meats, along with a basket of miniature pretzel rolls.

Carly found herself diving into the cheeses. Thin slivers of black truffle cheddar melted on her tongue like heavenly nectar.

"Gina, tell me about yourself," Tara said brightly. "I know you own a specialty stationery store."

"I do." Gina happily described her store and some of the new stationery designs she was working on. "If you get a chance, please stop in someday."

Tara took a sip of her wine. "I absolutely will, but you have to promise to come to my grand opening at Pugs and Purses." She slid a slice of spicy sausage meat into her mouth.

"I'm there," Gina said, plucking a purple grape off the board.

"Oh . . . my God," Tara blurted, almost choking on her sausage bite. She gawked at Gina's purse as if it had just been lowered from outer space. "Is that the bag Carly told me about? It's an Hermès Kelly Thirty-Two, isn't it?"

"It is," Gina said with a smile. "I was hoping you'd notice. It belonged to my mom, so it's very special to me. I checked it out online, so I know it's authentic."

Carly knew the "mom" part was a fib, but Gina pulled it off with her usual panache.

Tara pressed a hand to her chest, her eyes glassy. "My mom loved handbags, too. Of all the ones she collected, this is the only one I have left." She lifted her purse from under the table and held it up.

Carly drew in a sharp breath.

The bag Tara displayed was an exquisitely made tapestry purse with a silver chain handle. The design on the front was exactly like the one Ross had described—a woman lounging on a chaise, with a floral design around the border.

"That's . . . beautiful," Carly managed to choke out. "You've obviously had that a long time. I can understand why you treasure it."

Tara didn't respond. Instead, she looked down at her lap and set the bag on the floor. Then she waved in the direction of the server, who came over immediately.

"Would you please bring us an order of the steak and cheese spring rolls, please?" Tara held up her glass. "And I'll have another one of these. Ladies, more wine?"

Gina and Carly politely declined. The server nodded and strode away.

Carly sipped her wine slowly. She needed to get a picture of Tara's bag so she could show it to Ross. Unless there were two identical tapestry purses, which she thought unlikely, it had to be the same one he'd seen Octavia use. Which could only mean one thing.

Tara had been at her stepmother's home either close to or at the time of the murder.

CHAPTER 26

TARA WAS IN THE POWDER ROOM WHEN THE SERVER ARRIVED WITH THE spring rolls and her second glass of wine. She'd taken her purse with her, so Carly didn't have a chance to snap a photo of it.

She explained to Gina what she wanted, but before they could formulate a plan, Tara returned.

The spring rolls, paper-thin wafers wrapped around bits of shaved tenderloin and morsels of bleu cheese, were crisped to perfection. By the time Carly had eaten three, she felt stuffed as a Thanksgiving turkey.

"Thanks for ordering these, Tara," Gina said after she'd scarfed down the last one. "Best treat I've had in a long time."

Carly signaled her agreement, but her thoughts were elsewhere. Her mind kept shifting to Tara's purse. She tried to think of a tactful way to ask her about it without sounding accusatory. Unfortunately, any mention of it having been in Octavia's possession would probably make Tara shut down.

There were so many other questions Carly wanted to ask. Did Tara know anything about the fence dispute? How friendly was she, exactly, with Mark Hughes? Had Octavia seriously wanted the property line moved so she wouldn't have to rake leaves?

And then there was Sawyer, Tara's brother. By now the police must have questioned him about his whereabouts the day of the murder. How much did Tara know about that?

At Carly's prearranged signal—she rubbed her left eye—Gina excused herself to visit the ladies' room. If nothing else, she wanted to ask Tara about the will. As she was trying to find a tactful way to bring it up, Tara leaned over the table and said, "Carly, there's something I need to share with you, but I wanted us to be alone."

Carly nodded. "Of course."

"I got a call last Friday from my stepmother's lawyer. He filed her will in the probate court and asked me to stop at his office to pick up a copy."

"Oh." Carly tried to look surprised, but she felt a telltale flush color her cheeks.

"Oddly enough, the old witch left all her worldly possessions to me. Nothing whatsoever to Sawyer. Isn't that wild?" She gave out a nervous titter.

Proceed with caution, Carly told herself.

"Did that surprise you?"

"It did. Hugely," Tara added, frown lines pleating her brow. "I hadn't talked to her in ages. She tried calling me when word got around that I was opening my shop again, but I refused her calls. I couldn't think of anything she could say to me that I'd be interested in hearing."

"Do you think, I mean, could she have had something to give you? Maybe one of her purses for your shop? Maybe she realized she wasn't getting any younger and wanted to make amends?"

Tara's lips parted, and she stared curiously at Carly. "What would make you think that?"

Heart slamming her chest, Carly flailed for a response. "I don't really know. I guess my brain just works that way. You know, I thought . . . old age makes people reassess their priorities. Maybe she was reaching out?"

It sounded like a load of babble, but Tara seemed to consider it. She glanced around the wine bar as if taking in the scene, but then her focus returned to Carly. "I think you and I need to talk further, but I want to do it privately. I have another . . . issue I want to get your thoughts on. It's important. How about if I text you when I get home?"

"Um, sure. That'll be fine," Carly said, her nerves jumping like fleas.

It was exactly what everyone, especially the chief, had warned her about. Getting too close to a potential suspect.

Carly knew from experience that even the sweetest, loveliest person could be a deranged killer. But this time she'd be prepared. She'd tell everyone where she was, and with whom. And if she didn't return by a particular time, they should send in the cavalry.

"Tara, one last question, and you can refuse to answer if it's too personal. Did the attorney tell you how large the estate is?"

"Nope. It'll take some time to put the inventory together, but I should know within a few weeks. But the house is free and clear, so whatever it's worth, it'll be mine."

Gina returned from the restroom just then. After a few more minutes of small talk, they gathered their belongings and prepared to leave. Carly was happy to see that Tara had barely touched her second glass of wine. She didn't want to worry about her driving.

When the bill came, Tara insisted on treating, claiming they could "take turns." She was apparently hoping that girls' nights would become a regular thing.

They were nearing the doorway when Gina suddenly said, "Hey, you guys, this was *so* fun. I want to get a pic of you two, okay?"

Tara looked surprised but didn't protest. Gina tugged at Carly's and Tara's arms, positioning them under the canopy of faux grapevines near the entrance. Tiny lights, woven among the leaves, cast a warm glow above them. Like a real photographer, Gina prodded and pushed at the two until she got the pose she wanted.

"Take the picture already!" Carly said with a playful roll of her eyes.

"Okay, say grilled cheese!"

Click.

Gina held up her phone and studied the shot. "Perfect! I'll text it to both of you later."

In the parking lot, they all hugged, wished each other a great night, and promised to do it again soon. Once inside the car, Gina buckled her seat belt. With a crafty smile, she handed her cell to Carly.

One look at the photo and Carly burst into giggles. Gina had gotten a perfect shot of her and Tara. Hanging from Tara's left hand, in clear view, was her vintage tapestry purse.

Carly pulled out her cell to let Ari know they were on their way home. "You and I make a great team, don't we?" she joked.

"Yes, indeedy we do," Gina said. "Just call us Cagney and Lacey."

• • •

After Gina drove Carly back to the eatery to fetch her car, they bade each other good night and agreed to chat in the morning. Weary from a long day, Carly headed home.

The sight of the man she loved stretched out on the sofa, Havarti curled on his chest, made her heart melt into a puddle. "Got room for me?"

Ari moved his legs, and she dropped down beside him. Not to be left out, Havarti jumped onto her lap and gave her face a thorough licking.

"So, how did the evening go?" he asked.

"Interesting," Carly said. She was telling Ari all about her evening when her phone pinged with a text from Tara. *How about 7:30 am tomorrow at my shop? This time I bring breakfast.*

"Tara wants me to meet her in her shop early tomorrow morning," Carly told him. "She said she'll bring breakfast this time."

"Carly, it's almost eleven now," he said, sounding frustrated. "You won't get much sleep."

"It's only about a half hour earlier than I'd normally go to work," she reminded him. "So if you could walk Havarti again . . ."

Ari sighed and squeezed her shoulder. "You know I'll always walk Havarti. I'm working in Hoosick Falls tomorrow, but I'll still have plenty of time."

"Hoosick Falls? That's a nice little town," Carly said. "I read somewhere that Grandma Moses is buried there."

"She is," Ari confirmed, "but don't try to distract me. I'm worried about you meeting Tara again. As far as guilt goes, I still think she's iffy. And after what you told me about the will, I don't get why the police haven't hauled her in already."

Ignoring his protests, she rested her head on his shoulder. He pulled her close. "So, you're okay with my meeting her then?"

His voice softened. "It's your decision, but I have an idea. How about if I wait in my truck in the parking lot while you're with Tara. The second you're back in your car, I'm out of there and on my way to Hoosick Falls. If you don't text me by, let's say, eight ten, then I'm going inside with my electric cattle prod."

Carly laughed. "You have one?"

"Nah. I was kidding. I'm just saying I'll be there in a heartbeat if I suspect even for a second that you're in trouble. Remember, I still have visions of murderers past."

"Comforting as that would be," Carly declared, "it's not necessary. I'll let my posse at the eatery know exactly where I am."

Plans made, they called it a night.

But Ari's mention of murderers past invaded Carly's dreams, making for a restless sleep.

CHAPTER 27

EARLY TUESDAY MORNING, HAVING SENT A GROUP TEXT TO GRANT, Valerie, and Ross explaining her plan, Carly pulled into the parking lot adjacent to Tara's shop. The evening before, Ross had confirmed via text that the purse Gina had photographed was a "total look-alike" to the one he'd seen at Octavia's.

Aside from Tara's sporty red car parked near the building, the lot was empty. Overhead, thunderclouds were gathering in a murky sky. Downpours were predicted for later in the day, making Carly grateful she'd be working inside her restaurant.

At the front door to Tara's shop, she peeked through the glass. The lights were on, but there was no sign of anyone. Her gaze drifted to the empty shop next door. The rental sign had been removed from the window. Had someone already leased the space? Carly crossed her fingers for a chocolate shop, but she probably wouldn't get that lucky.

Carly hesitated for a moment and then tugged on the handle. It opened, and she stepped inside, staying close to the door.

She glanced all around, marveling at the transformation. The walls had been painted sea green with a hint of blue—a shade Carly found warm and soothing. Off to one side, near the far wall, was a rolled-up length of carpeting.

"Hello," she called out.

A thump from the back room echoed in the empty store, followed by a muttered curse.

"Tara, are you okay?" Carly took a few steps farther into the store.

"I'm back here!"

Carly followed Tara's voice to the back room. The card table had been hastily set with napkins, creamers, and sugar packets, along with two large paper coffee cups with lids. A box of donuts sat in the middle. A quick glance around the room revealed no sign of the tapestry purse Tara had carried the night before.

"Sorry for my bad language," Tara grumbled. Her hair had been scooped into a messy ponytail, and her eyes had a tired look. "I dropped a box on my foot." She kicked at a box labeled "office supplies" and shoved it farther away.

"No worries. The walls look great, by the way. I can't wait to see the store when the carpeting is installed." She sat down in one of the folding chairs.

"Yeah, me too," Tara said with a faint smile. "Gotta hand it to Sawyer, he really did a professional paint job, didn't he? Here, help yourself to goodies." She pushed the donuts toward her.

Carly snagged a glazed donut from the box and fixed her coffee. "Listen, I won't be able to stay very long, but I wanted to say how much I enjoyed our girls' night out last evening. Gina did, too."

"Ditto for me," Tara said, popping the lid off her coffee. "I don't have a lot of gal pals anymore, and you two were so easy to talk to. I hope we can do it again soon." She grabbed a pink frosted donut and set it on a napkin.

"I hope so, too."

"Um, speaking of Sawyer," Tara said, averting her eyes, "that's kind of what I wanted to talk to you about. I hope you don't mind, but he wanted to meet us here."

Carly's heartbeat sped up a notch. "Sawyer's coming here? I thought it was only going to be us."

"I know, and I'm sorry, but please let me explain." Tara heaved a weary sigh and rubbed a hand over her face. "Okay, so here's the story. When the police first questioned Sawyer, he told them he arrived in town the day after our stepmother was murdered. Unfortunately, someone spotted his car parked near her house shortly after her body was found. They even took a picture of his license plate and gave it to the police," she added testily.

Which, of course, Carly had known. Don Frasco took the photo.

"So, if I'm reading you correctly, Sawyer lied to the police and now he's a suspect?"

Tara nodded, her cheeks flushing pink. "I covered for him, so I'm in the hot seat, too. He's been questioned two more times, and each time he gets more frightened. But they don't have a shred of evidence, so they haven't been able to hold him."

Carly didn't know how to react or what to say. In one way, she was relieved that the police were focusing on Sawyer. It meant they weren't fully invested in proving Ross was the killer. But if Sawyer was the killer, she wanted to be as far away from him as possible.

"I can understand your need to protect your brother," Carly finally said, choosing her words carefully. "But did it ever occur to you that Sawyer might be the guilty party?"

Tara snapped her head up. "What? No! Carly, I'm telling you, Sawyer isn't capable of that. I would stake my own life on it."

"Okay, then why was he parked near your stepmother's house that day? How did he explain it?"

"Because he wanted to borrow money from Octavia. It was a crazy idea, but since he was driving up here to help me anyway, he thought it was worth a shot. He figured if he could scrape enough capital together, he could reopen his kitchen shop. I guess he loved that place more than I realized." She swallowed hard.

"Did he get to talk to her?" Carly asked.

"No, it was too late. The police were already there. He parked on the roadside, trying to see what was going on. Then the cops shooed everyone away.

When he realized something serious had gone down, he called me in a panic. I told him to meet me at my condo. My garage is under my unit, so I had him park there. That way he could stay inside and pretend he arrived the next day."

So many thoughts spun through Carly's mind, each one getting tangled in the others. If Tara's version was true, she'd gotten herself into quite a pickle by covering for her brother.

Carly took a slow sip of her coffee. Her initial hunger for the donut had waned. "Tara, did your stepmother know he was planning to stop by and see her?"

Tara blew a limp strand of hair out of her eye. "No, they hadn't talked in ages—and I mean like, decades. He thought a cold call would work best. A leftover tactic from his old salesman days," she said, her tone heavy with irritation.

Everything Tara was saying about her brother made a crazy kind of sense. But why did he happen to show up on the very day Octavia was murdered? Carly couldn't wrap her mind around that.

"Does Sawyer have any family of his own?" she asked Tara.

"No, he never married. For a while he had a girlfriend, but it didn't work out. I think he was so bummed it ended that he didn't want to take another chance. Poor guy. He's had a lot of lousy luck." She released a shaky breath. "And I haven't always been the best sister. Any time he whined about his troubles, I pretty much told him to suck it up and move on. Although I did bail him out of a mess more than once with his business."

"What kind of mess?"

"Oh, don't get me wrong," Tara quickly explained. "He was great with customers, and he had a beautiful shop. But when dealing with vendors, delivery people, you name it—he couldn't get his act together. One time he placed the same order twice for a huge box of hand-painted cookie jars. When the supplier refused to take back the duplicate order, Sawyer totally lost it. Threatened them with a lawsuit, bad reviews—you name it. I made one phone call"—she held up a forefinger—"one phone call and resolved the problem. All it took was a cool head and a courteous tone." She pressed her lips into a thin line.

"Sounds to me like you've been a darn good sister," Carly said, her thoughts drifting to her own sister. She hadn't heard from Norah since she'd left with Nate and his family for their whirlwind opera tour. She vowed to text her as soon as she got to the restaurant.

"So, let's skip to the chase," Carly pressed. "Why are you telling me all this?"

The fatigue lines around Tara's eyes deepened. "Because you know how to get to the truth, Carly. And don't try to deny it, because everyone in town knows you've helped the police find killers. Plus, I know you've been asking people questions. Don't try to deny it because it's true."

Oh no. Not this again.

"Who do you mean by people?" Carly said tightly.

"Well, Mark Hughes for one. I chatted with him Saturday on the town green, after I talked to you. In fact, he treated me to a popsicle." A smile formed on her lips, then instantly faded. "He told me the two of you talked about the murder."

Carly started to respond when her phone pinged with a text. "Excuse me a moment," she said, sliding the phone out of her tote. She noticed it was already ten minutes to eight. Was Sawyer still planning to meet them there? She wanted to leave Tara's no later than eight fifteen.

She looked at her cell and saw the text was from Grant: *All okay?* She texted back: *All good* and dropped the phone back into her tote.

"I'm sorry, Tara," Carly said. "You were talking about Mark Hughes?"

Another flush tinted Tara's cheeks. "I was only saying that I've known Mark forever, and he's a solid guy. So, if you were thinking of him as a suspect, you can cross him off your list right now."

"I didn't mean to imply anything," Carly said, feigning remorse. "Did you two ever date?"

Tara's eyes took on a dreamy look. "No, but when I was in high school, Mark had a huge crush on me. He's four years younger, so to me he was just the kid next door. But years later, when I came home for Dad's funeral, I saw the handsome dude he'd turned into. His father was living then, too, a real looker for an older guy. It was easy to see where Mark's good genes came from. Both of them attended my dad's service."

Carly broke off a piece of her donut. "So, you and Mark are just friends?"

Tara shifted on her chair, tucking one leg beneath her. "You have to remember—I wasn't around after college. When I finally moved back here after two failed marriages, I discovered he was still living in the same house with his mom. His dad was long gone. And yes, we're friends, though I wouldn't mind exploring a relationship with him. As far as I know, he isn't seeing anyone." She fixed Carly with a pointed look.

"I—"

"Hello, ladies." Sawyer's bulky form appeared in the doorway.

"Sawyer! I didn't hear you come in," Tara said, her voice rising. "Where's Paisley?"

He pulled out a chair and sat down. "I didn't bring her. She was sound asleep in her bed. She looked so comfy I didn't want to uproot her and take her into a stuffy car. I left her with plenty of water and a few treats."

"Hello again," Carly said, annoyed that he'd crept into the shop so quietly. Was he trying to sneak up on them?

"Nice to see you, Carly, and thank you for coming here." He helped himself to a jelly donut and plunked it onto a napkin.

"Sawyer," Tara said, "since Carly has to get to her restaurant, why don't you explain why you wanted to see her?"

Sawyer's heavy jowls reddened. He looked straight at Carly, then repeated the same story Tara had related about his arrival in town the day of Octavia's murder. At Tara's instructions, he parked his car in the garage at her condo and didn't show his face until the next day.

"I wanted you to hear my side of all this," he said by way of explanation. "Tara told me you helped out the cops in the past. I came here to look you in the eye and tell you I did not kill my stepmother. So please, if you have any pull with those cops, tell them that, okay?" His voice rose with impatience, but Carly sensed a sharp undercurrent of fear.

"Sawyer," Carly said evenly, "regardless of any rumors, I have no *pull* with the police. In the past I've pointed out things I noticed, things that might've sped up their investigations. But telling me you're innocent is not evidence. I don't know what I can do to help you."

As if Carly had lowered a guillotine, Sawyer's face dropped. "I see. Well, thanks anyway. I'm sorry I wasted your time." He wrapped his donut in the napkin, scraped back his chair, and stormed out of the room.

"Sawyer, get back here," Tara screamed after him. "Don't be such a baby."

Carly felt her blood simmer. She was less than pleased at the sneaky way Tara had sprung Sawyer on her. And now he acted as if Carly had wronged him.

"That's okay, Tara. I should be going anyway. I guess this was a bad idea."

"No. No, it wasn't." She curled her fingers over Carly's wrist. "I'm so sorry. I handled this all wrong. I should have told you first that he wanted to talk to you. I can't imagine what you think of me."

Carly forced a smile. "It's okay, Tara. If you want to talk later, we can. Right now, I need to get to work."

Before Sawyer's abrupt departure, Carly had planned to work the tapestry purse into the conversation. She couldn't help wondering if it was connected to Octavia's death. But the moment was lost—for the time being, anyway.

Tara pulled back her fingers and folded them in her lap. Neither one of them had eaten much. At Tara's insistence, Carly wrapped the rest of her donut in her napkin and shoved it into her tote.

"Know what the sad thing is?" Tara said, her green eyes dimming. "Whatever the size of our stepmother's estate turns out to be, I'm going to split it with Sawyer anyway. If only he hadn't gone there that day to ask for a loan, the police wouldn't be eyeballing him for the murder. And I could have given him money to start up his kitchen store again."

Carly felt a shred of compassion for her. Whatever the dynamic in their relationship was, Tara loved her brother. "Don't give up hope," Carly advised her. "The truth always comes out."

Tara's eyes welled and she sniffled hard. "I just hope Sawyer won't have to use his half of my inheritance to pay a lawyer to prove it."

CHAPTER 28

CARLY DIDN'T WASTE ANY TIME SCURRYING OUT TO HER CAR. THE MORE distance she put between herself and Tara's shop, the more relieved she'd feel. She shot off a quick text to Ari telling him she'd left Tara's, and another to Grant saying she was on her way.

Having started her engine, she was pulling on her seat belt when a knock on her driver's-side window startled her. She whirled around to see Sawyer Gray's face gaping at her through the glass. He motioned to her to roll it down.

Heart thumping, she powered it down about an inch. "Sawyer, I'm late for work," she said curtly. "What is it?"

"Please, can I just ask you a question?" Despite the plea in his eyes, Carly had no intention of letting down her guard.

"Go ahead, but I can only spare a minute."

He blew out a guttural sigh. "I know what you said in there, but I didn't tell you everything. I couldn't, not in front of Tara. I'm begging you, please. Just listen to my side of the story, okay?"

Carly fumed. "If you knew you couldn't be honest in front of Tara, why did you ask to meet me here? What was the point?"

"Because," he said, "from everything Tara said, I thought you would listen to me with an open mind. I should've known you were too smart to take me at my word." He looked close to tears.

Carly softened her tone. "Again, Sawyer. I can't help you. You need to work directly with the police. Now, if you'll excuse me—"

"But I did! I have," he said. "They still think I'm hiding something about Octavia's . . . death."

"Are you?" She kept her finger on the window button.

"No. I mean yes, but not about her death. That's why I need to talk to you." His face broke into a sweat, and for a moment Carly thought he would drop. He placed his palms on the roof of her Corolla, as if the car was keeping him upright. "I'm willing to come to your restaurant and tell you there. I'll order food and you can sit with me, as long as we can talk alone."

Carly considered his offer. In her eatery, with customers nearby—not to mention her loyal staff—she wouldn't need to worry about her safety.

"Alright. Meet me there at two. If I'm not in the dining room, ask for me."

Sawyer blew out a gust of relief that seemed to deflate him. "Thank you. And I promise you, Carly. I'm not the bad guy."

We'll see.

She powered up her window and peeled out of the parking lot. The darkening sky matching her mood, she drove faster than usual. When she pulled into the small lot behind her restaurant, she let out a huge breath.

Stepping inside her eatery, she paused for a moment, inhaling the scent of bacon and fresh-brewed coffee. Grant was busy at the grill—loyal, hardworking, irreplaceable Grant. How would she ever run the eatery without him?

A sudden urge to fall to her knees and kiss the floor washed over her. This restaurant was her safe place, her haven. She vowed never to take that for granted.

"Whoa," Grant said, studying her face. "You need some coffee."

"Do I look that bad?" Carly dropped her tote onto a stool and plopped down beside it.

Grant slid a steaming mug of java over to her. "Not bad, just . . . kind of like you've seen a zombie."

Or a killer.

Without asking, he began preparing a breakfast biscuit for her. The coffee, along with the delectable aroma wafting from the grill, gave her senses a much-needed jolt. It occurred to her that the coffee Tara had bought for her was still sitting on the card table back at her shop.

"Oh, good, you're back," Valerie chirped, emerging through the swinging door from the kitchen. Ross trailed at her heels.

Valerie moved Carly's tote and dropped onto the stool beside her.

Ross stood behind Carly. "We were like, kinda worried," he said awkwardly.

Carly smiled at all three of them. "Didn't I tell you not to worry?" she scolded.

"Oh you," Valerie said, waving a hand at her. "So, what happened? Did you find out anything from Tara? And don't worry, I won't share any of it with Fred."

"Thank you. I didn't really learn much." She felt bad fibbing to her crew, but the more she shared, the more they'd worry. At least that's what she told herself. "Tara's brother Sawyer showed up, which was kind of annoying. There's something private he wants to talk to me about. I agreed to meet him here after the lunch crunch."

"What?" Valerie squawked.

Grant frowned. "Yeah, Carly, what gives?"

"I'm not sure, but you'll all be here so there's nothing to worry about. Right?"

They all muttered in agreement, but not one of them looked happy.

Carly swirled her stool around. "Hey, today's Tuesday. Gina should be coming in for her biscuit."

"Maybe she's running late," Valerie offered.

Carly checked her cell, but there were no messages. She texted her friend: *Coming in for your biscuit?*

Gina's response came seconds later. *Sorry, buried in projects.*

Hmmm. That wasn't like Gina. Her texts were usually more chatty. Carly hoped her friend was okay.

After Carly finished her coffee and biscuit, they all went to their respective tasks. Before she started on the bathroom—it was her turn—she sent her sister a text asking how the opera tour was going. Norah's response was predictable.

Opera tour! Are you freaking kidding me? Mom told me about your latest escapade. Listen lady, STOP cavorting with murderers right now! Love you! BTW, it's not even 6 am in San Fran so plan your texts a little better! That ping woke me up!

Carly laughed. It was quintessential Norah—a drama queen all the way. And she did love her morning beauty sleep. Carly sent off a response dismissing her sister's concerns and instructing her to share some pics from the tour.

Grant was prepping the grill and Carly was wiping down the booths when Suzanne breezed through the door. "Hey, you guys, guess what?" She beamed like a full moon. "My kid and his two archery buds are coming in here today for lunch!"

"That's great," Carly said. "What are archery buds?"

"The other two kids taking archery lessons at the park this summer—Arlo and Paloma—and their instructor, Mrs. Roland. She'll be awarding each kid a certificate for completing her junior course with flying colors. Or flying arrows," she added with a snicker.

"That's cool," Grant said. "She sounds like a good teacher."

Suzanne accepted the steaming mug he gave her. "She's a battle-ax, but the kids love her. Anyway, they'll be in around one thirty. And get this. Paloma adores reading mysteries, so guess who her hero is?"

"Nancy Drew!" Carly offered.

With a sly smile, Suzanne said, "Actually, it's you."

Carly gawked at her. "Me? But she doesn't even know me."

"Well, she's read plenty about you." Suzanne took a gulp from her mug. "The kid's not even a teenager yet and she reads the paper every day. Her mom, who's a history teacher, says she's a glutton for news."

"Smart girl," Grant said.

"Turns out, they live on the same street as Imogene Hughes. Just a few houses down, in fact."

"That's interesting," Carly said warily, propping a hand on one hip. "And you mention this why?"

Suzanne shrugged. "I don't know the details, but Paloma has something to show you. You'll have to be patient until then."

Shortly after eleven, customers began trickling in. Three calls came in from seniors for delivery. Don, luckily, was happy to accommodate. His tips had apparently been large enough to keep him swimming in root beer.

When he arrived for his first round of deliveries, Carly gave him his insulated carrier and pulled him aside. The past due notice on Imogene's kitchen table had stuck in her mind like a thorn.

"Don, after you're done with deliveries, can you go to the property records at the town hall?"

He shrugged. "I guess so, but I *do* have a paper to get to the printer by tomorrow," he reminded. "Why, what's up?"

"Look up the Hughes property, see what you can find out. Whose name the house is in, if it has liens, whatever else you can learn."

"Okay, but for what reason?"

"Because that past due notice bothers me. If Imogene Hughes's son supposedly has such a great job, why did Imogene miss a payment?"

"Geezum, Carly," Don grumped. "It was probably an oversight. Haven't you ever forgotten to pay a bill?"

"Once, but humor me, okay?"

"Okay, okay. I'll do it. Did Mrs. Hughes call in an order today?"

"No, why?"

"Because I want another chance to cozy up to her to see what I can find out about her son. She seems to like me, so next time I want to hang around for a little chitchat." He gave her a toothy smile. "I can tell her how delicious her cakes smell, how pretty her kitchen is, stuff like that."

"That's fine, so long as you don't overdo it. But she hasn't called in, so it's a bust for today." Carly sent him on his way.

The lunch crunch flew by with nearly every booth filled. Around twenty past one, Josh and his archery buds filed in. A lanky, stern-faced woman wearing a green tee and black jersey shorts followed in their wake.

"Josh, my man, it's been a while!" Grant said as the two did a fist bump across the counter.

Glowing with pride at being on a first-name basis with the grill cook, Josh politely introduced their instructor first, and then Arlo and Paloma. Suzanne stood by and grinned at her son, apparently impressed with his manners.

"I'm Carly, and I'm happy to see all of you." She escorted the group to a booth and handed out menus. "And in recognition of you all earning your certificates today, your drinks are on the house."

"Thank you," Mrs. Roland said. "We appreciate your generosity. Don't we, kids?"

"Yes, Mrs. Roland," they chimed in unison.

Paloma, a petite girl of about eleven with dark brown curls and caramel-colored eyes, stared at Carly with stark admiration. "You know what?" she chirped. "Someday I'm gonna be a detective like you. I'm already working on a case."

The girl was so sincere that it squeezed Carly's heart. Carly explained that she wasn't really a detective, but that didn't diminish the awe in Paloma's gaze.

"Since Miss Carly is very busy," Mrs. Roland said crisply, "why don't we order before we start telling tales."

With that they chose quickly, and Carly gave their orders to Grant.

"Aren't they sweet?" Valerie said wistfully, coming up behind Carly. "So adorable at that age. Makes me kind of sad that I missed out on being a mom."

An invisible clamp pinched Carly's insides. Was being a mom in her *own* future? At thirty-three, was she creeping past the ideal age for having a child?

Her musings were interrupted by a familiar face entering the restaurant. Sawyer Gray was early—it was only twenty to two. Spotting Carly immediately, he nodded and waited for her to approach.

She grabbed a menu and made a beeline for him. "You're early," she said without preamble.

Looking chastised, he swallowed. "I know. I'm sorry. Should I—"

"There's a free booth near the back. I'll seat you and you can take your time looking over the menu."

Sawyer followed her to the booth, and she set his menu on the table. His doleful expression made her feel bad for being so short with him. The man might well be innocent of his stepmother's murder.

He might also be a killer.

She asked Valerie to bring him a glass of water, but not to take his order right away.

The archery buds, meanwhile, were laughing over a shared joke. When their sandwiches arrived, they squealed with delight.

"All right, kids, phones in your pockets. And let's not eat like barbarians," Mrs. Roland admonished with a sharp glance at Arlo. The poor kid had shoved a huge bite of his Sweddar Weather into his mouth and was struggling to wash it down with apple juice.

Suzanne, meanwhile, fluttered around them like a mother hen, ensuring they had everything they needed. Carly had never seen her in quite that mode. It was truly fun to watch.

Aware that she'd been ignoring Sawyer, Carly excused herself and shuttled over to his booth. "Have you decided on your order yet?"

He nodded and ordered a Smoky Steals the Bacon and a diet cola.

"I'll be back in a while," she promised, and went off to give his order to Grant.

By that time, most of the lunch customers had trickled out. Carly went back to check on the kids and their teacher. Judging from their grins and giggles, they were all having a blast.

"Miss Carly," Paloma said softly, after pushing aside her empty plate. "Can I show you what I found while I was investigating?"

"Paloma, Miss Carly is a busy woman," her teacher said. "It's not fair to impose on her time that way. Especially after she's been so generous."

"That's okay," Carly assured the teacher. "Honestly, I'd love to see it."

Mrs. Roland nodded, and Paloma's face lit up like a chandelier. She dug her cell phone from her pocket and tapped at her photos. When she found the correct one, she showed it to Carly.

Carly took the phone in her palm. She wasn't sure what she was looking at, but she wanted to sound impressed. "Wow. What is that? A piece of metal?"

"Sort of. Make it bigger and you'll see."

Carly enlarged the photo and the object came into view. It was a silver cross, rusted and weathered with age. "Paloma, this is quite a find," Carly said, unsure why the child was so excited over it. "How big was it?"

Paloma held up her thumb and forefinger about three inches apart. "My mom thinks it's from a rosary, but I think it's kinda big for that. It was like, pressed into the ground. I had to loosen the edges with my fingers to see it better."

Carly knew the young girl was proud of her find, so she complimented her for having a detective's "eagle eye." "Where was this? In your backyard?"

"Nope. A couple months ago, I was riding my bike around the neighborhood. I saw some guys taking down a fence in the yard down the street, so I rode down and asked what they were doing. They said a lady wanted her fence moved and they were stuck with the job. They called her a crackpot."

Octavia!

Carly's heart thudded. "Um, where exactly was this cross?"

Paloma scrunched her face in thought. "I'm pretty sure it was near the big tree that was there, like maybe four feet away?"

"Maybe there's a dead body there," Arlo chimed in brightly.

"That's exactly why I left the cross there," Paloma pointed out in a very grown-up tone. "In case the police have to dig it up. Plus, those fence guys told me I couldn't hang around while they were working 'cause they didn't want me to get hurt."

It couldn't be a coincidence, Carly thought. It had to be the Hughes property—formerly Octavia Gray's.

"Paloma," Carly asked, "tell me again, how long ago was this?"

"Um, it was like, in the early spring. I remember because it was school vacation that week. I was ten then, but I'm eleven now."

"Did you show this to anyone else?"

"Just my mom," the child said glumly. "She told me it was only junk and to forget about it. But when I found out we were eating here today, I knew I wanted to show you the picture. I read all about you in the paper and how you're a cool detective!"

"Alright," Mrs. Roland cautioned, "let's not get carried away. It's fun to imagine things, but let's get back to the real world. I have certificates to give out."

Fun to imagine a dead body?

Mrs. Roland opened her purse and withdrew three laminated cards, the borders made from colorful arrows. She presented the achievement certificates to each of the kids, who all hooted with joy.

But as Carly rang up their order, her mind was still hung up on the cross. *Could* something be buried there? Or did someone just happen to lose the cross in that particular spot?

Shaking her head, she printed out their slip. At the bottom she wrote, *Lunch is on the Eatery!*

"Much appreciated," Mrs. Roland said, ushering her charges out of the booth. "I will be back again. Count on it."

"I was happy to do it." Carly beamed at the kids. "After all, earning those certificates is something to celebrate. And Paloma, thank you for sharing your story with me. It's obvious you have an eye for detection."

Paloma nodded absently and crooked her finger at Carly, who bent toward the little girl. "Miss Carly," she said in a tiny voice, "do *you* think there's a body there?"

"Oh, no, Paloma, I don't think so. If it will make you feel better, I have a friend who's a policeman. Would you like me to ask him to check it out?"

The child's face morphed instantly into one of utter relief. "Yes! Thank you. I knew you'd know what to do. Can you take a picture of my picture to show the policeman?"

Carly smiled at the girl. "Now why didn't I think of that?"

Paloma pulled out her phone again, and Carly used her own cell to get a photo of the cross. If nothing else, it gave the child the comfort of knowing it would be shared with the police.

Suzanne hurried over and said goodbye to the troupe, ruffling her son's hair. "See ya back at the ranch, kiddo. I'll be home in a few."

Josh straightened his mussed hair, and they all trekked out. Carly hurried over to Sawyer. Suzanne had delivered his sandwich, but he hadn't touched it yet.

"Sawyer, you didn't have to wait for me," she said, sitting opposite him. "Don't let your grilled cheese get cold."

She'd brought along a mug of coffee for herself so he wouldn't feel self-conscious eating alone. After she took a small sip, he nodded and bit off a corner of his sandwich.

"Delicious," he pronounced without much enthusiasm.

"Now," Carly said, setting down her mug. "What is it you haven't shared with Tara?"

His eyes widened. "Wow. You don't waste time, do you?"

"Quite frankly, I don't have time to waste," she said, not unkindly.

Sawyer glanced around to be sure no one was within earshot, then said, "That day, when Octavia was . . . killed, I actually *did* see her."

"*What?*" Carly's mug nearly slipped from her fingers. "But I thought—"

"I left Connecticut real early that morning. I got to her house around . . . I don't know, maybe nine? She looked pretty shocked to see me. It'd been a while, for sure."

Carly could only imagine.

"I told her I was in town for a few weeks to help Tara. She didn't ask me to sit or anything, so for a minute I stood there like a lump. I finally asked her, very politely, if she could give me a small loan. I explained that I wanted to reopen my kitchen store now that the economy was back on track."

"And by a small loan you meant . . ."

"Ten thousand, minimum," he grated out. "Anyway, she said she'd be right back and left the room. After a few minutes, she came back and handed me a check. I almost choked when I saw the amount—five hundred dollars. Five hundred dollars!" He rubbed his stubby fingers over his face.

Carly shook her head, trying to read between the lines of his story. It felt as if he was skipping parts, giving her only the highlights. "In all fairness, Sawyer, did you ask to borrow a specific amount?"

"No," he said with a groan. "I've never been good at asking for what I need. I've always had my sister to step up to the plate for me. It's the only reason my store lasted as long as it did. And it's not that I'm dumb," he defended, "because I'm not. I'm just, well, a lousy communicator."

"Okay, so what happened after that?" she asked, more gently this time.

"I came close to telling Octavia where she could shove her five hundred bucks," he spat out, "but I said I'd pay it back as soon as the shop was up and running. She just nodded. No smile, no wishing me luck. I thanked her and left, but inside I was dying."

Mulling it over, Carly was surprised Octavia gave him any money at all. They'd had no contact for years—decades, according to Tara. Maybe what Octavia gave her stepson was all she could afford. Aside from that, it seemed Sawyer had been hanging all his hopes on a loan from a stepmother he hadn't seen in ages. That alone made zero sense.

"Sawyer, forgive me for saying this, but wasn't popping in and asking her for a loan a long shot? I mean, after all the years of estrangement, did you seriously think she was going to hand you a big chunk of cash?"

Sawyer's face reddened. "Look, I get it now—how dumb the idea was. But at the time I didn't think of it that way. I . . . tend to act first and think later. Tara says it's my curse."

"Is that why you didn't tell Tara you'd seen Octavia, because you were afraid of her reaction?

He nodded wretchedly. "After I found out Octavia had been . . . murdered, I was worried Tara would rip my head off for going there in the first place. I've been on the receiving end of my sister's brutal tongue-lashings too many times. I didn't want to subject myself to another one." He gave a slight shudder.

Carly felt a twinge of pity for him. "Sawyer, I can't help wondering why you didn't just ask your sister for a loan instead of asking your long-estranged stepmother?"

He held out his hands. "How could I? She's starting up her own business again, and that takes dough, lots of it. If only—" He cast his gaze downward.

"If only?"

His expression was bereft. "If only I'd had a crystal ball that day. Did you know Octavia left her entire estate to Tara? And that Tara intends to split it with me?"

So, Tara had already shared that news with him.

Instead of responding, Carly switched gears. "Sawyer, that day, do you recall seeing a cast iron pan in your stepmother's kitchen?"

"I sure do. It was on the stove. I recognized the brand immediately. I sold the same model in my store. Beautiful pan, made to last a century."

"Did you touch it?"

"No, ma'am," he said briskly and raised his right hand. "And that is the God's honest truth." He lowered his hand and took another bite of his grilled cheese. Carly waited for him to swallow.

"So what did you do with Octavia's check?"

He dropped his forehead in his hands. "I zipped it into a pocket inside my suitcase. I was going to destroy it, but I was afraid if my stepmother made a checkbook entry, the cops might find it and think I'm hiding something."

Carly wanted to scream in frustration. "Sawyer, you *are* hiding something. But here's what I don't understand. Why did you go back there in the afternoon? Your car was seen parked on the street shortly after all the police cars got there."

"I know, I know," he whined. "I'm such an idiot. I decided to man up, to go back and tell Octavia how big a loan I really needed. I figured if she gave me five hundred bucks with no questions asked, there had to be more where that came from."

Carly felt as if her head was going to blow off her neck. Sawyer's story was so convoluted, it was impossible to extract the truth from all his circular explanations.

A customer scurried past them on her way to the restroom. Carly waited until she closed the door and then said quietly, "Sawyer, you need to tell the police everything you just told me, okay? The longer you wait, the more guilty it'll make you look, especially if they find out about the check. I have no way to help you because I have no proof of anything. Anything I tell them would be hearsay."

His gaze clouded and then he hung his head. He looked like a man who'd been handed a one-way ticket to eternal damnation.

"Thank you for listening," he said in a resigned voice.

"You're welcome, and your lunch is on me. And I'll tell you the same thing I told Tara. The truth will come out. It always does."

CHAPTER 29

By the time Don returned to the eatery, it was after three o'clock. The clouds had finally opened their gates, letting loose a pounding rain that drenched everything in its path.

"My luck the deluge had to start the minute I left the town hall," he groused, shoving the door closed behind him. He handed over his insulated carrier to Carly and then peeled off his saturated windbreaker. "To make it worse, I had to park in the lot across the street. I wish to heck you had your own parking lot, Carly."

"You're preaching to the choir," she remarked.

Don hung his soggy windbreaker on one of the coat hooks adjacent to the refrigerated case at the front of the restaurant. "I have some intel, but first I want a bacon and tomato sandwich, with extra chips." He opened the refrigerated case and pulled out a bottle of root beer.

"Coming right up," Grant said, brandishing his spatula.

Don flashed him the peace sign. "Thanks, man. Carly, before you put that carrier away, I stuck a bunch of copies from the land records inside. It was the only way I could keep them dry in this monsoon."

Carly unzipped the damp carrier and removed a handful of papers. At the top of the first document, the words *Warranty Deed* were printed in a fancy script. Itching to peruse them, she tucked the carrier onto a shelf beneath the counter.

Don followed Carly to the rear of the dining room. Only two other booths were occupied, and they were near the entrance. She slid into the same booth she'd sat in with Sawyer. Don plunked himself down opposite her and snapped open his root beer bottle.

"I still feel like a drowned rat," he complained. "My pants are almost soaked through."

"Let's talk quietly," Carly said. "Do you want a towel?"

He shook his head and took a swig from his bottle, then looked past Carly with a smile. Grant was coming toward him with a bacon and tomato sandwich, along with a mound of chips that would put Stratton Mountain to shame.

"There you go, Don. Enjoy." Grant set his sandwich platter on the table.

"Whoa. That was fast. Thanks, man."

The two did a fist bump and Grant went back to the grill.

Don picked up a sandwich half. "I'm starving, so you might as well look that stuff over while I eat. I put them in chronological order."

While he chowed down his sandwich, Carly read through the Warranty Deed. Some of it was legalese, but she got the gist.

On September 8, 1973, Arnold R. Hughes and his wife, Imogene A.

Hughes, purchased their home for the sum of $23,500. Carly guessed it would be worth ten times that today, given the passage of time and the current housing market.

The next document was a mortgage to Balsam Dell Savings and Loan for $18,800. A subsequent discharge of the mortgage was recorded in 1988, leaving the home mortgage-free.

But in April of 2019, Imogene, by then widowed, took out a home equity loan with the same lender for $75,000. Which begged the question, what did Imogene do with that much cash only a little over five years ago? Did she make improvements to the home?

The last document was a Boundary Line Agreement and Deeds between Octavia Gray and Imogene Hughes. It established the new property line, giving Imogene an additional twenty-foot strip of land.

Carly flipped back to the Warranty Deed. A phrase had caught her eye. "The original deed to Arnold and Imogene says they're 'husband and wife as tenants by the entirety.' Do you know what that means?"

Don swiped his lips with a napkin. "I asked the clerk that very question. She said it means that if one dies first, the survivor owns the property outright."

The survivor being Imogene Hughes.

"I don't suppose you checked out the assessor's office?" Carly asked him.

"Then you suppose wrong because I did. The property is assessed at two eighty-nine five, and that's *with* the new strip of land tacked on. And because the additional land gave her a higher assessment—"

"It also gave her a higher tax bill," Carly finished.

So why, she wondered, did Imogene, or Mark, if it was his doing, agree to adjust the property line? What earthly benefit did they acquire?

Carly recalled the day she first questioned Mark about the fence dispute. His response had been a terse "water over the dam," after which he'd quickly changed the subject to the tour of England he was putting together.

She was beginning to wonder if Mark Hughes was at the heart of the Octavia mystery. But why? What motive would he have to kill her?

It was time to find out the truth about Mark's whereabouts on the day of the murder. That meant approaching Chief Holloway, if he would even agree to see her.

"This is good work, Don. Did you get a copy of the assessment card?"

He dug his phone out of his shirt pocket and gave it a few taps. "Here you go. I got sick of paying a buck a copy for everything, so I made my own copy. I'll text it to you later, when my fingers aren't so greasy. By the way, can you reimburse me the seven bucks I shelled out for the other copies?"

Carly laughed. "Not a problem. I'll even add seven extra bucks to cover your gas."

"Now you're talking." He crunched a large potato chip between his teeth.

In the next moment Grant rushed over to Carly, his eyes wide with alarm. "Hey, listen, I'm sorry to do this, but I gotta leave. My dad just called. Mom was rushed to the hospital. She might have a burst appendix."

"Oh, no," Carly said. "I'm so sorry to hear that. Never mind about us—you just go. But please keep us informed, okay?"

"You got it." Grant tore off his apron and plunked it on their table. In a flash he was out the front door.

Don shook his head. "Poor guy. I hope his mom'll be okay."

"Yeah, me too," Carly said, thinking how she'd feel if it were her own mom. Even the thought of it made her stomach curdle like spoiled milk. She snatched up the document copies and held them aloft. "All of a sudden, none of this stuff seems to matter, does it?"

"Not a bit," Don agreed. "Not a single, solitary bit."

She bade goodbye to Don, then grabbed Grant's discarded apron and hurried into the kitchen. Valerie was on a short break, sipping the last of her iced tea. Carly described Grant's emergency to her and Ross.

"Oh, no, I hope she'll be okay," Valerie fretted. "I can take over for Grant." She set her glass in the sink and pushed through the swinging door.

"I'll go out there if you need me," Ross offered. "I'm kinda sick of hiding from the public anyway."

Carly thanked him and returned to the dining room. Valerie was already behind the grill, and a threesome was waiting to be seated. She grabbed three menus and smiled at the women, who were shaking out their umbrellas. "Still coming down hard?"

"Like cats and dogs!" one of them said and laughed. "I'm so glad we spotted this place. We're from out of town and didn't have a clue where to eat."

"Well, you've come to the right place." Carly led them to a table. "I'll be back in a few for your order."

"May we all have some hot coffee?" one of them asked. "It might not be cold out, but that rain is chilling my bones." Her thin shoulders gave up a tiny shiver.

"You got it. Coming right up."

After the women ordered, Carly's thoughts returned to Grant's mom. Aware that a burst appendix could be deadly serious, she sent up a silent prayer for Raynelle Robinson. She hoped that whatever had sent her to the hospital would turn out to be minor.

Carly was pouring seconds on coffee for the threesome when a woman clad in a glossy red rain hat and a turquoise, hip-length raincoat swept into the eatery. Her shiny shoes matched her hat to a T, and over one arm she carried a rectangular plastic container with a yellow handle.

"I'm wet," she announced to Carly with a grin, who'd hurried to return the coffee pot to the burner. "Can you hold this while I shed my gear?"

"Um—"

"Thanks!"

Carly held the dripping container at arm's length while the woman removed her outerwear. After slinging her hat over her coat on one of the hooks at the front of the restaurant, the woman relieved Carly of the container. "Good thing it's waterproof, right?" she said with a tinkling laugh.

"It sure is." Carly smiled at the bubbly woman. With her rainwear removed, she looked to be about thirtysomething, with wide-set green eyes and short, upswept hair the color of a canary. "Would you like to be seated?"

"I do, but first I'd like to see Carly Hale? I'm Nina Cyr. I called yesterday?"

"Ah, yes. You're the cookie baker, right?"

"In the flesh. Are you Carly?"

"I am, and I'm happy to meet you, Nina. At the moment, though—"

"Excellent! I know you're probably super busy, but can I show you the samples I baked for you?"

Carly didn't want to disappoint the woman, but she'd chosen the worst possible time for a sales pitch.

"Nina, I would love to see your cookies, but our grill cook had to leave for an emergency, so right now it's all hands on deck. I'm afraid I'll have to give you—"

"A rain check?" Nina chirped with an infectious giggle.

"Exactly." Carly smiled. "In the meantime, would you like a booth?"

"Sure thing. I am *dying* for an ooey gooey grilled cheese."

Menu in hand, Carly was leading Nina to a booth when the front door burst open with a thud. A horde of bright yellow rain slickers thundered into the restaurant, their excited squeals echoing in the dining room. After a moment of panic at the size of the group, Carly excused herself and hustled over to greet them.

The kids, meanwhile—who looked like second- or third-graders—had made a mad dash for the booths, filling them in groups of four. Carly did a quick head count—seventeen, all totaled—with an extra kid squished into one of the booths. Two harried-looking adults—a man and a woman who looked barely twenty—pushed their waterproof hoods away from their heads.

"Kids! Hold on a minute!" the young man called out. "We need to be seated first."

His companion, whose own rain slicker was dripping, shot him a look. "Too little, too late, don't you think?" she retorted, but Carly sensed it was mostly in jest. "I'm sorry," the young woman said to Carly. "It's been a day. We're camp counselors, and we were supposed to be having a nature hike this afternoon, but as you can see—" She waved a hand at the front window.

"Well, we're delighted to have you here," Carly said. "If you're okay with it, the kids can stay right where they are. And you can grab any booth you'd like."

The man sagged with relief. "Thank you. That'll be great."

Carly hurried back to Nina, who she'd left standing there with her container. "Sorry for the interruption. You want to grab a booth near the back?"

After a momentary hesitation, Nina said, "Carly, let me help you, please. I was the dining room manager at the Pineapple Patch in Bennington before the owner closed down for health reasons. Give me an apron and a quick tutorial, and I'll take everyone's orders."

Touched by the offer of help, Carly stared at her. "That is so generous of you, Nina, but I couldn't let you do that. I have a kitchen helper who'll be glad to pitch in."

"Honestly," Nina pleaded, "I would love to help out. I really miss my old job, and—not to toot my own horn—I was darn good at it."

The idea was crazy, Carly told herself. How could she let a stranger walk in off the street and start waiting on customers?

Aside from what Nina had told Carly about herself, she knew virtually nothing. And yet, something about her was so genuine that she was sorely tempted to take her up on the offer.

The din in the restaurant rose as the kids grew more impatient. Was it a sign?

Carly made a snap decision. "Scrub your hands in the bathroom and I'll fetch an apron for you. I'll take your cookies into the kitchen for now."

"Yes!" Nina pumped her fist.

Once those tasks were done, Carly gave Nina an order pad and a one-minute crash course on the menu options. For the next hour, they worked together at warp speed. Valerie handled the grill, Carly helped plate orders, and Nina delivered them with bright smiles for everyone.

By the time the kids and their counselors had left—all with happy faces—Carly felt as if she'd run a marathon. The three women she'd waited on earlier praised both the food and the service before leaving.

"Terrific job on the grill, Val," Carly said to her friend.

Valerie wiggled her shoulders at the compliment. "I'm in my element when I'm on grill duty. It's my favorite part of working here. Now, how about I whip up a couple grilled cheeses with bacon for you and Nina?"

"That sounds fabulous," Nina said, "except for the bacon. I never eat meat. Can I have tomato instead?"

"I'll have the same," Carly said.

"You got it. Two grilled cheddar and tomato, coming right up!"

Nina held up a finger at Carly. "I noticed those kids' rain jackets dripped water all over the seats in the booths. If you have a towel handy, I'll wipe them all down for you."

This woman is amazing, Carly thought. *But is she too good to be true?*

"Okay. Be right back."

In the kitchen, Ross was transferring a fresh batch of tomato soup into containers for freezing. Carly removed two towels from the supply closet.

"Sounded like you guys got pretty busy out there," he said with a slight pout. "Why didn't you ask me to help?"

"Long story, but you can help out right now. The cookie baker is here and I'm having a late lunch with her. Can you be server for a half hour or so?"

Ross's eyebrows shot upward. "You mean like, take orders and serve food?"

"Yup. You know the menu, and you have a pleasant way with people."

"I'm on it! Wait. Better get a clean apron first." He tugged off his apron and replaced it with a fresh one.

Carly grabbed the cookie container and followed him into the dining room. A man garbed in a long raincoat and safari hat was standing near the entrance, carefully folding his umbrella. "There's a customer waiting to be seated," she whispered to Ross.

Ross gave her a thumbs-up and strode toward the front. Carly tossed Nina a towel, and together they made short work of wiping down the booth seats.

"Let's sit." Carly indicated the booth where she'd left the cookies. Moments later, Valerie came striding toward them with their sandwiches.

"Your lunch, ladies." Valerie set their plates in front of them with a flourish. "And to drink?"

"Hot coffee for me, please," Nina said.

Carly grinned. "A woman after my own heart."

As they ate their sandwiches, the two fell into a relaxed conversation. Nina was easy to chat with. They shared some of their personal favorites—dogs, cheese, and cookies being high on the list.

After they'd finished their sandwiches, Nina rubbed her hands together. "Can I *please* show you the cookies now? It won't take long, and I'll leave them here so you can share them with everyone."

"Of course!"

Nina snapped the lid off the container, and Carly's jaw dropped. Each cookie was shaped like a sandwich, frosted with precision to look like a grilled cheese. Yellow cheese made from icing oozed at the edges, some with faux bacon peeking out from the sides.

"I studied your menu," Nina explained. "I wanted the cookies to resemble some of your special sandwiches, like Grant's Vermont Jammin'." She pointed at one of the cookies. "That's a smidge of real fig jam around the edges."

Carly was gobsmacked. "Nina, these aren't cookies. They're works of art!" She wiggled her fingers. "Can I try one?"

"I'll be crushed if you don't."

Carly chose a Smoky Steals the Bacon look-alike and bit into it. Soft and buttery, frosted with royal icing, the cookie was sheer heaven. She swallowed and said, "This is the best cookie I've ever eaten, and I'm serious when I say that."

Nina's grin stretched across her face. "That's music to my ears." She pulled a business card out of her pocket and gave it to Carly. "I'll come back for the container in a few days. In the meantime, I'd love it if you'd check out my website and read the reviews. I also list the ingredients in my cookies, in case you care about that."

"I do," Carly said, "and I'll check out your site when I get home. But I want to pay you for today. You were a lifesaver taking all those orders and keeping those kids fed."

Nina held up a hand. "Absolutely not. You can repay me by sampling my cookies and sharing them with your friends. And now, I'm going to get out of your hair so you can tend to your restaurant!"

After giving Carly a quick hug, she said, "Hey, listen, if you ever need someone to fill in as server, I hope you'll keep me in mind. I know some people think it's a thankless job, but I totally love it."

Then she donned her rainwear and was gone.

Valerie was smiling when Carly went behind the counter. "That gal was a real worker, wasn't she?"

"She was," Carly agreed, "and wait till you taste her cookies. Best sugar cookies I've ever had. But give yourself some credit, too. You whipped up more than twenty grilled cheeses in amazingly short order."

"Don't be silly. I enjoyed it. I'll grab one of the cookies later. Any word yet from Grant?"

Carly blew out a worried sigh. "No, but I wish he'd text us with an update."

Her cell rang, and Ari's face appeared on the screen. "Hey," she said in a soft voice. "How are things in Hoosick Falls?"

"Coming along. I'm working with another contractor, and we're hoping to finish up today. He told me the local diner here has great food. If you don't mind, after we finish up, I thought I'd join him for a blue plate special and a slice of pie before heading home." The smile in his voice was evident. Ari loved diner food.

"You know I don't mind. Take your time and enjoy your dinner."

"You got it. Love you."

They disconnected, and Carly slid her cell into her pocket.

Ross was seating an elderly couple when the man sitting solo in the front booth waved at her. "Carly?"

She looked across the counter. His safari hat and neatly folded raincoat resting beside him on the seat, Mark Hughes was signaling to her to come over and join him.

CHAPTER 30

"MARK, WHAT BRINGS YOU IN HERE ON SUCH A SOGGY DAY?" CARLY FORCED a light tone, but she knew it sounded false. Why did she always feel so uneasy around him? Was it because she felt weird about refusing his dinner invitation?

He smiled and extended his hand toward the seat opposite him. "Can you sit for a minute?"

"Sure. For a minute." Carly sat down and placed her palms on the table.

Mark reached into the inner pocket of his folded raincoat and pulled out a manila envelope. His eyes glittered like a kid's who just spotted Santa Claus dropping down the chimney. "I had the printer make a mock-up of the final brochure. I wanted you to be the first to see it. Tell me what you think." He removed a folded paper and slid it over to her.

Carly tried not to fidget, but his unwavering gaze made her antsy. On closer inspection, she saw that his eyes were slightly bloodshot.

"Thanks, Mark, but I'm not sure I'd be the best judge. I'm afraid I haven't traveled very extensively."

"Ah, then that makes you the perfect judge."

Carly unfolded the paper, which was about twelve by twenty-four inches. She felt her eyes widen at the magnificent photos of quaint English villages, twisty cobblestone lanes, and medieval castles. The descriptions were enticing. She could easily imagine herself there with Ari, ambling over ancient roadways trod by long-dead kings and queens.

"These photos are gorgeous, Mark. I can't imagine anyone not wanting to sign up for a vacation like this. Funds allowing, of course," she added.

He blinked. "Well, sure. It's not intended as a bargain vacation. My company specializes in high-end luxury tours." His tone was a tad defensive.

She folded the mock brochure and gave it back to him. "Thank you for sharing that with me."

He nodded and slipped it back into the envelope. Keeping his voice low, he leaned forward and said, "Have you heard anything new from the police?"

The sudden change in topic sent a tingle through Carly's nerve endings. She faked a smile. "In spite of what you might've heard, the police don't consult with me. I'm as much in the dark as you are."

He nodded. "I understand. I only ask because my mother is going nuts with worry. She's convinced herself there's a killer out there preying on old people. In a few days I'll be heading back to the UK, and she's terrified of being alone. I bought her the taser she wanted, but I'm not sure it gave her any comfort."

"Can't you postpone your trip?" That's what Carly would do if it were her mom.

"I wish I could, but this time it's impossible." He pulled a folded twenty out of his coat pocket. "Listen, it was great seeing you again. This is for my lunch. What's left is for that young man who served me."

"That's very generous, Mark. I'll be sure to give it to him." She wondered if he knew his server was the person who'd discovered Octavia's body.

Mark was unfolding his raincoat when Carly's cell rang. The call was from Grant. "Excuse me. I have to take this." She shot out of the booth and hurried behind the counter.

"Grant? We've been waiting to hear from you!"

"I know. I told Dad you guys would be worried. Listen, Mom's in surgery but it's not her appendix. She's having her gall bladder removed. The doctor doesn't anticipate any complications, but I'll text you when she's in recovery, okay?"

"Yes, please," Carly said, "and give your mom our best once she's awake. Let me know if there's anything we can do."

After they disconnected, Carly let out a breath of relief. She relayed Grant's message to Valerie and Ross, who were equally relieved at the news. She remembered that Don had also been concerned, so she sent him a quick text.

By early suppertime, the rain had lessened to a mild drizzle. Business was light, which gave Carly time to think. A kaleidoscope of faces swirled in her mind's eye—images of people who had reason to want Octavia dead.

Sawyer Gray, Tara Shepard, Lois Feeney, even Helen Quigley could not be discounted. Mark Hughes should probably be added to the mix, except she couldn't imagine what his motive would be.

Ross had returned to the kitchen. He was wiping down the work counter with lemon-scented cleaner when Carly went in with a tub of dirty dishes. She shot him a grateful smile.

"Hey, thanks for helping out in there today. You did a super job."

"No prob," he said tonelessly. "I liked doing something different."

Carly set the tub next to the sink and faced him. "Is something wrong?"

He shrugged and said, "No, it's just . . . I don't want to accuse someone of doing something if I'm not like, totally sure they did it, you know? I know how that feels," he added bitterly.

"Is it something you can share with me?" Carly went over and stood beside him.

For several moments, Ross was silent. Then, "I'm not sure, but that man I waited on in the front booth? His voice sounded kinda familiar. Except, it wasn't the *exact* same voice. That's why I can't say for sure."

"What do you mean by exact same voice?" Carly wished he would get to the point.

"Remember I told you? When I first started my delivery gig, one of my customers was Mrs. Gray. When I went there to deliver her sub, I overheard her arguing with a man. He said something like, if she didn't give it back she was going to regret it."

And suddenly, Carly did remember. How had she let that slip her mind?

"You thought his voice was the same as the one you heard threatening Octavia Gray?"

"That's just it—I don't know! This guy today had like, a normal voice. Not nasally, like the other voice. It was the tone, I guess. They sounded similar."

Carly shook her head wearily. Ross had only heard the other voice once, and it was almost a month earlier. Was he grasping for answers so he could finally be free from suspicion?

"Ross, that man in the front booth was Mark Hughes, Imogene Hughes's son. When Octavia was murdered, he was still in the UK on business." *Supposedly.*

His brow furrowed in thought. "So like, even if he was the guy I heard arguing with Mrs. Gray, he couldn't be the killer?"

"That's how I see it. When the police talked to you—"

"*Interrogated* me," he snorted.

"Okay, interrogated you. Did you mention it to them?"

"Maybe. I'm pretty sure I did. But they had me so confused, and I was so tired, I could've told them I saw a purple cat that day."

Carly smiled. "That's okay. If the chief ever decides to talk to me again, I'll mention it, okay?"

"Yeah. Thanks." His face brightened. "I feel a little better now."

There were so many odd parts to the puzzle. If only Carly could piece them together, she'd have a clearer picture of the killer.

The big problem? Some key pieces were missing, leaving gaping holes in the picture. In her mind, two of those pieces topped the list.

First was Tara's tapestry purse. Had it been the same one Ross had seen at Octavia's? If so, why did Tara have it now?

Second, Carly still hadn't confirmed Mark Hughes's whereabouts on the day of Octavia's murder. She didn't seriously believe he'd killed his neighbor. Since the fence matter was a done deal, what other motive would he have?

An idea struck Carly. After what Ross had just told her about the man he'd heard arguing with Octavia, maybe she could use it to get to the chief. She'd have to humble herself, even grovel a bit, but it would be worth it to get the answer she needed. If Mark Hughes's passport showed he'd arrived home two days after the murder, she'd cross him off her list and move on from there.

At a little after six, only a few customers lingered in the dining room. Both were finishing up their meals and preparing to pay.

Since she'd left things a bit strained with Tara that morning, Carly decided to text her rather than call. *I feel bad about this morning. Would you like to pop over for a grilled cheese?*

Carly didn't really feel all that bad, but she wanted to put Tara at ease.

Tara's response was instantaneous. *I'm ravenous! Be there in 10!*

Carly pulled in a calming breath. With Grant gone, only Valerie and Ross remained, and it was getting close to closing time. When she told them that Tara would be there shortly, she expected them to protest.

Instead, they both crossed their arms and stared at her. "Fine," Valerie said. "I'll man the grill, and I'm not leaving until she's gone."

"And I'm staying in the kitchen," Ross declared, "and *I'm* not leaving until she's gone and I've walked you to your car."

Carly felt tears prickle her eyes. "You guys, you're the best." She hugged them both.

True to her word, Tara came through the door nine minutes later. They sat in the booth Carly was beginning to think of as the "interrogation booth." A flowered cross-body purse hung over Tara's shoulder. She set it down on the seat beside her.

"You're not carrying the tapestry purse today," Carly noted.

Tara smiled, her cheeks turning pink. "I save that for special occasions."

Valerie grilled up a Farmhouse Cheddar Sleeps with the Fishes for Tara, and Carly fetched two mugs of coffee.

Tara swallowed a bite of her sandwich. "Sawyer told me everything, and I mean *everything* you guys talked about this afternoon." Her lowered gaze skimmed the table. "Truth be told, I'm a little embarrassed. You must think I'm some horrible ogre who verbally beats up on her big brother any time he does something I don't approve of."

Carly shook her head. "I don't think that at all, Tara. Families are complicated. From what I've seen, you care very deeply about your brother."

Tara's green eyes misted. "He was wrong, you know, when he said I'd have gotten angry. If I'd known he'd accepted a check from Octavia that morning, I would have taken him right to the police station and made him tell them everything. I'd have stood by him, like I always have. Like I always will." Her voice faded to a shaky murmur. "I can't stress this enough, Carly. My brother is not a killer."

Carly gave her a few moments, then said, "Will he go to the police now, tell them everything?"

Tara gave a slight nod. "We're going to do it tomorrow, together."

"Good plan," Carly said, although she wished they'd do it sooner. After a pause she added, "Do you have anything *you* need to tell them?"

Tara's head came up sharply. "What . . . are you talking about?"

"I'm talking about your tapestry purse," Carly said quietly, "how long have you had it?"

Tara's mouth dropped open, and a flush crept up her neck. "What do you mean? I told you—it was my mom's."

"You also told me Octavia either donated or kept all your mom's purses. So where did that one come from?"

"Did it ever occur to you," Tara said in a clipped tone, "that my mother might've given it to me when I was a girl?"

Carly looked at her but said nothing.

"Okay, okay," Tara admitted. "It was one of the ones Octavia kept. How did you even know about it?" she asked crossly.

Carly explained how Ross had noticed it missing the day he found Octavia's body.

"Which technically means nothing. A million other bags could look like that." Tara took a long pull from her mug, her hand shaking slightly.

"I know," Carly said gently. "I'm not trying to accuse you of anything or upset you. I'm only trying to figure out what happened that day. For your brother's sake, if nothing else, don't you want that too?"

Tara slumped in her seat. She looked defeated. "Okay, I'll explain it as best I can. You can believe me or not. I don't care anymore.

"The night before Sawyer drove up here, we were talking on the phone about a lot of things. Mom, Dad, the days when we were a happy family. Well, Sawyer was almost happy then."

"Why *almost* happy?"

"As a teenager, he was chubby and shy. Not one to make friends. He'd come home from school, and instead of watching TV he'd make a batch of brownies. I was only a little girl, so to me it was great. Sometimes he made entire meals for the family. They were always delicious, but heavy on the carbs. Although back then, I didn't know a carb from a frog," she said with a rueful chuckle.

Carly smiled. "Sounds like his interest in kitchens started early on."

"It did. But then he was off to college. I was still a kid, and I really missed him. When Mom died, I felt so alone. Dad couldn't get past the grief."

A lump rose in Carly's throat, but Tara was getting off track.

"So, the night before he drove up to Vermont, you were reminiscing on the phone? Is that what made you think of the purse?"

"Exactly. I guess I was feeling nostalgic. After we hung up I made a decision. I'd go to Octavia's the next day and ask if I could have one of mom's purses to display in my new shop. In return, I was going to give her a one-hundred-dollar gift card."

"The next day," Carly murmured. "You mean the day her body was found?"

"Yes, but I got there midmorning, before all of that . . . awful stuff happened. What's weird is that I had no idea my brother had already been there. I must've just missed him." She took a small bite of her sandwich.

"I gather she gave you the purse?" Carly said.

Tara swallowed. "Not exactly. When I got there, the front door was open. I called her name through the screen a few times, but she didn't answer. So, I went inside and walked to the back where the kitchen was. The table was messy as all get-out, but Mom's tapestry purse was right there, hanging on the back of a chair. My heart clenched when I saw it—it was Mom's favorite one. She had no right to be using it!"

At Tara's raised voice, Valerie glanced in their direction.

"It brought back memories, didn't it?" Carly said softly.

The anger in Tara's eyes was intense. "Yes. I—I got so furious. I opened the purse, dumped out the contents on the table, and booked it out of there like my shoes were on fire." She looked suddenly drained.

Carly didn't want to press her any further. Tara's confession, for what it was worth, had come at an emotional cost.

"I know that was hard for you, Tara. I appreciate you telling me. I'm only trying to put the pieces together. I'm not trying to accuse anyone of anything."

At that, Tara gave her a tiny smile. "I know. I get that you're only trying to help. And I'm glad I got that off my chest." She wiggled her fingers over the remains of her grilled cheese. "Well, after that confession, I'm going to enjoy finishing my sandwich. Best tuna melt I ever had."

Carly was awed at Tara's knack for mood shifting. She'd gone from penitent to perky in the space of a few seconds. Was she acting? Or was it simply how she dealt with stressful situations?

After changing the subject to her new shop, Tara finished her sandwich in record time. To the relief of Valerie and Ross, she left right before closing.

"I'm still walking you to your car," Ross declared to Carly, his jaw set in a firm line.

Carly laughed. "After everything that's happened today, that's an offer I won't pass up."

CHAPTER 31

WHEN CARLY PULLED INTO HER DRIVEWAY, SHE SAW A FAMILIAR SEDAN parked behind Becca's old Lincoln. Her heart hammered. Why was her mom here? Was something wrong?

A million horrible scenarios hopscotched in Carly's mind—from Norah getting mugged in California to Ari getting injured on the job site.

She took the stairs two at a time, stumbling on the top step. When her key turned in her lock she nearly fell into her apartment. "Mom?" she squeaked.

She dropped her tote in the hallway and flew into the kitchen. A warm, tantalizing aroma tickled her taste buds.

Rhonda Hale Clark was standing at the counter, dropping cherry tomatoes into Carly's large glass salad bowl. Havarti was busy scarfing down the last dregs in his food dish. He barely noticed Carly's presence.

"Hi, honey!" her mom said cheerily. Sporting a red and white polka-dot tee and cherry red Bermuda shorts, she was the picture of summer casual. "Aren't you running a bit late?"

"Um, no. This is my normal time. I just didn't expect you. What's . . . happening? Havarti didn't even greet me at the door."

"That's because I cheated a bit when I fed him," her mom admitted. "I added some cooked burger and cheese to his kibble. I know you're not big on giving him people food, but he deserves a treat too, right?"

"Sure, but why are you here? I mean, I'm happy to see you, but . . ." She trailed off.

Rhonda went over and hugged her. "Honey, I've been texting you for days, and all I get in return is 'Everything's fine! No worries!' Those messages alone made me worry myself sick." She wagged at finger at her daughter. "I know when you're fudging the truth, Carly Hale. Now, sit down and I'll pour you some wine. I picked up a nice Riesling on my way over."

Carly dropped onto a chair. His dish depleted, Havarti trotted over and sniffed her knees, and she lifted him onto her lap. As he licked her face vigorously, suspicion crawled into her mind. "Did you know Ari wouldn't be here?"

Rhonda opened the fridge and pulled out a bottle of dressing. "Actually, I did. I called him and asked if he'd have dinner out this evening. I told him I wanted some alone time with you. This was the only way I could think of to get it." She poured two glasses of wine and gave one to Carly.

Now Carly felt truly bad. Had she been so dismissive of her mom's concerns that she'd triggered a major worry episode?

She gulped back a mouthful of the sweet wine and inhaled a deep breath. "What's in the oven?"

Rhonda winked at her. "What goes best with taco salad?"

"Corn bread?"

With that Carly's taste buds segued into a salsa dance. Cold taco salad was a favorite of hers, something her mom only made during the hot summer months.

Rhonda added the final ingredients—sauteed burger, shredded cheese, and crumbled corn chips. She tossed it all with Ranch dressing, set out the warm corn bread, and they sat down to dine.

By the time Carly's stomach had reached its fill line, she saw anxiety slip into her mom's eyes.

"What's really wrong, Mom?" she asked. "Is it because of the murder?"

Rhonda rested her elbows on the table and folded her hands. "No, and I didn't come here to talk about that." Her gaze softened. "My dear child, you've been very out of sorts lately. I'm not sure what's happening, but I'm concerned about you."

Carly shrugged. She started to deny it, but she knew it was useless. Rhonda Hale Clark was no fool. Especially when it came to her daughters.

"I don't know how to explain it," Carly finally said. "I guess, partly, it's that I don't know where Ari and I are headed. I'm confused, and I'm kind of in limbo. The thing is, I put *myself* there. Ari had nothing to do with it. I think that's why I'm struggling."

Her mom ushered her into the living room, taking their wineglasses along with her. Havarti scampered in ahead of them and secured his position in the center of the sofa.

Rhonda sat down and handed Carly her glass. "Why do *you* think you're in limbo?"

Carly swallowed hard. How could she explain it when she wasn't sure herself? "I keep thinking, you lost Dad when you were so young. I mean, I was only seven when he passed so I barely remember him. Norah developed a bond with him that I never had."

Rhonda chuckled. "Wanna know the truth? Norah was the quintessential daddy's girl, but you were a momma's girl all the way."

"I was?"

"Absolutely. But why does it still trouble you?"

"Well, I was barely thirty when I lost Daniel. Almost the same age you were when Dad passed. Without you and Norah, but especially you, I don't know how I would have muddled through those awful days. You and Gary flew up from Florida in the dead of winter to stay with me. I can't think what I'd have done without you."

"That's one of the million things moms are for. What families are for." She tilted her head at Carly. "Are you worried that if you marry Ari, you'll lose him at a young age, too?"

Carly rested her head on the back of the sofa. Is that what was nagging at her? Ari's job was dangerous at times, but she knew he used every safety precaution.

"Maybe? I know it sounds nuts, but it already happened to both of us. What if it's some sort of family curse?"

Narrowing her eyes, Rhonda made one of her *get real* faces. "I know you don't honestly believe that. You're far too smart for such nonsense."

Carly gave her mom a lukewarm smile. "You're right. I don't. Not really." She reached over and stroked Havarti's furry face.

The real truth was poking at the surface, trying to break through. For a long time she'd managed to tamp it down. Now that she and Ari were officially moving in together, it'd finally burst through the cracks.

After a long silence, Carly said, "Mom, do you think Daniel would be disappointed in me or mad at me for wanting to be with Ari?"

Rhonda plunked down her wineglass on the side table. Her voice was soft, but firm. "Now, you listen to me, Carly Hale. Do you seriously think Daniel, who adored you, would want you to spend the rest of your life without love? Think about it. He died a hero, trying to save a young family from freezing to death. Would that kind of man want you to mourn him forever? To go through life never having that kind of love again?"

Carly felt her throat tighten. Her mom had hit the nail, right on target. She shook her head.

"That's right. No more than Dad would've wanted me to never meet Gary."

"But this is different," Carly protested. She shifted on the sofa to face her mom. "You didn't meet Gary and get married again until you were much older."

"Did you forget I had two daughters to raise?"

Carly stared at her mom. "Is that really why you waited?"

"It's exactly why." Rhonda's eyes twinkled. "Make no mistake. I had plenty of chances back then. But I made the decision not to allow anyone into my life until you and Norah were out on your own. *And* thriving."

Carly's thoughts whirled, and then a huge breath left her lungs. It felt like a cleansing—a release of all the unspoken doubts and worries she'd built up over the past months.

"Mom," she said, because she couldn't resist, "do you ever regret not having a romance or two back then?"

Rhonda's face beamed. "Not for a single second. I knew the moment I met that sweet, blue-eyed pimple popper he was the one I'd been waiting for." Her cheeks colored. "And believe me, he was well worth the wait."

Carly didn't want to delve too deeply into that declaration. She reached over Havarti and squeezed her mom in an awkward hug.

"Don't squish your dog," Rhonda scolded, still clinging to her daughter.

"I won't." She sat back and felt a smile touch her lips. "Mom, I do have some news. I wasn't going to tell you until it was a done deal, but I know Ari won't mind. We're going to buy a house and move in together."

Rhonda squealed, and the sofa cushion bounced. "Yesss! Does that mean—"

Carly held up her hand. "It means we're making a commitment to create a home together. Right now, that's all. In fact, we're pretty sure we're buying this house and turning it back into a one-family, like it was decades ago. Joyce is planning to make us a very generous offer."

Her breath coming in gasps, Rhonda pressed a manicured hand to her chest. "OMG, I'm hyperventilating." She drained her wineglass, leaped off the sofa, and jitterbugged her way into the kitchen. "I'll clean up," she called. "In the meantime, think about what you want for a housewarming gift!"

Carly sat back and hugged Havarti. Even if she tried, she couldn't erase the silly grin she felt sprawling across her face.

Her mom poked her head into the living room. "By the way, if you ever tangle with a killer again—which I forbid you to do—tell them that if they so much as harm a hair on your head, I'm going to reach into their throat, rip out their heart, and roast it over an open flame."

CHAPTER 32

CARLY AWOKE WEDNESDAY MORNING WITH A RENEWED SENSE OF PURPOSE. Ari had stayed at his own house the night before, and while she missed his presence, it had given her a chance to gather her thoughts and reassess her priorities.

Determined to pay Chief Holloway a surprise visit, she'd set her alarm for an hour earlier than her normal wake-up time. The chief was a creature of habit, and Carly knew that early morning would be her best chance to pin him down.

After the pounding rain of the day before, the sight of the sun's rays rising above the slopes of Vermont's green mountains lifted Carly's spirits. In the distance, a hawk soared low over the treetops, seeking a tasty morsel.

When she reached the police station, she lucked out and found a parking spot on the street in front of the building. In the reception area, a portly officer with slicked-back graying hair was seated behind the bulletproof barrier. He performed a two-fingered dance on his keyboard for at least half a minute before looking up. "Help you?"

"Hello, I'm Carly Hale," she said with the sweetest smile she could muster. "I'd like to see Chief Holloway, please. I'll only need a few minutes of his time."

The officer picked up the phone and jabbed a button. "Chief? A Carly Hale is here to see you." After a few seconds he hung up. "Take a seat. He'll be right out."

"Thank you."

Crossing her fingers at her good luck, Carly sat in one of the molded plastic chairs in the small waiting area. She'd assumed, at the very least, she'd get a royal runaround. That he agreed to see her was a near miracle.

About ten minutes later, the chief stepped into the lobby and motioned to her to follow him. His expression was unreadable—the unsmiling face of a seasoned interrogator.

Okay, so he's not in a good mood, she thought. But at least he was willing to talk to her. It was a start.

Instead of going toward his office, he led her down an offshoot of the main corridor, which led to a door that required a code to enter. The chief flipped on the overhead light, ushered her inside, and closed the door behind her.

The room was small. A plain metal desk graced with a phone and a computer sat in the center. Also atop the desk was what appeared to be a gift bag.

Opposite the desk was the structure that made her stomach flip.

A jail cell.

Her legs wobbled. Was the chief arresting her?

Without a word, he pulled out a set of keys and unlocked the cell door. "If you want to talk, we'll talk in here. Those are my terms."

Carly halted. She crossed her arms over her chest. What was the chief trying to pull? Was this a scare tactic?

Finally, she stomped inside the cell. It was small, about ten feet by eight. The only place to sit was a narrow bed covered with a thin nylon mattress. Weighing her options, she chose to stand.

The chief followed her into the cell but left the door unlocked. "You can sit. This is a temporary holding cell. It gets cleaned every day."

"Why are you doing this, Chief?" she said furiously. "Are you trying to embarrass me?"

"No, Carly. That's the last thing I want to do." His face relaxed and his voice softened. "I'm trying to show you what can happen when you compromise an investigation *and* risk your life trying to squeeze information out of potential murder suspects." He waved a hand to his right. "Now, please sit. The mattress was sanitized this morning."

Carly looked at the so-called bed. It did look pretty clean. A mild disinfectant scent hung in the air. She sat down on the edge and rested her tote in her lap.

The chief sat at the other end. "I know you've been wanting to ask me questions because you want to help Ross Baxter. I get it. We've been down this path before. Too many times, as I recall."

"Even so," Carly said, with a bold lift of her chin, "you can't deny that I've been *some* help to the police in the past."

"You're right. I would never deny that. But you can't deny that you came close to losing your life on more than one occasion because of the risks you took."

"Yes, but I didn't take risks intentionally. I never knowingly walked into a killer's trap."

Holloway folded his hands over his knees and blew out a sigh. "You said last week you had a question for me about Mark Hughes. Without rehashing all the chances you took in the past, I'll agree to answer it under one condition. Until Mrs. Gray's killer is in custody, you will not talk to anyone connected to this case. That includes the stepkids—*especially* the stepkids. And before you ask, Valerie didn't share any of that with me. She's too loyal a friend to tattle on you."

"Then you've been watching me," Carly said flatly.

He gave her a crooked smile. "Carly, more than once I've seen your car parked next to Tara Shepard's new place. I drive that way on my way to work, but lately I've made it a point to swing past it pretty routinely."

Carly fidgeted on the mattress. "Okay, I admit Tara and I met a few times for coffee. She's a fellow businesswoman and we have a lot in common.'"

"And Sawyer Gray?"

"I spoke to him, too," Carly conceded, "only because he begged me to. He seemed to think I could convince the police of his innocence. I told him I couldn't help him. I urged him to take his concerns to the investigators."

Holloway rubbed his hand over his eyes. "All right. Is there anything else you want to tell me?"

"Quite a bit, but I'll start with what happened yesterday because it relates to my question."

She explained what Ross had told her about recognizing Mark Hughes's voice as the one he'd overheard arguing with Octavia. "He said the voice he heard was more nasal, but it sounded very similar to Mark's. The voice threatened Octavia to 'give it back or she'd be sorry.' Something like that, anyway."

The chief looked thoughtful. "Hughes was questioned a couple of times. For logistical reasons, he's been ruled out as a suspect."

"Does that mean you have proof that he was out of the country the day Octavia was murdered?"

"We do. Both his passport and the airline's passenger log show that he was in the UK that morning. Unless he crossed the ocean both ways in a teleportation machine, he's not a suspect in the murder."

"Thank you, Chief," Carly said. "You've answered my question. It's one more worry off my plate."

"Carly, listen to me. You don't have a plate. You're off the case, understood? Right now, you need to back off before someone decides you're getting too nosy. *Again.*"

She nodded. "I understand, and I promise I will. But you *do* know Ross still works for me, right?"

Holloway cracked a smile. "I'm going to tell you something, but if you ever repeat it, I'll deny I ever said it. I never seriously considered Ross a suspect. The investigators questioned him repeatedly, mainly because they were coming up empty. But in my book, there's no way that kid's a killer."

Carly gave him a weak smile. "At least we agree on that."

"Anything else?"

At the risk of incurring his wrath, Carly gave the chief a recap of her evening out with Tara and Gina, and the details of her discussions with Tara and Sawyer. The one thing that still bothered her most was the tapestry purse. Tara's explanation had sounded reasonable enough. But it also sounded too pat.

She also shared Paloma's story, and the photo of the cross the child had found semi-buried on the strip of land at the rear of the Hughes property. It probably had no relation to the murder, but she'd promised Paloma she'd pass along the info to the police.

Lastly, she told him about her and Ari helping a distraught Lois Feeney into the church on Sunday to confess her sins to the pastor.

"Poor woman," Holloway said. "She really thought she'd caused Octavia's murder by wishing her dead?"

"She was convinced of it." Carly twisted her fingers over her tote. "You know what bugs me about the day of the murder, Chief? The lack of witnesses. I mean, didn't anyone report seeing anything that morning? A neighbor, a delivery person, a kid on a bike?"

"Every neighbor within a mile was questioned. The subdivision behind Octavia's yard is pretty much all working folks, so they're not home during the day. The couple across the street are in their eighties. They claim they keep their shades drawn day and night. Sad to say, but these days a lot of people are simply afraid to get involved."

"What about Imogene Hughes?"

"According to her, she didn't notice anything until she saw all the flashing lights in Octavia's driveway."

She'd pretty much told Carly the same thing.

Carly gathered up her tote. "Well, it's getting late. I'd better—"

"Carly, wait," the chief interrupted. "Can you give me another five minutes? I'd like your help on an unrelated matter."

"Um. Sure, okay."

Perplexed, Carly waited as the chief retrieved the gift bag from the desk and came back into the cell. He set the bag down on the mattress between them and cleared his throat. "I want to give one of these to Valerie when I"—he flushed deeply—"ask her to marry me."

"M-marry you? Oh my gosh, Chief!"

"I realize we've known each other less than a year, but I also know she's the person I've been waiting for. I'm pretty sure she feels the same about me."

I think she does too, Carly wanted to say, but she kept her opinion to herself.

"The jeweler let me take two rings, but I have no idea which one she'd like better." He lifted two velvet boxes out of the bag and opened them. "They're both set in eighteen-karat white gold. What do you think?"

Carly hitched in a breath. Both rings were stunning. "These are both . . . unreal, Chief." She examined them closely. "I love the one with the diamonds around the band. But I think Val would choose the one with the sapphires set on either side of the solitaire diamond. It's a more classic style, and in my opinion, it's more to her taste."

"Whew," he said, and blew out a breath. "I thought the same thing, but I wanted to get a woman's opinion." His eyes grew shiny. "That is, a woman who really knows Val." He quickly secured the rings back in the bag.

Carly couldn't stifle a grin. "Gotta say, this makes my day. And I promise, my lips are sealed. When are you going to, you know . . ."

"Saturday. I made a reservation for a private dining room at the inn."

Carly thought a moment. "If I hadn't come by here today, were you still going to ask my opinion?"

"Probably not. That's why I was relieved when you stopped in to see me."

"You were relieved? You certainly hid it well," she said dryly. "Did we really need to go into a jail cell?"

"A holding cell," Holloway corrected. "And it was merely a precaution. For privacy," he added.

"Gotcha." *Sort of.*

After returning the bag to his office, he walked Carly out to the waiting area. A red-faced uniformed officer waved his arm and intercepted them.

"Chief, we've been looking for you. We got a huge break in the Gray case. Someone just confessed to the murder. She's in the first interview room."

Carly's insides dropped to her knees. The officer had distinctly said *she*. Did Tara confess to killing her stepmother?

Holloway morphed instantly into cop mode. He turned to Carly. "Thank you for coming in today. I'll be in touch." He turned on his heel and followed the officer.

Pretending to fish around for something in her tote, she perked her ears and moved closer to where the chief had trailed after the officer.

"Who is it, Jarvis?" she heard Holloway inquire.

"You won't believe it, Chief. It's that kid's grandmother, Helen Quigley. She just confessed to murdering Octavia Gray."

CHAPTER 33

CARLY COULDN'T GET TO HER RESTAURANT FAST ENOUGH.

Helen Quigley killed Octavia? How can that be? There's no way. No way . . .

The words thrummed repeatedly in her brain until she swung into her parking space behind the eatery. She noticed that Gina's car was gone. Not surprising, since her friend had claimed the day before to be "buried in projects." But it wasn't like Gina to have sent off such a dismissive text.

One more thing for Carly to worry about.

She killed her engine and dashed inside.

The sight of Grant standing behind the grill gave her an unexpected rush of emotion. She walked past the booths and paused in front of the counter, then plopped her tote on a stool and started to cry.

Grant raced around the counter and cupped her shoulders. "Carly, what's wrong? Did something happen?" His brow crinkled with worry.

Embarrassed by her breakdown, she shook her head. "Don't mind me. How's your mom? Is she okay?"

"She's doing great. Her gall bladder is history. They're gonna release her from the hospital this afternoon. But what's the matter? Why are you crying?"

Carly swallowed. "I was at the police station talking to the chief this morning. When I was leaving, I heard someone say that Ross's grandmother just confessed to murdering Octavia Gray."

Grant's mouth dropped in shock. He released his grip on her shoulders and took a step backward. "How . . . how can that be?"

"I don't know. *I don't know.* I need to find out if anyone's told Ross yet."

"Right now you need coffee." Grant's tone left no room for argument. "And a biscuit."

Carly slid onto a stool. "Coffee, yes, but I don't think I could choke down any food right now."

Grant poured her a mug of coffee, added one creamer, and set it down in front of her.

"Thank you." She teared up again. How would she ever replace this wonderful, kind, talented, extraordinary young man?

"Carly, take it easy," Grant soothed, as if he'd read her mind. "You know we'll do everything we can to help Ross. You want me to see if I can reach him?"

She felt her throat clogging again. She hated feeling out of control this way. "That would be great. Thanks."

Grant tapped Ross's number on his cell. "Voicemail," he mouthed to Carly. "Hey, man, it's Grant. Can you give me a call when you get this? Thanks."

Just then Valerie came in. Garbed in a loose-fitting coral top over baggy white pants cinched at the ankles, she was the poster girl for casual chic.

"Hey, guys, good mor—" The greeting died on her lips. "Something's wrong. I can see it in your faces." She dropped her belongings on a table.

Carly told her what she'd overheard at the police station.

Valerie looked baffled. "No. This isn't right. She did it to protect Ross. I'd bet anything!"

"Grant tried calling Ross, but he didn't answer." Carly took a long sip from her mug.

Valerie sat down beside Carly. "Your eyes are puffy." She slid an arm around her.

"Thanks," Carly said with mock offense.

Grant handed Valerie a steaming mug of java. After blowing on it and taking a tiny sip she said, "Okay, listen, guys. We can't do much to help Ross, or his granny, until we know what's happening. I think we should all go about our day as we normally would. If Fred calls, I'll try to get more information."

"Sounds good to me," Grant said.

"I agree." Carly smiled at her friend. "As for me, I need to get my act together. I can't run a restaurant if I'm falling apart like some damsel in distress."

"Carly," Valerie said seriously, "everyone has the right to fall apart now and then. It means you're human. It means you care. What's important is that you have people in your life to prop you up when you falter. In that way, my friend, you are very, very blessed."

"Oh, sure, make me cry again."

Valerie clapped her lightly on the shoulder. "Come on. Let's get to work."

By eleven, the eatery was spotless and ready to open. They still hadn't heard from Ross. Suzanne had arrived a few minutes before opening time. Carly gave her a brief recap of what she'd overheard at the police station.

Suzanne slung a hand on one hip. "She confessed? Well, I don't believe it for a minute. She probably did it so the cops will stop badgering poor Ross."

"Totally possible," was all Carly said.

During the morning, Carly had taken a few minutes to text Ari with the news about Helen Quigley's confession. She also texted Gina, who'd replied with a brief *Sorry to hear that.* When Carly asked her if she was okay, she responded with an emoji of a frazzled face followed by *Yup. Super busy.*

Carly shook her head. Something was up with Gina. Maybe after work she'd pop upstairs and pay her a visit—see what was really going on.

Shortly after they'd opened, four separate orders came in from seniors asking for delivery. Word was getting around that delivery was available to folks who didn't want to order online.

Carly was surprised to see that one of the orders came from Imogene Hughes. What bugged her was that Mark had been in the restaurant the afternoon before. If he was home, why couldn't he pick up his mother's lunch?

She texted Don, who was happy to accommodate the deliveries. He'd apparently been getting surprisingly good tips from some of the seniors. Aside from that, Carly suspected he'd been enjoying the praise a few of her homebound customers had been lavishing on him.

She was in the kitchen slicing a round of Gouda when Ross trudged through the swinging door. Dark circles ringed his eyes, and his cheeks looked sunken into his face. She wiped her hands on her apron and went over to hug him.

He flopped onto a chair as if his limbs were numb. "I'm sorry I didn't text you this morning. I guess you heard about Gram."

"We did." Carly sat down opposite him. "Is she still at the police station?"

"Yeah, but they're gonna release her and send her home this afternoon. I'll have to go back and pick her up. Is it okay if I skip work today?"

He'd already skipped half a day, but Carly saw no reason to mention it. "Of course it's okay. So, what's happening with your grandmother? Are they charging her?"

He looked at his sneakers and shook his head. "No, but they're super PO'd that she wasted their time. Once they started questioning her, it was so obvious she didn't know anything about the crime." He gave a mirthless laugh. "She told them she got fed up with Mrs. Gray tormenting me and went to her house to confront her. She said when Mrs. Gray laughed in her face, she grabbed a saucepan off the counter and smacked her with it."

"A saucepan?"

"Gram was so rattled she didn't remember the weapon was a frying pan." Ross groaned and ran a hand through his curly hair. "It was all downhill from there."

It pained Carly to see Ross looking so desolate. She rose and packed a container with several of Nina Cyr's sugar cookies. She'd never had a chance to check out Nina's website, but for now the scrumptious cookies spoke for themselves.

Carly gave him the container. "You need to go home and take care of your grandmother and yourself. Call me if you need anything, okay?"

"Thanks," he said dully. "Tell Grant I'm sorry I didn't call him back. I was just, like . . ." He threw up his hands.

"That's okay, and don't worry about tomorrow," Carly said as he was leaving. "For the time being, let's take things day to day."

Ross gave her a two-fingered salute and left.

In one way, Carly was relieved that Helen Quigley couldn't be the killer.

The downside?

It looked like Tara and Sawyer were running neck and neck toward the top of the suspect list.

• • •

"Busy day," Suzanne noted, removing her apron. She tossed it into the laundry bin and grabbed her purse from the closet in the kitchen. "Anyway, I'm outta here. We promised Josh he could have his own archery set, so I'm taking him to the sporting goods store this afternoon."

"So, it's totally safe for kids to do at home?" Carly asked.

"It is, if they've had proper training. Believe it or not, it's considered one of the safest sports for kids. Plus, Jake is going to practice with him, so he'll get the hang of it, too." Her warm smile spoke volumes. "I'm really glad he wants to do that. Father-son bonding and all that. Anyway, see ya tomorrow!"

Carly wished her luck and went back to feeding chunks of sharp cheddar into the shredder. Suzanne's mention of archery reminded her of Paloma.

As she'd promised, Carly had told a policeman about the cross half-buried in the ground on the Hughes property. From the chief's casual shrug, she didn't think he'd placed much importance on it. But at least Carly had kept her word to Paloma.

The cheddar shredded, Carly shoveled it into a plastic container and sealed the cover. After stashing it in the fridge, she took a short break to check her cell for messages.

None from Gina, but Ari had texted a few times to see how things were going. After a few back-and-forths, they agreed to have leftover taco salad for dinner, along with watermelon sherbet that Ari would pick up on his way there.

By three thirty or so, the dining room had quieted down. Only two booths were occupied, so Carly insisted that Grant take a break. He'd been working straight through all day. Valerie had taken hers earlier to shop for new earrings to wear on her date with the chief on Saturday. If she had any inkling about his secret plan, she showed no sign of it.

Grant wiped his hands on a towel. "I won't be long. I just want to head home and see if Mom needs anything. Dad drove her home from the hospital about an hour ago."

Carly smiled. "You're a good son. Give her my best wishes, okay? Why don't you take home some of those sugar cookies?"

"Whoa. Good idea. Mom's diet will probably be restricted for a while, but Dad and I won't have any problem powering through them," he said with a grin.

The moment he was out the door, Valerie scurried behind the counter to take over for him. Three teenaged boys wearing shorts and tees sauntered in. Carly seated them near the front, took their orders and then clipped the orders above the grill.

As assistant manager, Valerie's duties were varied. But at that moment, watching her whip up sandwich plates, Carly was struck by something—working the grill was Valerie's favorite part of the job. Carly suspected she'd do it full-time if she could, instead of just being Grant's "fill-in."

Carly was cleaning dirty dishes off the tables when she realized she hadn't heard from Don Frasco.

"Hey, Val," she called out, "did Don ever come back with the takeout carrier?"

Valerie paused, then gave Carly a puzzled look. "No, I haven't seen him, unless he popped in when I was at the jewelry store. But now you've got me wondering. He always brings our money in as soon as he's done delivering. Maybe he got tied up somewhere?"

A sliver of worry shot through Carly. She brought the tub of dishes into the kitchen, set it next to the sink, and pulled out her cell. She frowned when she saw that she'd missed an earlier call from him while she was busy helping out in the dining room. Fortunately, he'd left a voicemail. She played it.

"Hey, Carly, I won't be able to get back today, but I'll bring your money over tomorrow. I have to get to the printer ASAP. There's a glitch with tomorrow's edition." He made a scratchy sound in his throat. "And, um, don't worry about the sandwich you promised me. I'll make my own grilled cheese when I get home."

His own grilled cheese? Don hated grilled cheese!

Worried now, she called his cell number. It went directly to voicemail. She left a message for him to call her as soon as possible.

She rinsed the dirty plates and flatware and loaded them into the dishwasher. After that, she pushed through the door into the dining room. Grant had returned and was back behind the grill. Valerie was seating a fortysomething couple in a booth near the back.

Carly went over to Grant. "How's your mom doing?"

"She's great. Hurting a little and moving kind of slow, but that's normal after surgery."

"I'm glad to hear everything went well. Listen, Don called me a while ago and left a weird message." She described it to him.

Grant shrugged. "The grilled cheese part does sound odd, but I wouldn't read too much into it."

Carly made a face. "I guess you're right."

She reached under the counter and retrieved the slips for the day's delivery orders. In the kitchen, she sat at the table and called the first three customers. She used the excuse that she was checking to be sure they were pleased with the delivery service.

Each customer she spoke to said they were thrilled with both the food and the delivery. Don received so many glowing compliments she wondered if he'd sprouted a halo.

She'd saved Imogene Hughes for last. Unfortunately, her call went straight to an answering machine. She left a message asking Imogene to call her.

Then she remembered. Don had said he was heading to the printer. Could he still be tied up there?

Carly googled the name and called the number. The man who answered sounded baffled.

"Don was here this morning to wrap up tomorrow's edition, but he hasn't been in this afternoon. And there's no glitch with the paper. Not that I know of."

After thanking the man, she glanced at the clock and then hurried out to the dining room.

"Grant, I'm really concerned about Don. I'm going to drive by his apartment, see if his car is there. Will you and Val be okay for half an hour or so?"

"Yeah, sure. But you—"

She didn't wait to hear the rest, which she was sure would be a lecture. She soared out the back door and hopped into her car. Maybe Don was home sick and didn't want to admit he needed help.

She hoped that's all it was.

His apartment was located above a garage in an older neighborhood several blocks from the main drag. The yard in front of the two-story home was neat, if sparse, with a driveway large enough for three cars. One glance told her Don's car wasn't there. The garage door was open, but the only vehicle inside was a sit-down mower.

Carly mulled her next move. The printer was a bust. They'd already confirmed they hadn't seen Don since morning.

Don's last food delivery had been to Imogene Hughes, the one person she hadn't reached yet.

It was probably a waste of time, but it would only take a few extra minutes to pay her a visit.

CHAPTER 34

Minutes later, Carly parked on the street in front of Imogene's ranch home. The driveway was empty, the garage door closed. Either Mark Hughes wasn't home or his car was inside the garage. Either way, at least she knew that Mark couldn't have killed Octavia Gray.

She slid her cell phone into her pocket and climbed out of her car. Before she had a chance to ring the bell, the front door swung open.

"Carly, what a pleasant surprise!" Looking flustered, Imogene opened the screen door. "Come in, come in." One hand on her walker, she motioned Carly inside and locked the front door behind her. "For obvious reasons, I've been locking up every day. Let's go in the kitchen and have a glass of cold iced tea."

Carly didn't want any more of Imogene's oversweet iced tea, nor did she have time for a social call. She followed her into the kitchen hoping the woman could shed light on Don's whereabouts.

"Please don't go to any trouble," she told Imogene. "I can only stay a few minutes."

"No trouble at all. Sit," Imogene urged, opening her fridge door. She pulled out a plastic pitcher half full of iced tea. "Would you bring that to the counter, dear? Glasses are in the cupboard. You can pour a glass for each of us." She plunked down onto the nearest chair.

Nervy, Carly thought, but she did as Imogene asked. She brought the glasses over to the table and sat down. "I called earlier and left you a message, but apparently you didn't see it."

Imogene glanced over at her wall phone, the lines in her wrinkled brow deepening. "That's odd. There's no message blinking. Well, you're here now. What was it you wanted, dear?" She took a noisy sip from her glass.

"I'm wondering if you remember what time Don Frasco left here after his delivery. I haven't been able to reach him."

Imogene blinked several times, then tapped a finger to her chin. "Let's see, I think he left around . . . one thirty, quarter of two? Since I was his last delivery, he stayed and had some iced tea and a slice of cake. Oh, how he gushed over my sponge cake!"

Carly knew that Don disliked iced tea. He probably choked it down so he could score a slab of cake.

"When he left, did he say where he was headed?" she asked, struggling to quell her impatience.

"Well, yes, as a matter of fact, he did. He said something about going to the printer. After that he was going home to make himself a grilled cheese." She gave Carly a sweet smile. "I thought that was odd, since *your* grilled cheeses are so wonderful. But to each his own, right?"

Carly's insides knotted. Why would Don tell a casual acquaintance he was going home to make a grilled cheese—a sandwich he loathed?

He wouldn't.

Which meant Imogene had been with him when he called Carly and left the message on her cell.

"Excuse me," Carly said, "I need to check my messages."

She started to pull her cell phone from her pocket when she noticed something. The tail end of a neon yellow stylus pen was sticking out from underneath the fridge. Leaning forward in her chair, she squinted to get a better look. "Isn't that Don's pen?" She rose to retrieve it. When she turned, the barrel of a gun was aimed directly at her chest.

Carly dropped the pen and sat down again. Every muscle in her body tensed. "Im . . . Imogene, what are you doing? Where did you get a gun?"

Imogene smiled. "It was my husband's. I thought he sold it ages ago, but I found it in a box in the garage. He knew I hated guns, so I guess he humored me. Or maybe he knew one day it would come in handy."

Gone was the sweet, warbling voice of a kindly senior. In the space of an instant, she'd morphed into a cold and calculating woman.

"I don't understand." Carly's voice sounded like gravel to her own ears. "Why are you doing this?"

"Because I didn't want to be forced to tase you, like I did to your delivery boy. He got a bit too nosy, I'm afraid. He figured out I didn't need my walker to get around. After he left, he sneaked back in through the back door and started poking around."

"Where is he?" Carly demanded. "Did you hurt him?"

"Only temporarily. The taser was very effective on him."

"But why . . . *why?*"

Her gun leveled directly at Carly's face, Imogene sighed heavily. "My son is responsible for all of this. When he gets home, I'll let him explain it. Then he'll have to deal with both of you."

Stay calm, Carly told herself.

"What did Mark do, Imogene? Did he kill Octavia?"

"Don't be stupid," she scoffed. "He was in London that day. It *is* his fault she's dead, though. If he hadn't started doing that day trading thing and lost all his savings, he wouldn't have gotten us into this mess. The more he lost, the more he invested to try to make it up. I tried to help him by mortgaging my home, but he squandered that, too." Her eyes darted back and forth but her gun hand remained steady.

Day trading. Carly had read of people who'd made a fortune that way. The practice was risky, though, especially if you didn't understand the intricacies of the stock market.

Her cell phone was still in her pocket. Slowly, she reached her hand toward it.

"Put it on the table," Imogene ordered. "Now."

Heart pummeling her chest, Carly did as she was told.

With her free hand, Imogene picked up the phone and threw it across the kitchen. It landed with a *thwack* at the back of the counter.

So much for that.

"Can you tell me what happened? Please?" Carly said gently. "Maybe I can help—"

"It's too late for that," Imogene said, her tone laced with despair, "but I'll tell you anyway. On one of Mark's trips back from England, he was in the airport restroom when someone sneaked a package into his carry-on. He'd already gone through customs. He was just waiting to board his plane."

Carly swallowed. "Don't tell me. Drugs?"

Imogene looked shocked at the question. "Absolutely not. He'd have gone to the authorities if it was that. No, it was a packet of rare emeralds, along with ten thousand dollars in American money. He didn't find it until he got home."

"I assume the emeralds were stolen," Carly said. "But why would they risk passing them off to a stranger?"

"Because their original contact didn't show up—at least that's what they told Mark afterward." Imogene rubbed one eye with her fingers but kept the gun steady.

"But . . . how did they know where to contact him?"

"While he was washing up at the sink, he set his carry-on down. Whoever slipped him the packet took a copy of his luggage tag with his business card on it."

Slick operation, if it was true.

Carly skimmed her gaze around the kitchen. Unfortunately, she didn't see anything she could use to disarm Imogene. Nothing within reach, anyway.

She needed to keep her talking, empathize with her, until she could figure out something.

"So, when Mark got home and found the package . . ." Carly prompted.

"The thieves," Imogene continued, "called Mark from a number that couldn't be traced. They told him where to ship the jewels. It was my idea to hide them inside a sponge cake. We designed labels making it look like a home business."

Which made Imogene an accessory.

"If there were no problems, he could keep the cash. If something went wrong"—Imogene hitched in a breath—"they reminded him they knew where he lived. And with whom."

Carly was stunned. The scope of it was mind-boggling. Even more horrifying was the threat to Mark's life. Would they have hurt Imogene, too?

"Was that the only time Mark did that?" Carly asked her.

After a hesitation, Imogene said, "No. It worked so well they contacted him again. They've got him in their clutches now. He's in too deep."

And you are, too.

"I still don't get how it happened. I thought airports had all kinds of security."

"There's a way around everything, if you're clever enough," Imogene said bitterly. "The transfers were made by someone dressed as a custodian cleaning the bathroom. Maybe he was a real custodian, who knows?" She lowered her gun slightly but caught herself and raised it again.

"So how did Octavia get involved?"

Imogene's eyes dimmed. "One of those days when we had windswept rain, Mark didn't secure the trash can cover when he put it out for pickup. The cover blew off and some of our trash blew into that witch's yard. After the rain ended, she stormed over here like a crazed woman, holding some of our soggy trash—empty powdered sugar and flour bags, mostly. She barged into my kitchen so fast I didn't see her till she was right in my face!"

Carly could guess the rest. "She caught you making one of your *special* cakes, didn't she?"

Imogene nodded. "I turned so fast my hand slipped, and a handful of emeralds scattered on the floor. Before I could get them all, she grabbed one of the larger ones and raced out the door, laughing all the way."

"She put the pieces together and then she blackmailed you," Carly supplied. "Forced you to move the property line so she could get rid of the maple tree she hated. And Mark went along with it because he couldn't afford not to."

Imogene hitched in a ragged breath. "She promised to give back the emerald if we did that. But even after we complied, she still refused. Every one of those gems has to be accounted for! If Mark doesn't find it pretty soon—" She made a throat-cutting gesture across her lined neck.

"But that fence was moved in the spring," Carly pointed out. "I'm surprised the thieves have been this patient."

Imogene's lips twisted. "Mark keeps putting them off, making excuses for how it got misplaced. They gave him a deadline, and it's coming up soon."

Ross had been right all along. The man demanding that Octavia "give it back" was Mark. She recalled Mark telling her he'd postponed a trip because of a summer cold. That would've accounted for his nasal voice.

"Mark went over and demanded she give it back, didn't he? The threats were escalating. He was getting desperate."

"Yes, but she still refused. I got so scared. Three times I saw a strange car drive by my house—slowly, like they were watching. And always when I was alone."

In a quiet tone, Carly said, "You had every reason to be afraid. You went over to Octavia's yourself and tried to reason with her, didn't you?"

Outside, a car door slammed shut. Carly's pulse spiked, but she kept her voice even.

"And when she refused again, you picked up the skillet. But you didn't mean to kill her, did you?"

Imogene's eyes took on a wild look. "No! I only wanted to scare her into giving me the emerald. And then . . . and then she laughed at me. She said she could see why my husband chose her over a dried-up hag like me." A bubble of spittle formed on her lips.

"She was only trying to get under your skin," Carly said.

"No." Fury darkened Imogene's eyes. "He did go to her. Many times."

A wronged woman has a long memory.

Imogene's own words.

And suddenly it all made sense. Imogene had not one motive but two.

At the front door, the sound of a lock turning caught Carly's attention. Imogene seemed oblivious, so Carly forced herself not to react.

"She made the mistake of turning her back on me," Imogene went on. "Her frying pan was on the stove, so I grabbed it and smashed the back of her head. I thought she was just . . . knocked out. I started straightening up that disgustingly messy table, hoping the emerald was hidden there. But I gave up. It was taking too long, and it could've been anywhere in the house. She still wasn't moving, and then I remembered I'd touched the handle of the frying pan. I pulled a tissue from my pocket and wiped the handle clean, then I hurried back to my house as fast as I could."

Her face went slack, her eyes unfocused. The gun wavered only slightly. Not enough for Carly to risk leaping off her chair.

"Please let me help you, Imogene," she said, injecting calm into her voice. "I know the chief of police. I'll explain what happened."

She shook her head. "It's too late."

"At least tell me where Don is," she pleaded. "I need to know he's okay."

"Don't worry, he'll survive," Imogene said with a sneer. "At least until my son figures out what to do with both of you."

"Put the gun down, Mother."

Carly swung her head around sharply. Mark Hughes was standing behind her, his gaze fixed on Imogene.

"Mark! You're finally home," Imogene cried. She dropped the gun on the table and jumped up to embrace him.

Carly reacted instantly. She retrieved the gun and shoved it into a drawer, then called 9-1-1 from Imogene's landline.

Mark's handsome face contorted with anger and revulsion. He grasped his mother's shoulders and shook her roughly. "So all along it was you who killed her. So much for needing a walker, right, Mother?" He shoved her away from him.

Imogene stumbled backward, but she caught herself. "How else could I get any attention from you? You've lived in my house for years, but you don't care a fig about me. You're just like your father—Mr. Get Rich Quick. Did you know that's what people called him? He left me with nothing but this house, but you took that away, too, with your idiotic schemes. Where will you go when the bank forecloses?" she shrieked.

Mark looked as if he'd been sucker-punched. He covered his mouth with his hand and closed his eyes.

Veins bulging in her neck, Imogene continued her tirade. "How could you be stupid enough to let criminals use you for a patsy? Mr. high and mighty travel consultant. You couldn't even keep track of your bag in an airport washroom!"

Mark's blue eyes seethed with contempt. "Now who's being stupid, Mother? Can't you figure it out? I was in on it from the beginning."

With a cry of utter defeat, Imogene slid to the floor, sobbing. The steady blast of a car horn, very close by, made Carly jump. Mark's face registered confusion, and then he raced toward a door that led from the adjacent laundry room. Carly followed at his heels.

Mark opened the door and flipped on a light switch.

There in the garage was Don Frasco's car. Don's face bobbed in the driver's-side window, his eyes wild, his mouth sealed with duct tape.

"Don!" Carly yanked open the car door and his head dropped to the seat. He lay across both front seats, his wrists and ankles tightly bound with the same gray tape.

In the next instant, the high-pitched wail of multiple sirens echoed in Carly's ears.

"Hang in there, Don. Help is on the way." She loosened a corner of the duct tape that covered his mouth.

Barely a minute later, she heard pounding on the garage door. "Police! Open up!"

Mark stood there, frozen, his face a sickly shade of yellow.

"Open the door!" Carly screamed at him.

He finally stumbled to the switch that lifted the garage door. It was halfway open when a swarm of police officers ducked underneath it and rushed inside.

Carly turned back to Don. As gently as she could, she removed the tape from his mouth.

"Ow! That hurt!"

Carly laughed through the tears that were streaming down her cheeks. "I've never been so happy to hear you complain." She began removing the duct tape from his hands.

"That Imogene woman—she's bat-crap crazy," he bellowed. "You know what it's like to be tased? Twice?"

An officer opened the passenger-side door. She helped Carly remove the remaining duct tape.

"Thanks," Don said, and then to Carly, "After she tased me, she taped me up and dragged me into my car. Oh, yeah, first she drove my car into her garage. She left me on the floor in the back. Do you know how long it took me to wiggle onto the backseat so I could work my way onto the front seat?"

Carly let him rant. After what he'd been through, he deserved to let off some steam.

Freed from his bonds, he rubbed his wrists. He sucked in several deep breaths. "This is the second time you saved my bacon, Carly. What's that saying? Déjà vu all over again?"

"I guess so, but let's *never* do this again. Deal?"

"Deal." His freckled cheeks flushed. "I'm glad you're okay. You are, aren't you?"

"I am for now," Carly said with a groan. "But when Chief Holloway finds out what happened here, I'm pretty sure he's going to kill me."

CHAPTER 35

TWO DAYS LATER, CHIEF HOLLOWAY SUMMONED CARLY AND DON TO HIS office. Carly tried not to fidget in her chair, but she had no clue what the chief was going to say.

His expression blank, Holloway folded his hands on his desk blotter. "Well, it's good to see you two looking rested after your ordeal. How are you both doing?"

"I'm doing fine, Chief," Carly said, "grateful it's over. I have to say, though, the whole thing really messed with my head. I never could have imagined anything like this."

"Same here, Chief," Don said with a sheepish look at Carly. "I guess having Carly for a friend isn't a bad thing."

"Gee, thanks," she said dryly.

"Well, that's good to hear." The chief opened a folder. He put on a pair of reading glasses. "I want to update you both on what's happening. There's much more to the case than I can reveal, but I'll give you the highlights.

"Mark Hughes got involved with a band of international jewel thieves. The authorities are still trying to piece together how it worked and what Mark's role was. They suspect he was a minor player in a huge operation. They also believe that this little episode will barely put a dent in it."

Carly was astounded. "Even with Mark testifying?"

"Mark's contacts were all low-level cogs in the wheel. The real kingpins have layers of protection between themselves and people like Mark. Mark's frequent trips to Europe, along with his financial woes, made him an easy pigeon. It's sad that he got his mother involved. She was trying to protect her son, but it only made matters worse."

"I still feel bad for Imogene," Carly said. "I honestly believe she didn't mean to kill Octavia."

Imogene admitted to the police that after recovering fully from her hip surgery the year before, she continued to "need" her walker so that her son would lavish more attention on her. She was actually quite sprightly, and also fairly strong.

That's what Carly had struggled to remember. The first day she delivered food to her, Imogene didn't grab her walker until after she came out of the kitchen. It didn't strike a chord until now.

"If it's any consolation," Holloway said, "my daughter's partner Erika is going to be representing her. Believe me, Imogene couldn't do any better."

"That's a relief," Carly said. "What about Mark Hughes?"

The chief sat back in his chair. "His case is a lot more complicated, but he's got one thing in his favor. He never used any of the cash that came with the gems. He stashed it in a metal box and hid it under a floorboard—probably planning to flee to the Cayman Islands at some point. If the authorities can trace it back to the source, it could provide some valuable leads."

"Wow," Carly murmured, "I'm glad I'm just a lowly grilled cheese cook. By the way, has there been any sign of the missing emerald?"

"No, but the authorities are hiring a team to do a thorough search of the Gray property. Something like that is easy to hide, and Octavia wasn't exactly a neat freak. One last thing," the chief said, a mysterious smile on his lips. "Carly, this is for you. We dug up the spot where the cross was buried on what's now the Hughes property."

Carly's ears perked. "And?"

"There was, indeed, a body buried there. But I'll let Tara Shepard tell you all about it."

"But—"

"And now, if you'll both excuse me, I have paperwork coming out of my ears, so I will bid you both goodbye." Holloway rose from his chair.

"That's it?" Carly said incredulously. "No lectures, no backlash?"

"Not this time," the chief said. "In this case, it all worked out the way it was supposed to."

How fatalistic of him, Carly thought. Or maybe he was just in a *really* good mood.

She and Don stood to leave.

"Chief," Carly said, hoisting her tote over her shoulder, "Ari and I are having an informal open house at my apartment on Sunday, starting around one. We'd love to see you and Valerie there."

He smiled broadly. "Then I expect we will be. And thank you very much for the invite."

CHAPTER 36

"THAT IS ONE SPECTACULAR CHEESEBOARD," GINA SAID, HER GAZE sweeping over Carly's kitchen table.

Looking adorable in a sixties-style, poppy-print sheath that barely skimmed the tops of her knees, she removed her bowtie salad from the fridge and set it on the opposite end of the table.

"It's a summer charcuterie board," Carly said, a touch of pride in her tone. "I made it myself. Deviled eggs, cherry tomatoes, pickled carrots, jalapeño wontons, homemade salsa, garlic crisps, and a selection of cheeses to suit every taste. Mom's bringing her famous fruit trifle, which I *love*."

"Yum, me too." Gina lifted the see-through cover of the charcuterie board and snatched a cherry tomato.

"Hey! No sampling!" Then, "So things are okay with you and Zach?"

"They are, but I still feel so bad about how I acted. Zach understood completely. Except . . . you know what? It actually *did* help bring his mom and me closer."

Gina had thought Zach was making excuses about having to stay with his mom so often. She'd assumed it was a prelude to a breakup and was prepared for the worst. When he finally explained the situation, she felt terrible.

During Mrs. Bartlett's recent colonoscopy, several lesions were removed. Zach and his mom had been worried sick waiting for the results. Mrs. Bartlett had asked Zach not to share with Gina because she felt it was too personal. A good son, he respected her wishes. After the results came in and all was well, Zach's mom wanted Gina to know. A new phase of their relationship was born, and things were better than ever.

"We're even attending a fancy tea together," Gina said brightly. "Just the two of us. It's at a historic place in Brattleboro and she's already made the reservation."

"Gina, I'm so happy for you. Oh, that's the door. Can you get it? I hope we have enough chairs."

Carly had decided to close Havarti in her bedroom for the duration of the open house. He was a sweet dog, but she wasn't sure how he'd react to so many people at once—or if he'd beg them for food. She'd left him snoozing on her bed, with plenty of fresh water and kibble available.

Ari and Zach had set up fifteen or so rented folding chairs around Carly's living area. It was a squeeze, but they all fit.

Joyce and Becca were first to arrive, Becca keeping her arm firmly wrapped around Joyce's. In her multihued, loose-fitting top and neon pink orthotic shoes, Joyce resembled a view through a kaleidoscope.

"Whew! I haven't climbed those stairs in years," Joyce wheezed as Becca led her to a chair.

In the living room, Carly had set up a corner table with a bowl of raspberry punch. David Parlee had kindly shared his recipe. She'd added only a *touch* of champagne to it. It wouldn't do to have any of her guests tumble down the stairs from over-imbibing.

"Carly, it's us," Rhonda Hale Clark called through the door.

Gina was hurrying to open it when Rhonda and Gary strode in. Hugs were exchanged, and Gina relieved Rhonda of the covered trifle bowl, in which vanilla pudding, strawberries, whipped cream and fresh blueberries nested in perfectly even layers.

Another knock at the door. Gina rolled her eyes. "What am I, the butler?"

After ushering in Ross and his grandmother, who both looked thrilled to be there, she found a sheet of paper in Carly's hallway table and wrote, in huge letters: *Come in!*

Carly was setting out cups and napkins around the punch bowl when Gina went over to her and said, "Where's your tape?"

"Kitchen," Carly said. "Third drawer down next to the fridge."

After finding the tape, Gina started to open the apartment door when it opened on its own.

Ari and Zach came in carrying cold beer and soda, along with an ice chest. "We didn't know if there'd be room in the fridge, so we came prepared."

Gina kissed Zach briskly on the lips, then taped the sheet of paper to the door.

The two men set up their wares on a card table next to the punch stand. Then Ari went over to Carly and gave her a kiss on the cheek. "Everything looks great!"

"Thanks, but I had lots of help." She winked at him and handed him two paper cups filled with red liquid. "Can you bring these over to Joyce and Becca?"

"You got it."

Suzanne swept through the door and greeted everyone, then went over to Carly. "Hey, this is great, Carly. First time I've seen your digs! My dudes bailed on me, so I'm flying solo. They're doing some sports thing at the park. Just as well. Josh gets bored if he has to spend more than ten minutes with 'old people,' as he calls them."

"We are rather ancient," Carly said jokingly. She gave Suzanne a cup of punch.

"Spiked?" Suzanne grinned.

"Just a touch."

Suzanne joined the others. Ross and his grandmother came up to Carly.

"Carly, you have a lovely place," Helen said, a sparkle in her eyes.

"Yeah, cool crib," Ross said with a toothy smile.

"I don't know what we'd have done without your support," Helen went on, her eyes misting, "not to mention your"—she leaned forward—"detective work."

"It wasn't that much," Carly said, "and I didn't do it alone. Mainly, I always knew Ross was innocent. I'm just grateful everything worked out."

The chief and Valerie came in next. Carly's breath caught in her throat.

Valerie was a vision in a shimmery, pale blue sundress and white peep-toe sandals. Her topknot was highlighted and fluffier than ever. She discreetly raised her left hand to show Carly the ring.

Carly hugged them both, then whispered to Valerie, "Announcement soon?"

"Absolutely," Valerie said. "I'll probably cry, so I'll let Fred do it."

He squeezed Valerie's shoulder and gazed at her as if she'd single-handedly strung the planets.

Everyone began to mingle, and Carly smiled at the gathering. This was her first open house. So far, people seemed to be enjoying themselves. She had a few announcements of her own to make, but those would wait until after Fred and Valerie made theirs.

Don ambled in next and waved at everyone. He seemed overly pleased by all the warm greetings, almost as if he hadn't expected them.

"Hey, Carly," he said, weaving his way over to her. "I can't wait till you see Thursday's edition." He puffed out his skinny chest.

"I'm anxious to read it." Carly smiled. "Did you make me look good?"

"Of course!"

Don's and her encounter with the killer that past week was bound to be a blockbuster story—at least for Balsam Dell. Carly knew Don was hoping to be noticed by one of the prominent newspapers in the region. For his sake, she hoped it would happen.

Don went in search of a root beer and Carly stood before her guests. "Everyone," Carly called out. "We're setting up food in the kitchen, so start eating whenever you'd like. You'll find plates, flatware, and napkins. But leave some room, because Grant will be making us all a special treat when he gets here."

After everyone had fixed plates for themselves—Becca doing one for Joyce—Carly and Ari put their own together. They sat side by side in two folding chairs, their elbows nearly touching. A warm, comforting silence fell over them.

That is, until Grant came in and everyone called out a greeting. With him was a young woman with shoulder-length, loose brown curls and a ready smile. Her periwinkle crop top highlighted her lovely eyes, and she waved shyly at everyone.

Carly set her near-empty plate on her chair and went over to welcome them.

"This is Ellie," Grant said, the admiration in his eyes obvious. "She'll be going to school in Boston in the fall, studying music therapy. Since I'll be close by, we plan to spend some of our free time together."

Ellie's eyes lit up. "Thank you for inviting me," she said to Carly. "Grant speaks so glowingly of you. I'm glad I'm getting to meet you in person."

"You are so welcome, Ellie. Please help yourselves to food and beverages."

"If you don't mind," Grant said, "I want to start working on the sandwiches now. Ellie wants to help me."

"Then the kitchen is yours. The ingredients are in the fridge."

Ten minutes later, Grant emerged from the kitchen holding a large tray of sandwiches, each one cut diagonally into quarters.

"Hey, everyone," Grant said to the group. "We're going to be introducing two new sandwiches at the restaurant—one with cream cheese and raspberry jam on whole-grain, and the other with basil pesto and provolone on crusty Italian. Let us know if you like one over the other."

Ellie handed out napkins as Grant went from one guest to the other with the tray. Before long, oohs and aahs rose from the group.

"Raspberry for me!" Suzanne called out.

"Oh, man, this pesto is like, unbelievable," Ross piped up.

Carly and Ari sampled theirs. "Grant, you've gone above and beyond with these," Carly told him. "I can't wait to add them to the menu."

When her guests had eaten their fill, Carly got up and addressed them. With the exception of three people, everyone she'd invited was there.

It was time.

"Hey, everyone. Fred and Valerie have an announcement to make," she said. "Chief?"

He and Valerie rose together. Valerie looked flushed, and incredibly happy.

"I'll be brief." The chief cleared his throat. "I have asked this wonderful woman to marry me. I don't know what I ever did to deserve her, but to my sheer amazement she accepted."

Screams and hoots filled the apartment. Everyone rushed over to hug them, and Valerie displayed her ring.

Over the clamor, Carly heard a tentative knock at the door. Before she could get there, Nina Cyr came in clasping a large container. Her short, canary-colored hair had been brushed high, and her slender neck was graced with several strands of colored beads.

Carly led her into the living room and took the container from her hands. She stood in front of her guests. Valerie murmured something to Fred and went over to join her.

"For those of you who haven't met her," Carly announced, "this is Nina Cyr. She makes the best sugar cookies I have ever tasted. I know you'll think so too, after you sample them."

With that, Grant touched Ellie's elbow and went over to stand beside Valerie.

"Starting in mid-July," Carly continued, "Nina will be joining our restaurant crew. She's had a lot of experience, and we all feel she'll be an ideal addition to our happy staff."

"So she'll like, replace Grant?" Ross asked.

"No. Valerie is going to take over as head grill cook. She knows the job, and she's a pro at it—and it's what she wants to do. Nina will be our new assistant manager. I'm confident she's perfect for the role."

The day before, they'd all gathered in the restaurant for a lengthy meeting. Nina was there for much of it, but after she left it was Carly, Grant, and Valerie who'd come to an agreement. Suzanne had been less enthusiastic, mainly because she felt it happened too quickly. But Nina's references had been impeccable, and Carly felt sure she'd made the right choice.

Suzanne moved forward from the back of the room and went over to Nina. "Welcome to the world of grilled cheese, girl. You're gonna love working with us." She squeezed her in a hug and everyone cheered.

After that, the guests began to gather in small groups. Some went for seconds on food. Nina mingled comfortably among them, passing around her cookies for everyone to sample.

Observing them, Carly felt herself overflowing with joy. *How lucky am I to be blessed with all these wonderful people in my life!*

Her mom, though, had been oddly quiet. Carly went over to where Ari was chatting with Gary and squeezed his arm. "Maybe it's time for our announcement."

Ari smiled and wrapped his hand around hers. He beckoned their guests toward the window that faced the front yard. Behind them, the lush greenery of the warm summer day framed them, as if in a portrait.

In a sudden flashback, Carly's mind traveled back to the day, in a freezing cold parking lot, when a desperate killer had tried to end her life. Ari had raced to the scene at the speed of sound, terrified he might be too late. She could still see him, sprinting toward her like a heat-seeking missile and sweeping her into his arms. *I love you, Carly Hale.*

It was the first time he'd uttered those words, and she'd repeated them, almost verbatim. *And I love you, Ari Mitchell.*

Now that she'd made the decision she'd known all along was right, her heart felt lighter than a helium balloon.

"Hey, everyone, Ari and I have some news," Carly said when everyone quieted. "Our dear friend Joyce has agreed to sell us this house. She and Becca have plans of their own, but I'll let them tell you all about it themselves." Feeling herself choking up, she squeezed Ari's hand.

"This lovely home," Ari explained, his gaze fixed on Carly, "was at one time a one-family. It's going to be that again. Carly and I plan to make it our permanent home."

Carly swiped at one leaky eye. "We are so excited, and so grateful to Joyce for all she's done for us."

"As soon as the permits are in place," Ari said, a mischievous glint in his eye, "we'll start the rehabbing. After it's completed, you'll all be invited back here to attend our official engagement celebration."

Shouts of congratulations erupted from the guests, Rhonda's being the loudest. She rushed over to Carly, losing one high heel in the process and nearly knocking over a chair.

Gina was grinning and doing a crazy dance at the same time. Then she raised a glass of punch and led everyone in a toast to Carly and Ari.

Eventually, the guests began to trickle out. Carly squeezed Joyce fiercely, thanking her again for the house.

Zach and Ari loaded the folding chairs into the back of Ari's pickup. Gina went over to Carly and hugged her again. "I'll probably bawl like a baby at your wedding, you know," she warned.

Carly laughed. "We won't worry about that now."

Rhonda sniffled. "I am so happy for you, sweetie. You and Ari are so perfect for each other. I only wish Norah could've been here."

"I know, but the three of us will celebrate together when she gets home. Just us girls."

When everyone was finally gone, Carly released a breath of pure bliss. Ari wrapped her in his arms and pulled her close. "So far, this has been the best day of my life," he murmured.

"With many more to come," she said, just as a light tap on the door reached her ears.

"Late guests?" Ari said.

Carly opened the door to find Tara and Sawyer standing there. Tara was clutching her beloved tapestry purse, and Sawyer was holding a cellophane-wrapped gift basket shaped like a bone.

"I'm sorry we didn't come earlier," Tara said, her cheeks pinking. "We just felt—"

"I'm thrilled you're here," Carly said, inviting them to sit on the sofa. She introduced them to Ari, who greeted them warmly.

Sawyer gave Carly the gift basket, which was packed with dog treats and toys. "This is for Havarti."

Carly slapped her forehead. "Havarti!"

Ari laughed and headed to the bedroom. Seconds later, Havarti raced into the living room. He jumped on the sofa between Tara and Sawyer, and then settled in Sawyer's lap. Smiling broadly, Sawyer rubbed the dog's face. "Well, aren't you a good boy?" he cooed.

"Carly," Tara said, "Sawyer and I want to thank you—for everything. It's because of you that we got our lives back, not to mention our sanity."

"Tell them the news," Sawyer urged, tickling Havarti's chin.

Tara's green eyes beamed. "Sawyer and I are teaming up. We've signed a lease for the space next to Pugs and Purses. Sawyer will set up a cookery-style shop. We'll add a doorway so that people can move easily between both shops without having to go outside. We've come up with some fun ideas we hope will attract shoppers to both stores."

"We also found out that the space above both shops is empty," Sawyer added. "It used to be an apartment, but no one's lived there for a few years."

"At the moment it's a bit dusty," Tara said, wrinkling her nose, "but once we get it spiffed up and furnished Sawyer will move in." She looked at her brother. "Ironically, Octavia's estate turned out to be substantial enough to fund our venture. It was the ending to this whole nightmare I could never have predicted."

"Tara's hiring a manager to handle both businesses," Sawyer said. "Thank heaven for that."

Carly was almost speechless. Relieved of the stress created by recent events, the brother and sister were like two different people.

Ari jumped up and offered them some of Nina's remaining cookies.

"Thanks," Sawyer said, nabbing two.

"Tara and Sawyer, I'm so happy for both of you," Carly said. She looked over at Ari. "We have some news, too. When our guests were here earlier, Ari and I announced our engagement."

Tara squealed. "Yay! I'm so happy for you. For both of you." She looked at Carly's left hand. "What, no ring?"

"It's on our agenda," Ari said, squeezing Carly's hand. "We're going shopping this week. With everything that's happened, there wasn't a lot of time."

"Tara," Carly said, "the chief mentioned you had news about a body that was dug up?"

Tara chuckled. "It's a strange story. When Octavia had Ziggy put down all those years ago, she told me she left his remains with the vet. Turned out she didn't—she buried them near the maple tree. Ziggy's little bones were in the box, but something else was too." She opened her tapestry purse and pulled out a plastic bag that, though severely degraded with age, was intact. She handed it to Carly. "Read what she wrote. The ink is faded but it's still legible."

Carly's jaw dropped as she read the message.

> Dear Tara,
> Although you'll never read this, it will relieve my mind to put it
> in writing. I know I've not been the kindest or warmest person. I had

terrible parents and I treated people the way they treated me. It wasn't until I married your father that I realized I might enjoy having a daughter. You seemed to like me at first, and my fondness for you grew. Ziggy was the catalyst that helped us bond, and I began to hope you might think of me as a surrogate mother. When Ziggy became terminally ill, I was as heartbroken as you were. I thought ending his pain without you having to witness it would be easier on you. I see now it was the worst thing I could have done. You hated me for it, and I deserved it. I reacted badly to your anger, unforgivably so. I told you I gave away all your mother's treasured belongings. But I didn't. After I pass, the house will be yours, if I'm still living in it. You'll find all your mother's things in boxes in the attic. It was the one thing I could do to show you how sorry I am.

Octavia

"So all this time, your mom's things were in the house?" She showed the letter to Ari.

"They were. We found several boxes of her stuff. Everything was surprisingly well-preserved."

Carly thought about the twist of fate that led to Tara finding the letter. "I can't help wondering—did Octavia expect one day you'd find the grave?"

"I honestly don't know. One thing I know for sure, though. That cross wasn't there when I left to go to college. I think Octavia wrote the letter and buried it with Ziggy's remains long after I was gone."

"Maybe she hoped you'd find it and wonder if something was buried there?" Carly mused aloud.

"Possibly." Tara frowned, and her voice softened. "It makes me sad for what might've been. Maybe Octavia really *did* want me to think of her as a mom. But after I treated her so . . . viciously, she knew that would never happen."

"You were a teenager," Carly gently reminded her. "You can't blame yourself."

Tara shook off the sudden gloom and smiled. "That little girl who spotted the cross—I'd like to thank her personally. In a way, it gave me some closure with Octavia."

Carly grinned. "I'm sure you can. She lives in the neighborhood."

"As for Mark Hughes," Tara said with a snort, "I totally misjudged him, didn't I?"

"I'm sure a lot of people did," Carly said. "He could turn on the charm when he wanted to."

"Anyway," Tara said, "I came here to give you a gift." She unlatched her tapestry purse and dug around inside. "Oh, for heaven's sake, where is it? Sawyer, I brought the gift card with me, didn't I?"

He shrugged. "I thought you stuck it in your pocketbook."

Looking perturbed, she felt all around the bottom of the purse. And suddenly, her expression changed. She slowly pulled out her hand and opened her palm.

"I bet this would make a nice engagement ring."

Carly leaned closer for a better look. A dazzling green gem, rectangular in shape, winked at her from Tara's palm. "Oh . . . my gosh. That must be the missing emerald!"

Tara nodded slowly. "That day, when I dumped the stuff out of Octavia's purse, it must've gotten stuck in the lining."

Ari gave a low whistle. "That is one gorgeous gem. With your permission, Tara, I'd like to ask Chief Holloway to come over."

She laughed. "Yes, please. I want nothing to do with it." She gave the emerald to Carly. "I'll bring your gift card to the restaurant tomorrow."

After handshakes and hugs of congratulations, Tara and Sawyer departed.

Ari took Carly's hand and led her over to the sofa, where he wrapped her in his arms and pulled her close. Not one to be left out, Havarti squeezed onto Carly's lap.

"I was thinking," Ari said, his gaze capturing Carly's. "I haven't called the chief yet. Shall we take the emerald and make a run for it?"

"Hmmm," Carly said, "I had a similar thought, except for one thing. Well, two things. I'm not sure how well Havarti would travel. And I'm not terribly keen on wearing orange on my wedding day."

"Ah, both good points," he said seriously.

Carly hadn't shared it with anyone, but she'd already imagined herself in a sage green gown, layers of chiffon over satin, dotted with tiny, embroidered daisies.

Ari pulled his phone out of his pocket. "Oh, well, it was fun to pretend. I'd better call the chief."

Carly closed his hand over his phone. "Wait a minute. That emerald's not going anywhere, right? Why don't we enjoy being alone for a while."

"Now that," Ari said in a throaty voice, "is the best idea you've had all day."

RECIPES

Raspberry Sizzle

Summer is raspberry season, and Grant loves to experiment with cheese and bread combos when creating a new sandwich. He tried this one with Brie, but ultimately it was the cream cheese he selected. The blend of smooth cream cheese and sweet raspberry jam makes this the perfect choice for jam lovers. And, as Grant says . . . it's so simple, it's sinful.

Yield: one sandwich

2 slices whole-grain bread (sourdough works well, too)
Salted butter
1 to 2 tablespoons cream cheese (depending on your preference and the size of the bread)
2 tablespoons raspberry jam

Butter one side of each slice of bread evenly with the salted butter. (Try not to skimp on butter, as you want the sandwich to have that crispy, crunchy outside.)

On the un-buttered side of one slice, spread the cream cheese, then evenly spoon the jam over that.

Place the other slice on top, butter side facing out. Press down *gently* so that the two slices stick together.

Place in a skillet over medium or medium-low heat. Grill each side until browned to perfection and the cream cheese and jam are warm.

Enjoy with a cup of your favorite tea, or any other beverage that makes you smile!

Tips:

Softened butter spreads more easily.

Be sure the bread you use is not too thick; you don't want to detract from the flavor of the cream cheese and jam.

Zesty Pesto

Pesto isn't a flavor savored by every palate, but for those who enjoy it, this grilled cheese is for you! Grant insists on using only the best-quality pesto to make this tangy treat. Fortunately, there are several available brands to choose from. Basil pesto should contain basil, pine nuts, Parmesan cheese, garlic, and extra virgin olive oil. You can also make your own pesto, using one of the many recipes found online.

Yield: one sandwich

2 thick slices of crusty Italian or artisan bread
2 to 3 tablespoons of good-quality basil pesto (if the pesto is oily or the consistency thin, drain it through a sieve first)
4 slices provolone cheese
Softened butter

Butter one slice of bread, then place it butter-side down in a skillet with the heat *off.*

Place two slices of provolone atop the buttered slice (depending on the size of your bread, you can fold the provolone slices to make them fit).

Spoon the pesto evenly over the provolone; top with the remaining slices of provolone.

Butter the other bread slice and place it, butter-side up, atop the provolone.

Press the sandwich lightly, then grill each side over low heat for a total of 5 to 6 minutes, until the cheese is melted and the sandwich is golden brown.

Served with Grant's tomato soup, this sandwich is a flavorful delight. You can add your own variations, such as sun-dried tomatoes or crispy bacon. Just be sure any extras have been patted dry so as not to make the sandwich oily. Make it your own and you'll have a meal fit for royalty!

About the Author

As a child, Linda Reilly practically existed on grilled cheese sandwiches, and today they remain her comfort food of choice. Raised in a sleepy town in the Berkshires of Massachusetts, she retired from the world of real estate closings and title examinations to spend more time writing mysteries.

A member of Sisters in Crime, Mystery Writers of America, and Cat Writers' Association, Linda is also the author of the Deep Fried Mysteries and the Cat Lady Mysteries. Her first Cat Lady mystery, *Escape Claws*, was selected by *Modern Cat* magazine as a "must read." Linda lives in southern New Hampshire with her two feline assistants, both of whom enjoy prancing over her laptop to assist with editing. When she's not pounding away at her keyboard, she can usually be found prowling the shelves of a local bookstore or library hunting for a new adventure—or at the stove whipping up a delectable grilled cheese. Visit her on the web at lindareillyauthor.com or on Facebook at facebook.com/Lindasreillyauthor/. She loves hearing from readers!

Made in the USA
Middletown, DE
20 May 2024

54580071R00116